CRESCENT CITY COOKING

Crescent City Cooking

Unforgettable Recipes from

Susan Spicer's New Orleans

SUSAN SPICER WITH PAULA DISBROWE

Alfred A. Knopf   New York   2007

THIS IS A BORZOI BOOK
PUBLISHED BY ALFRED A. KNOPF

Library of Congress Cataloging-in-Publication Data

Spicer, Susan.
Crescent City cooking : unforgettable recipes from Susan Spicer's
New Orleans / by Susan Spicer with Paula Disbrowe.
p.   cm.
Includes index.
ISBN 978-1-4000-4389-7
1. Cookery, American—Louisiana style. 2. Cookery—Louisiana—
New Orleans. I. Disbrowe, Paula. II. Title.
TX715.2.L68S68 2007
641.59763—dc22   2007013834

Manufactured in China
First Edition

To my mother, Alice:

I learned most of what I know about love,
life and cooking just by watching her.

Contents

Acknowledgments

I guess publishing a first book is a little like winning your first Oscar—there are *so* many people to thank.

Let me begin with Janis Donnaud, my agent, whose combination of Southern quirkiness and New York smarts was just what I needed. I appreciate her confidence on my behalf and her patience with my leisurely Louisiana ways.

To Paula Disbrowe (Norman), my co-writer and friend: it was so much fun to work on this with you. Thanks for working through my angst and helping me say what I wanted to say in a better, smarter, and funnier way. I look forward to granitas and pedicures for years to come . . .

Thanks to all the folks at Knopf, but especially Paul Bogaards and Sarah Robinson for taking the chance on a first-timer almost past her prime. They embraced the book, gave me lots of creative freedom, and helped me make the most of my personal style.

Thank you to my photographer, Chris Granger, who did a beautiful job of visually conveying not only my food but the charm and funk of the French Quarter.

And to Maria Wisdom, food stylist and recipe tester, for her eye, her enthusiasm, and her friendship.

Many thanks to my partner and friend of seventeen years at Bayona, Regina Keever, who wonders why this book took so long! I am proud of the beautiful restaurant we have created together, and grateful for a partnership that works so well.

Thanks to all my siblings: Tom, for sourcing the mud; Alice (and Kent), for stepping in when Maria couldn't be there; Bettina, for all the computer hours; Hank, for all the advice (wanted and unwanted!); Diana, for lifting me up early on; and Doris, for your acuity and perspective. But mostly, thanks for all the love, laughter, and support through the years. I love you all.

Thanks to my stepfather, Joachim, for bravely stepping into the family, for all his many kindnesses to me, and for making such a happy life with my mom.

In addition, special thanks to:

My in-laws, the Martinsons (especially Rita and Billy, and Allen and Mimi), who welcomed me into the family and opened their homes and hearts after Katrina.

My partners in Herbsaint: Donald Link, Bill Hammack, and Janice Parmalee.

Sandy Whann, my partner at WildFlour Breads, and to Connie, Angelo, José, and Linda, for keeping it going.

The chefs who taught me and had faith in me, Daniel Bonnot and Roland Durand.

The folks at Bayona: Jane Ruppel, Ginger Havard, Jenni Lynch, Michael "Puck" Hopkins, Shannon Skarda, Jeremy Gresham, Hall Ford, Christy Phebus, Paul Chell, Thomas Baptiste, Mr. Burnett, Kirk Ricks, Lynell, Chris Meyers, Pablo, Cameron Magee, Jeff Eustis, Jerryca Faucheaux and Nat Carrier, Howard, Kerri Dean, Sam, James Cannon (father and son), Charles, Stephen, Heidi, JP, Chris E., Bubbles, and all our wonderful cooks, waiters, bartenders, and hosts, past and present. Damon and Frank, we miss you.

Megan Roen, my long-time pastry chef who inspired us all and helped me test the dessert recipes.

All my former sous chefs (and friends): Loretta Keller, Michelle Nugent, Jody Naccarato Bush, Greg "Hoss" Collier, Ashley Hykes McGee, John Harris, Adam Yorty, Stephen Hassinger, Scott Freer, Corbin Evans, Kate Paterson Applebaum, Jim Morris, Ronald Carr, Pat King, Andy Friend, Dimitri Phyllos.

Daniel Walters, John Arbizzani, Jim Bremer, Ken Jackson, David Payne, Shannon Fristoe, Mark Hightower, Dan Brown, Glen Vesh.

All our "regulars"—thanks so much for keeping us going all these years.

All the purveyors who send me the good stuff. . . .

But most of all, love and thanks to Chip, Evelyn, and Kelly, for giving my life meaning.

CRESCENT CITY COOKING

Crescent City Gal

On a warm spring evening in 1979, in a relatively quiet corner of the French Quarter of New Orleans, I ambled down Rue Dauphine, past a restaurant housed in a 200-year-old Creole cottage. I was drawn to its windows by the warm glow emanating from the place and the happy bustle inside. I remember peering in and wondering *what goes on in such an enchanting place?* I happened to be on my way to my first cooking job. At that point in my fledgling career, the excitement, romance, and chaos of the restaurant world were still mysterious—but they were already intoxicating. Little did I know that several years and countless gastronomic adventures later, that restaurant would become my own.

But I'm getting ahead of myself. Born in Key West, Florida, I was one of seven well-fed children. I first learned the pleasure of cooking from my Danish mother—she was in the kitchen all the time, but her work there never seemed like drudgery. My family settled in Holland for several years on account of my dad's job as a naval officer, and Mom learned to cook everything from Indonesian stir-fries to French crêpes and Danish open-faced sandwiches. Thanks to her, I developed a taste for exotic flavors early on.

We moved to New Orleans when I was seven. As a kid, I always felt a little bit offbeat, a little left of center. I loved music, books, movies, art, and of course food. I dreamed of a bohemian lifestyle, which New Orleans seems to foster. When I played Barbie, it was "Career Girl Barbie" with an apartment, a cool job, and a convertible. I never fantasized about getting married. I was independent and I meant to stay that way.

After high school, I actually toyed with the idea of becoming a cook, but my father put the kibosh on that—no daughter of his was going to have a mindless blue-collar job. So I left home at seventeen and spent several years trolling for the right outlet for my passions. I lived in San Francisco and Massachusetts. I worked in a record store, got jobs as a waitress, secretary, and typesetter, but nothing engaged me. I also traveled throughout Europe, eating curry and fried fritters in London, and crudité plates and crêpes in France—now, that I enjoyed!

But I could never stay away from New Orleans for very long. I made a point to come back each spring, for Mardi Gras, Jazz Fest, and the food (plenty of fried oysters, crayfish, and sweet shrimp), and because that's when the city is at its most lush and the sweet olives are in bloom. During one such spring, my father had health problems, so I stayed on to take care of him. And then I needed to find a job.

I didn't start cooking until 1979, when I was twenty-six, first for fun, then professionally. I started catering with a girlfriend of mine. When she got her first job as chef at a downtown restaurant, she called and said, "Come work with me!" I never looked back.

From the get-go, I found cooking mesmerizing. I was captivated by the colors, aromas, textures, and tastes, and found the process both sensual and fascinating. Cooking was something I seemed to do well, and the results were satisfying and fun. I had found my calling.

My first job in a true French kitchen was at Louis XVI Restaurant in the French Quarter. I was terrified. The head chef, Daniel Bonnot (my mentor, my tormentor), basically ignored me for the first couple of weeks. So, desperate for some direction, I began to pore over the cookbooks in his office. Then I started to ask questions. "How do you 'turn' an artichoke?" "What is a tournedo?" I began to memorize classic dishes from *Le Guide Culinaire* and *Larousse*. Soon I had the "privilege" of turning two cases of artichokes and making two cases of *pommes soufflés* every day. (I still bear the scars from shaking the potatoes in two bubbling pots of hot oil.)

I continued to be inquisitive, and Daniel responded by giving me more responsibility. He taught me to mince shallots with a razor-sharp paring knife, make duxelles (a finely chopped mixture of mushrooms and herbs), and wrap Beef Wellingtons in puff pastry. My days got longer. There was always something that needed doing, and I was eager to do it.

In 1982, Daniel helped me arrange a stage or apprenticeship at the Hotel Sofitel in Paris. I worked day and night during that incredible summer. It was the beginning of nouvelle cuisine, so I was exposed to a whole new style of cooking. Roland Durand, the head chef there, would become another mentor. He and his staff created extraordinary food that was more ingredient-oriented (showcasing a flawless piece of fish, for instance), with flavors that were more distilled and a presentation that was more refined. His staff raised the bar for me: I was in awe of their dedication. I could have stayed a lot longer, but at the end of the summer Daniel called and urged me to come home to accept a job as chef. It was at Savoir Faire, a sixty-seat bistro in the St. Charles Hotel.

Daniel and I created the bistro menu (classic in France but still new to New Orleans) that included crudités plates, terrines, sweetbreads, lamb chops, *assiettes anglaises* (cold meats), steak frites, a killer lemon tart.

Then it came time to hire cooks, which was unnerving because everyone who submitted a résumé seemed more qualified than I was. Still, I managed to put together a crew. I remember giving them tasks that I thought would take hours, and they'd be back in twenty minutes, saying, "What next?" I'd be thinking, *Go away. I hate you!*

As Savoir Faire came into its own I realized I had a strong sense of how the food should taste and be presented, and that I was setting a standard for an exciting style of cooking. When I understood this, it gave me confidence and I felt more like a leader.

After Savoir Faire, I was hungry for more learning and exposure to new things. So, I traveled and worked as a cook in California and Europe. But it wasn't too long before I once again heard the siren call of New Orleans.

In 1986, refreshed and inspired from my travels, I again put on the chef's toque when I was hired to open the Bistro at Maison de Ville in one of the city's treasured small hotels, the Hotel Maison de Ville. Little did I know when we opened that first night, with one oven, four burners, a refrigerator in the alley, and our salad greens packed in ice chests under the counter, that this would be a launching pad for me, and so many other talented chefs, in the years to come.

Our forty seats were filled every night, and soon no one could get a reservation. Ideas that had been percolating, such as Grilled Shrimp with Black Bean Cakes and Coriander Sauce (p. 75), Seared Duck Breasts with Pepper Jelly Glaze (p. 264), and my Epiphany Lemon Tart (p. 340), emerged as signatures.

I learned how to cook with folks watching (our small kitchen had a large window that guests could peer into), enjoying that connection to what was happening in the dining room. I saw each plate go out *and* come back, so I knew which dishes worked and which did not.

During my three years as chef there, I learned to be demanding of my crew and of myself. As a result, I was deemed a "prima donna" and a "perfectionist." Like that was a bad thing!

I received several offers to open my own place, but I ignored most of them—that is, until the enchanting space on Rue Dauphine captured my attention once again. I fell in love with the big, romantic courtyard and the three cozy but not cramped dining rooms inside. I noticed a tiled marker on

the side of the building, CAMINO DE BAYONA, from when New Orleans belonged to Spain. I immediately thought "Bayona" would be a warm and beautiful name for a restaurant.

I had become friendly with a particularly enthusiastic and savvy customer, Regina Keever, and she offered to back me in my endeavor. The night we signed our agreement, it snowed, which is a rare event in New Orleans. It seemed to me an auspicious and festive omen. Michael Fisher, the sommelier at the Windsor Court Hotel, agreed to come on board as dining room manager. With this charismatic, ebullient man—boasting a brilliant palate and sterling connections—in our corner, how could we lose! Add to the mix a talented sous chef and a fun-loving (and disciplined) office manager, and it's no wonder we felt on the verge of something extraordinary.

There is some confusion about whether we officially opened Bayona on March 31 or April Fool's Day, 1990. I like to think it's the latter—because it seems appropriate. Thanks to loyal friends, family, and customers, we started off with a bang. We're approaching twenty years, and after surviving floods and hurricanes, I still get an absolute thrill when I walk into the dining room on any given night and see customers eating and drinking and having a wonderful time.

Being a chef is a job and a half, but it also demands that one travel to continue the education of the palate. Over the years, I've cooked at The Oriental Hotel in Bangkok, the Lanesborough Hotel in London, and across the seas for Cunard and Crystal cruise lines. I've slurped curries in Malaysia and sipped pisco sours in Peru. I've served hundreds of Crayfish Croque Monsieurs (p. 158) at Jazz Fest, and developed countless recipes for cooking classes and charity benefits, as well as many television shows and magazine articles.

Back home in New Orleans, I fell in love with the warehouse district and its energy, and thought it would be the perfect spot for a casual fine-dining restaurant similar to my favorites in San Francisco and Chicago.

I joined forces with partners Ken Jackson, Donald Link, and Donald's in-laws, Bill Hammack and Janice Parmelee. We found a beautiful, sunny space on a busy corner of St. Charles Avenue (with the streetcar running past), and Herbsaint was born. We opened in October 2000, and Donald kicked me out of the kitchen in May 2002. With a great staff and a strong menu, he was ready to run it alone and has been doing a fantastic job ever since. These days when I'm there, I get to sit at the bar, drinking wine and indulging in his perfect French fries.

And now, on balmy nights in my relatively quiet corner of the French Quarter, I find myself back at Bayona. After almost two decades, thousands of guests, and hundreds of employees, we're still at it. We've survived hurricanes, fires, New Orleans summers, even having the street out front torn up for two years! We've had at least a dozen employee marriages and lots of babies (some from folks who were practically babies when they started), and many customers have become good friends. This constant but ever-changing family has sustained and supported me, and made Bayona the success that it is today.

My reputation has been built on the efforts and strengths of this family. They have weathered the wrath of an overcaffeinated, overworked, stressed-out chef with a bone to pick, and they have danced at my wedding. Every day (well, most days) I look forward to working shoulder-to-shoulder with them, laughing with them, turning out great food together, and wishing them good night.

Perhaps that's why it's taken me another twenty-six years to tackle my first cookbook. We were busy cooking, securing our reputation, doing what we love. I never wanted to slap together a string of recipes. I needed to nurture Bayona, and to lay its foundation as a vibrant and vital part of New Orleans.

Then I needed to meet Chip, the man I was meant to marry, and experience the pride of putting a home-cooked meal on the table, and the delight of watching him relish every morsel. And I had to learn how to cook for my step-kids, Evelyn, eleven, and Kelly, ten, which is a whole different ball game.

I needed to travel and expand the range of my palate, then condense my wild, delicious ride into a selection of very personal, hand-chosen recipes—from my restaurants (labeled appropriately as "Best of Bayona" or "Herbsaint") and my life. Finally, I wanted to share what I learned from my mentors, and make them proud of me. My mother taught me the sheer joy of cooking and the gift of entertaining. Daniel Bonnot showed me classic and essential techniques, and gave me the confidence to push myself. Roland Durand instilled a love of fine ingredients and the desire to make every plate beautiful. All this takes time; and timing, I believe, is everything.

I hope you enjoy the selections I've made, and next time you're in New Orleans, do come by. Chances are, I'll be there cooking.

The Spicer Pantry

When I was a little girl, I loved to watch *Captain Kangaroo*. Every now and then he read a story called "Stone Soup" that had a profound impact on me. You're probably familiar with it too. It's about a soldier who comes into a village asking for food, but all the villagers have hidden and locked up their meager supplies. So he sits down in the middle of the square, makes a fire, and puts on a kettle of water with a small stone in it. He sits there, watching the kettle simmer, gleefully rubbing his hands over it in anticipation. Eventually, one of the hungry villagers comes out to see what he is cooking, and he says, "Stone soup!" He talks about how delicious it is going to be, and promises to share it when it's done. The villager says, "Oh but think how much better it would be with a little onion" and runs to bring out a little shriveled onion that he was hiding. Gradually, a second villager comes out and eventually says, "But a potato would make it really tasty." You get the picture. Eventually the whole village comes out and adds carrots, herbs, a bit of dried meat, and so on. In the end, they have a wonderful, brimming pot full of savory soup that feeds everyone.

That story made me understand the power of food and community, of sharing, of being clever and resourceful—and of making the whole process fun. And, of course, of having the right ingredients in the cupboard!

As for equipment, you will want to invest in a couple of good kitchen knives, such as a paring knife and an 8-inch chef's knife, as well as a steel to keep them sharp. (Make sure you learn how to use it.) What a difference you will find, not only in the ease of cutting and chopping, but also in the look of what you're cutting. It will be much cleaner and less ragged than the work of a dull blade. An extra electric coffee grinder is great for grinding spices. And though I'm not much of a gadget person, I like having my blender, food processor, and heavy-duty electric mixer around when I need them. There's not much you can't do with that lineup.

I would also encourage you to think more about *technique* than *recipes*. Use your powers of observation and your senses (including common sense) to notice how the food cooks and how the ingredients come together when you go through the steps of a recipe. Then apply this awareness to other dishes. But most important, try to relax and enjoy the process as much as the end result.

I have always been drawn to bold and faraway flavors, so I have always been a proponent of a well-stocked larder, with an assortment of sauces, spices, and pastes that allow me to make dishes more interesting in a flash. Had that soldier found his way to my town, I would have swirled in a spoonful or two of *sambal oelek,* a spicy red chile paste, for a sassy and complex result.

The following is a suggested list of staples and flavor makers that I rely on. They are certainly not all essential. But the more variety you have, the easier life will be when you need a little inspiration . . .

ASIAN SAUCES Varieties are hoisin, plum, oyster, and sweet chili sauce (sold in a large clear bottle). Hoisin and plum sauces make quick and easy glazes for fish, chicken, or veggies, such as eggplant. They are usually very sweet and benefit from the addition of a little rice wine vinegar or lime juice. Sweet chili sauce is great straight from the bottle as a dipping sauce for tempura or fritters, although it's even better with some lime juice, cilantro, and scallion.

BUTTER I always use unsalted. Like most chefs, I'm a control freak, and I want to control the amount of salt I put in a dish. Also, unsalted butter tends to taste fresher and sweeter. If you want to splurge on a European or European-style butter (which has a higher butterfat content that delivers a richer flavor and texture), use it for finishing sauces, in mashed potatoes, or in baking. For the freshest possible option, seek out butter from a local dairy if possible. I also like to use clarified butter for sautéing because it has a higher smoke point. To make clarified butter, melt a pound of butter in a small saucepan over low heat, skimming any foam that rises to the top. The milky water will sink to the bottom of the pan and the golden (clarified) butter will remain on top. I like to pour the clarified butter into a tall, clear container, because it makes it easier to see (and skim) any remaining solids that rise to the top after the heating process. I always clarify butter a pound at a time, because it lasts forever in the fridge.

CANNED TOMATOES   These can be whole tomatoes in juice, crushed, or pureed. My favorites are from the San Marzano region of Italy and are readily available. Essential for quick tomato basil sauces, soups, and stews.

CAPERS, ANCHOVIES, OLIVES, AND HORSERADISH   These provide big flavors for instant pasta dishes, jazzing up tuna salad, flavoring mayos, and more.

CHUTNEYS, RELISHES, SALSAS, PICKLES   These are essential because you can use them to add sweet and spicy flavors to so many things. I'm never without Major Grey's chutney (for a curried chicken sandwich), New Orleans's famous olive salad, pickled jalapeños, and Indian lime pickle (try a little dab with the curried crayfish turnovers).

CURRY PASTE   Try Patak's Indian and Thai red and/or green. A spoonful of one of these can add instant flavor complexity to any number of sauces or creamy condiments. I call for the warm, subtle spice of Indian curry paste in dishes like my Crayfish and Curried Cream Cheese Turnovers. Thai curry pastes and a can of unsweetened coconut milk make a super-easy chicken or shrimp curry with jasmine rice and scallions (or a vegetable curry with eggplant, mushrooms, and other vegetables).

DRIED FRUIT   These include raisins, cherries, apricots, figs, sweetened cranberries. Keep just a few varieties on hand to make grain salads, chutneys, cookies, and pan sauces more interesting.

FLOUR   Unless specified, assume I mean all-purpose unbleached.

HONEY   Choose a good basic variety and then one or two specialty flavors, like lavender, thyme, or chestnut. Beyond tea and biscuits, I use honey to give sweetness (without the grittiness of sugar), flavor, and body to numerous salad dressings, marinades, and sauces.

HOT SAUCE   It's no secret that hot sauce is a staple in New Orleans kitchens. It remains one of the most popular souvenirs from the Quarter. Crystal or Louisiana, two of my favorite brands, can be used as an ingredient during the cooking process or as a seasoning at the end. I think Tabasco is more intense, and best reserved for finishing a dish. Most hot sauces strike a balance between chile flavor, vinegar, and heat, so in the end it's a personal question of which flavors you prefer.

CRABMEAT

CRABMEAT

Parsley Scraps

O LUMP CRABME

rst. red
Pepper

NET WT. 16 OZ (1LB)
PERISHABLE, KEEP REFR

BLEU
VIN.
9.3

PERISHABLE

Roasted
Ess Plant
10-5

JAMS AND JELLIES   I'm a huge fan of pepper jelly, which I use in signature duck recipes. But it's also great spooned over cream cheese and served with crackers—a quintessential southern hors d'oeuvre. I often use apple and other jellies to sweeten sauces. Apricot jam and red currant jelly are great for glazes on sweet or savory tarts. Lemon curd makes an easy dessert with crêpes. I've become addicted to Bauman's Tomato Butter (see Sources, p. 384), which has the texture of apple butter. Dark, slightly sweet, and clove-scented, it's delicious with bagels and cream cheese, or pork and meat loaf sandwiches.

KETCHUP, BARBECUE SAUCE, CHILI SAUCE   Slightly sweet and tomatoey, these sauces are essential for more than just French fries. I use ketchup for cocktail sauce, homemade barbecue sauce, and some Asian sauces. Prepared barbecue sauce (I like Stubb's) does wonders for leftover chicken, beef, or pork. I love chili sauce mixed with mayo and other flavorings as a dipping sauce for fritters.

MAYONNAISE   I use Hellman's when I don't make my own. The French don't call it a "mother sauce" for nothing. You can add just about anything to mayonnaise to create a perfect condiment for any grilled or roasted meat or even a platter of grilled vegetables. Try adding a spoonful of canned chipotle chile, with a squeeze of lime and a touch of garlic, for a spicy spread for burgers. Or swirl in delicate herbs such as tarragon and dill with lemon zest for a topping for fish. There's no limit to what you can do with mayo and many of the condiments on this list.

MUSTARD   When I was a kid, I used to love yellow mustard sandwiches on white bread. I think I may have eaten one too many, because I don't really use it anymore. In my pantry at home and at the restaurant I stock several, such as Dijon, Creole (a mustard flavored with horseradish), and spicy brown, such as Gulden's. There are myriad flavors out there, so have fun picking your own (my absolute favorites are the gourmet mustards from Fauchon, www .fauchon.com). Good mustards are essential for creating classic vinaigrettes, bold sandwiches (Chip loves jalapeño mustard with salami), and more vibrant pan sauces when whisked with pan drippings, water, and stock. Mustards can also replace sauce—I love a spoonful next to steak, lamb, or pork.

NUTS   Look for pecans, walnuts, pistachios, peanuts, pine nuts, hazelnuts, pumpkin seeds. Buy in small amounts and store in the freezer to keep them fresh (they'll last up to six months). These are pesto and baking staples, but I also sprinkle nuts on salads and grind them as a coating for fish.

OILS   Unlike some chefs, I don't use extra-virgin olive oil for everything. I find its flavor too intense for many dishes. Instead, I tend to go with "pure" olive oil, which has a milder taste and is more versatile. I use it for cooking, in mayonnaise, and in most vinaigrettes. Reserve the more expensive, good-quality extra-virgin olive oil (and use it in smaller quantities) for finishing dressings and sauces, or for drizzling on pasta or bread. Unless I call for extra-virgin, assume that "pure" will suffice. I use vegetable oils, such as canola, peanut, or corn, for frying. For added flavor, I rely on sesame oil, and nut oils (walnut, hazelnut) for Asian dressings and vinaigrettes (particularly in salads that call for nuts). These are quite intense, so start with just a couple of drops and add more as you like.

PEPPER   I use freshly ground black pepper. I never got into the habit of using white, though some chefs swear by it for things like béchamel, seafood, and cream soups. I focus more on freshness (buy from a reliable source that has a high turnover) than fancy varieties, but I most often use Tellicherry, because it has a wonderful perfume. Use any pepper mill that you're comfortable with and gets the job done. Crushed red pepper flakes are never far from reach for a quick hit of heat.

RED CHILE PASTE   I love the clean, intense flavor of red chile pastes and stir them into all sorts of curries, stir-fries, pasta, and soups. Red chile paste provides the heat of small fresh Thai chiles, which are hard to find, tricky to handle, and don't last nearly as long. *Sambal oelek* is my favorite variety. I use it in many Asian dishes, such as Vietnamese *nuoc cham* dipping sauce (with sugar, fish sauce, and lime). *Sriracha* is a puree, almost like spicy ketchup. For staff meals at the restaurant, we squeeze it onto just about everything, including meat pies, fried rice, and roast chicken and pork. *Harissa* can be purchased in a tube. I use it more for Mediterranean preparations, such as couscous broth or rouille, a spicy mayonnaise.

SALT   Kosher salt is the workhorse in my kitchen. When I call for salt in my recipes, that's the variety I reach for. I also love slightly crunchy sea salts, like Maldon and *fleur de sel* and *sel gris*. They are great for both quickly sautéed or slow-simmered fish dishes, and as a garnish on ripe tomatoes or spicy radishes with a dot of butter.

SOY SAUCE   Japanese is a given, and I think Kikkoman has the deepest, truest flavor. I also love a sweeter Indonesian soy sauce called *ketjap manis*. My favorite brand is Conimex (see Sources, p. 384), which my family has used for forty years. If you can't find it, you can make your own by sweetening soy sauce with molasses. Basically, the ratio is for every tablespoon of *ketjap manis,* substitute 2 teaspoons soy sauce plus 1 teaspoon unsulfured molasses.

STOCKS AND FLAVORFUL COOKING LIQUIDS   I store one- and two-cup containers of vegetable, chicken, beef, and fish stock (preferably homemade or a purchased organic brand) in the freezer so I always have them on hand. I love coconut milk, white and red wines, and fruit juices, such as apple cider or carrot juice (available frozen at most health food stores), for adding flavor layers to sauces.

TAHINI   This is for my Fast and Foolproof Lemon-Tahini Sauce and for hummus—two things I crave nearly all the time.

VINEGAR   My basics include apple cider, white and red wine, sherry wine (my favorite), balsamic, and rice wine. I love fruit vinegars such as raspberry, pear, and cherry. Specific grape varietals, like champagne, muscat, and chardonnay, also add intrigue and are fun to use when you want to add a particular nuance to sauces and dressings. For instance, drizzle some reduced, syrupy balsamic vinegar or muscat vinegar around roasted figs and prosciutto.

———————————

Let's Get the Party Started

Appetizers

Artichoke Dolmades

Cajun-spiced Pecans

Mykonos Taramasalata

Classic N'Awlins Shrimp Boil

Ashley's Pickled Shrimp

Spanish-style Shrimp with Smoked Paprika and Basil

Cornmeal-crusted Crayfish Pies

Slow-scrambled Eggs with Potatoes, Mushrooms, and Bacon

Bahamian Conch Fritters with Cat Island Cocktail Sauce

Smoked Salmon Beignets with Brandied Tomato Sauce

Asparagus Flan with Smoked Salmon–Potato Salad

Crabmeat Gratin with Mushrooms and Artichokes

Oyster, Eggplant, and Tasso Gratin

Poached Oysters with Leeks and Bacon

Pork Quesadillas with Ancho-Mango Sauce

Seared Scallops with Spinach, Bacon, and Tomatoes

Portobello Mushrooms Stuffed with Italian Sausage

Indonesian Pork Satés with Spicy Peanut Sauce

Pork and Shrimp Pot Stickers with Chile-Lime Dipping Sauce

Layered Crêpe Gâteau with Prosciutto, Ham, and Cheese

Peppered Tuna with Asian Guacamole and Hoisin Dipping Sauce

Spicy Shrimp with Tasso Cream and Green Chile Grit Cakes

Bayou "Chicken Wings" with Fines Herbes Butter

Goat Cheese Croutons with Wild Mushrooms in Madeira Cream

Grilled Shrimp with Black Bean Cakes and Coriander Sauce

Crayfish and Curried Cream Cheese Turnovers

Smoked Duck Hash in Puff Pastry with Apple Cider Sauce

In New Orleans, any time you get more than three people together it's a party—and a party in New Orleans means food and lots of it. As far as I'm concerned, appetizers are the most fun, both to eat and to put together. In small dishes, it's easier to work with intense flavors and textures that might be overwhelming as a main course. My appetizers tend to layer several different tastes and textures—I'm crazy for crispy, crunchy bites paired with creamy dips and fillings. The collection in this chapter represents a vast range of the things I love to eat. The dishes are sexy and eclectic, and they span the globe. What's more, your own supply of flavorful pantry staples will enable you to be more creative in a flash. There's something in this chapter for all tastes and skill levels, from Mykonos Taramasalata (p. 23)—a simple, silky puree of fish roe, lemon juice, and olive oil—to a Layered Crêpe Gâteau with Prosciutto, Ham, and Cheese (p. 61), which is fancier but absolutely irresistible and worth the effort.

I think it's fun to put together two small plates to make a full meal, like Crabmeat Gratin with Mushrooms and Artichokes (p. 42) and the Bayona Caesar with Arugula (p. 100).

Artichoke Dolmades with Lemon Sauce

MAKES 32 TO 34 STUFFED GRAPE LEAVES   PREP TIME: ABOUT 2 HOURS (INCLUDING 1 HOUR COOKING)

Don't let your opinion of dolmades, stuffed grape leaves, rest on the ubiquitous canned versions, which are tasty but forgettable. Take the time to make these and you'll be rewarded with a fragrant house and a satisfying savory snack for a party or simply for having on hand. Unlike most other versions I've had, this filling is brightly flavored and packed with aromatic ingredients—I add artichoke hearts, preserved lemon, and golden raisins. Pine nuts give these little guys a pleasing crunch, and I love the briny, herbal flavor that the grape leaves impart while they cook—this is the process that forms the sauce—in the lemony liquid.

RICE

1 tablespoon olive oil, plus more
   for greasing
¼ cup finely chopped celery
¼ cup finely chopped onion

2 cups white rice
1 bay leaf
½ teaspoon salt

In a medium saucepan with a tight-fitting lid, heat the olive oil over medium-high heat. Add the celery and onion and sweat for 5 minutes, stirring occasionally, until softened but not browned. Stir in the rice and add 2 cups water, bay leaf, and salt. Bring the rice to a boil, cover, reduce the heat to low, and cook for 15 minutes. Remove it from the heat, keep covered, and cool.

ARTICHOKE FILLING

½ cup golden raisins
3 tablespoons olive oil plus
   3 tablespoons extra-virgin olive oil
2 (14-ounce) cans artichoke hearts,
   drained and chopped
3 garlic cloves, minced
2 tablespoons finely diced Preserved
   Lemon (p. 194)
½ cup pine nuts, toasted and coarsely
   chopped

2 tablespoons fresh lemon juice,
   plus more to taste
3 tablespoons coarsely chopped
   fresh dill
3 tablespoons coarsely chopped
   fresh mint
½ teaspoon salt
¼ teaspoon crushed red pepper flakes
Rice

In a small bowl, cover the raisins with steaming hot water; soak them until plump, 5 to 10 minutes, and drain. Pat the raisins dry with paper towels and coarsely chop; set aside.

Heat the 3 tablespoons olive oil in a medium skillet over medium-high heat and add the artichokes. Stir and cook about 3 minutes, add the garlic, and cook 2 more minutes. Scrape the vegetables into a large bowl and add the diced lemon, pine nuts, lemon juice, dill, mint, salt, and red pepper, along with the raisins, extra-virgin olive oil, and the cooked rice. Stir with a spatula and taste for seasoning, adding lemon juice as needed.

TO ASSEMBLE

⅓ cup olive oil, plus more for greasing dish

16 ounces grape leaves from a jar or can, packed in brine

Artichoke filling

⅓ cup white wine

⅓ cup fresh lemon juice

Preheat the oven to 350°F. Grease a 13 × 9-inch baking dish with olive oil.

Drain the grape leaves in a colander. Place them in a medium saucepan, cover with fresh water, bring the water to a boil, then drain the leaves and cool. Take an individual leaf and spread it on a work surface, with the smoother, shiny side down and dull veined side facing up. The small stem should be pointing toward you; use a paring knife to trim it from the bottom of the leaf. Place a heaping tablespoon of filling about an inch above the bottom edge of the leaf. Fold the bottom edge over the filling and roll, egg-roll style, wrapping the sides of the leaf around the mixture starting approximately halfway up the leaf. The dolmades should be firm but not wrapped too tightly, as they will expand with further cooking.

Place the filled dolmades seam side down in the baking dish, arranged snugly together. Drizzle them with the olive oil, wine, lemon juice, and enough water to just cover. Place a weight, such as a plate or small casserole dish, on top (this will help submerge them in the liquid, which will finish cooking the rice). Cover the dish with foil or a lid and bake for 1 hour, or until the rice filling is completely cooked.

You can serve the dolmades hot or cold, but I like them best at room temperature. If you're not serving them immediately, let them cool completely, cover with plastic, and refrigerate for up to three days.

Cajun-spiced Pecans

MAKES 1 CUP   PREP TIME: 15 MINUTES

These lend a spicy bite to just about any green salad, particularly Crispy Smoked Quail Salad with Bourbon-Molasses Dressing (p. 127). But they're also a delicious snack to serve with any of the killer cocktails in the last chapter.

1 tablespoon butter

1 cup pecan halves (4 ounces)

2 tablespoons sugar

2 teaspoons Worcestershire sauce

¼ teaspoon salt

¼ teaspoon cayenne

Preheat the oven to 325°F.

In a medium skillet, melt the butter over medium heat. Add the pecans and remaining ingredients and toss to coat evenly. Spread the pecans on a baking sheet and bake for 7 to 10 minutes, until lightly toasted. Cool completely, then loosen from the baking sheet with a metal spatula. Store any leftovers in an airtight tin.

Mykonos Taramasalata

If you love mayonnaise as much as I do, you will love this silky Greek fish roe spread, since it's basically a salty, lemony mayonnaise made with coral-colored carp roe (also called tarama), which is available in most stores that sell Greek or Mediterranean products. It may sound unusual, but this aromatic puree is absolutely addictive. It's particularly satisfying with bone-dry white wine, Seasoned Pita Crisps (p. 89), and crunchy vegetables such as carrots, celery, and fennel. Or serve a creamy dollop with sliced smoked salmon on toast points. If you've never worked with tarama, you'll find it drier and more firmly packed than caviar, but it crumbles easily in a food processor.

4 ounces (½ cup) tarama, or
   carp roe
¼ small onion, minced
1 garlic clove, minced
6 tablespoons fresh lemon juice
   (about 2 medium lemons)

½ teaspoon paprika
2 cups olive oil
Hot sauce

Place the tarama, onion, garlic, lemon juice, and paprika in the bowl of a food processor and pulse for 30 seconds, until the tarama is crumbly and the ingredients are combined. With the motor running, slowly add the olive oil until all is incorporated and the mixture is the consistency of mayonnaise. Taste for seasoning, and add more lemon juice and hot sauce as desired.

Classic N'Awlins Shrimp Boil

No self-respecting resident of Louisiana will need this recipe! Everyone in this state has his or her own method (complete with secret ingredients—I know one guy who uses Tang, the powdered orange drink) for boiling shrimp, crab, and crayfish. For outsiders, here's a brief rundown of the basics.

Start with the freshest, sweetest shrimp available. I love to add spicy sausage and potatoes to the pot, but by all means, omit or add what you like (even Tang).

The peeling process may throw some people off, but that's part of the fun. This recipe calls for 2 pounds of shrimp, so you can get a feel for it before you move up to the more common 20-pound party batch. If you can get your hands on some crabs or crayfish, you will need to go a bit stronger on the seasoning and the cooking time, as those hard shells need more spice and more time to absorb the other flavors.

---

2 small bags "crab boil," *or*
    4 bay leaves
    1 teaspoon whole allspice
    10 whole cloves
    8 sprigs fresh thyme, or
       1 teaspoon dried
    2 tablespoons coriander seeds
    2 tablespoons mustard seeds
    1 teaspoon celery seeds
1 tablespoon salt
2 lemons, cut in half

1 tablespoon cayenne, or as much as
    you can stand
2 garlic bulbs, cut in half horizontally
1 onion, quartered
1 pound small potatoes, such as red
    bliss or Yukon gold
1 pound andouille sausage, sliced into
    8 pieces
2 pounds medium or large whole
    fresh shrimp

If you're not using the commercial crab boil, wrap the seasonings in cheese-cloth and use kitchen twine to secure the bundle. Place the spices, 1 gallon water, salt, lemons, cayenne, garlic, onion, and potatoes in a large pot (squeeze the lemons over the water as you throw them in), and bring to a boil. Reduce the heat and simmer at least 10–15 minutes, until the potatoes are just about cooked through. Return the heat to boiling and add the sausage and shrimp. Cook for 5–7 more minutes, until the shrimp are cooked through (they will turn bright pink).

Drain the pot carefully, to serve hot or at room temperature. Remove the cheesecloth bag and lemons, if desired, and then serve the shrimp, garlic, sausage, and potatoes in a large bowl, or just dump them out on a table covered with newspaper and get peeling! If you are using the shrimp for salad or another recipe, cool it completely, then peel and refrigerate until ready to use.

The easiest way to season boiled shrimp (and/or crabs and crayfish) is with purchased "crab boil" and plenty of salt, which creates the full flavor associated with a spicy boil. My favorite brands are Zatarain's and Rex, and they are widely available. Crab boil comes in three different forms: liquid, powder, and nifty net bags of whole spices, which is my choice at home. The liquid and powdered varieties tend to have additives, and while some people find them easier to use, I prefer the natural ingredients in the net bags.

Ashley's Pickled Shrimp

MAKES 4 TO 6 SERVINGS   PREP TIME: ABOUT I HOUR, PLUS MARINATING TIME

Who would have thought you could improve upon a good old-fashioned New Orleans shrimp boil? A former Bayona sous chef, Ashley Hykes, showed me it was possible. Serve these shrimp bathing in their colorful marinade in a pretty bowl, along with other appetizers, for a party, or serve them for lunch with deviled eggs, a big green salad, and some bread or croutons for soaking up the pleasingly tart juice perfumed with citrus and vinegar.

ASHLEY'S MARINADE

¼ cup fresh lemon juice

½ cup apple cider or red wine vinegar

2 teaspoons Dijon mustard

¼ cup sugar

1 garlic clove, minced

1 cup olive oil

½ teaspoon kosher salt

½ teaspoon freshly ground black pepper

1 large red onion, thinly sliced

3 tablespoons capers

2 bay leaves, preferably fresh

2 tablespoons chopped fresh flat-leaf parsley

Whisk everything together in a large bowl.

SHRIMP

1 lemon, quartered

1 bag crab boil (see page 25), *or*

    4 bay leaves

    1 tablespoon coriander seeds

    1 tablespoon mustard seeds

    1 teaspoon crushed red pepper flakes

    2 tablespoons kosher salt or coarse sea salt

2 pounds medium or large shrimp, peeled and deveined, leaving tails intact

Ashley's Marinade

Place a large pot containing about 1 gallon water over high heat. Squeeze the lemon quarters into the water, then drop them in. Add all the spices and seasonings and bring to a boil. Reduce the heat and simmer for about 5 minutes, then add the shrimp and return to the boil. Cook for 3–4 minutes, until the shrimp are cooked (they'll become opaque and the tails will turn bright pink). Drain the pot well and transfer the still-warm shrimp to the bowl of marinade. Marinate the shrimp for at least 15 minutes or store them, covered, in the refrigerator up to one day before serving.

Spanish-style Shrimp with Smoked Paprika and Basil

MAKES 4 APPETIZERS OR 2 ENTRÉES   PREP TIME: ABOUT 35 MINUTES

This recipe is based on the much-loved Spanish dish called *Gambas al Ajillo*, or shrimp with garlic. The basil is not a traditional ingredient, but I like how its fresh flavor pairs with the sweet, garlicky shrimp. Smoked Spanish paprika, or *pimentón*, has a unique flavor and is well worth tracking down. You can find it at most specialty food stores, or in Latin markets. It's typically much cheaper at the latter.

2 tablespoons olive oil

3 garlic cloves, thinly sliced

1 pound medium shrimp (21–25 count), peeled and deveined, heads kept intact

½ teaspoon crushed red pepper flakes

Salt

¼ cup dry sherry or white wine

½ teaspoon smoked Spanish paprika

2 tablespoons butter

1 tablespoon chopped fresh basil

Heat the oil in a wide skillet over medium-high heat until it's shimmering. Reduce the heat to low, add the garlic, and cook until light golden brown. Use a slotted spoon to remove the garlic from the oil; drain on paper towels.

Raise the heat to medium-high, add the shrimp and red pepper, and cook for 2–3 minutes, until the shrimp turn pink. Lightly salt the shrimp, then carefully add the sherry and paprika and mix well. Return the garlic to the pan, swirl in the butter, and cook 1 more minute, stirring. Add the basil, toss or stir to combine the ingredients, and taste to adjust seasonings. Serve immediately, preferably with good, crusty bread to sop up the warm sauce.

Cornmeal-crusted Crayfish Pies

MAKES 8 INDIVIDUAL PIES   PREP TIME: 1 HOUR 15 MINUTES, PLUS BAKING TIME

There's a reason Hank Williams was inspired to write and sing "Jambalaya and a crawfish pie and filé gumbo . . ." Crayfish (pronounced "craw-fish" in Louisiana) pies are a beloved New Orleans snack, and this recipe has more vibrant flavor than traditional versions. With a spicy, savory filling encased in slightly sweet cornmeal dough, these crispy little pies are a somewhat refined take on one of my favorite Jazz Fest treats. Serve them with plenty of cold beer.

CORNMEAL PIE CRUST

2½ cups all-purpose flour

¾ cup cornmeal

1 tablespoon sugar

1¼ teaspoons salt

½ pound (2 sticks) plus 1 tablespoon
    cold butter

⅜ cup sour cream

Place the flour, cornmeal, sugar, and salt in the bowl of a food processor. Pulse to combine. Add the butter in small pieces and pulse into the dry mix just until coarse pebbles form. Transfer the mixture to a large bowl. By hand, gradually work in the sour cream and ¼ cup ice water. The dough should be soft and pliable but not sticky. Adjust as necessary with flour or water. Chill the dough for at least 30 minutes (or up to a day in advance).

To prepare the pies, preheat the oven to 350°F. Divide the dough into 8 equal parts. Roll each part into a very thin (⅛-inch) round and drape it into a 4-ounce tart pan or individual gratin dish. Cover each shell with parchment paper or foil and fill with pie weights or dried beans. Place the pie shells on a baking sheet and bake for 10–12 minutes, until lightly golden. Remove the beans and parchment and bake 1–2 minutes longer. Don't let them color too much, because they will be baked again with the filling. Let them cool to room temperature.

CRAYFISH FILLING

1 tablespoon olive oil

1 tablespoon butter

½ medium onion, diced

1 celery stalk, diced

1 small green or red bell pepper, diced

½ fennel bulb, diced, optional

1 garlic clove, minced

3 scallions, sliced thin

3 tablespoons chopped fresh parsley

2 tablespoons flour

¾ cup Chicken Stock (p. 206) or
    Vegetable Stock (p. 204), or
    ½ cup stock and ¼ cup milk
    or cream

Zest and juice of 1 medium lemon
    (about 2 teaspoons zest and
    3 tablespoons juice)

½ teaspoon Worcestershire sauce

1 pound cooked and peeled crayfish
    tails, coarsely chopped

Salt and pepper

Hot sauce

Crispy bacon bits, diced pickled
    jalapeños, and sliced scallions, for
    garnish

Cornmeal Pie Crust

Heat the oil and butter in a large skillet over medium-high heat. Add the onion, celery, bell pepper, and fennel, if using, and sauté for about 5 minutes, until softened. Add the garlic, scallions, and parsley and cook for 2–3 minutes more. Sprinkle the vegetables with the flour and stir. Whisk in the stock, lemon zest and juice, and Worcestershire sauce. Add the crayfish and simmer for a few more minutes, until the crayfish is warm. Adjust the seasonings with salt, pepper, and hot sauce. Cool to room temperature or refrigerate until ready to make pies.

Fill each cooled shell with 3 ounces (about 6 tablespoons) of crayfish filling. Set them on a baking sheet and bake at 350°F until hot and bubbly, about 15 minutes. Serve warm or at room temperature.

Put your fear of pastry aside—this cornmeal pie dough is not sticky and is absolutely wonderful to work with. If you don't want to bother blind-baking pie shells you can simply prepare these as little turnovers. Roll each portion of dough into a 6-inch round, place a few tablespoons of filling on one half, fold the other side over the top, and crimp the edges together with a fork or your fingers. Brush them with egg wash, if you like, and bake at 350°F until golden, about 25–30 minutes, or deep-fry them—which is more traditional.

Louisiana Crayfish

I cook only with Louisiana crayfish—accept no substitutes! Frozen varieties are available from China, but they have no texture or flavor. That's because the fat that normally coats fresh crayfish does not freeze well (it tends to go rancid before the tail meat does), so it's rinsed off before freezing. But crayfish needs that fat to retain its sweet flavor. Your best bet is to choose a Louisiana source (see Sources, p. 384) whose crayfish are frozen close to the end of the January-to-June season. Better yet, buy a few pounds of fresh crayfish and freeze them yourself, but use them up within four weeks.

Slow-scrambled Eggs with Potatoes, Mushrooms, and Bacon

MAKES 4 SERVINGS   PREP TIME: ABOUT 40 MINUTES

For years, I would eat eggs only as an excuse to have bacon and hash browns. And then I made this discovery—the French method of slow cooking. The results of this technique are so good, I'd be perfectly happy to eat the eggs plain, without embellishment, but in this version I still get my potatoes and bacon. This dish requires patience: it's tempting to turn the heat up and finish the eggs quickly, but if you do, they will lose the creamy, custardy consistency that elevates this dish beyond breakfast. Try these eggs as a first course before something simple and light, such as a vegetable or chicken sauté, or grilled fish or beef. You can also serve them for brunch, with fresh fruit or a green salad.

POTATOES, MUSHROOMS, AND BACON

1 large potato, peeled and diced

Salt

2 strips thick-sliced bacon, diced

¼ pound button mushrooms, stemmed and quartered

Pepper

Put the potato dice in a small pot, cover with cold water, and add a pinch of salt. Bring it to a boil, then reduce the heat and simmer until cooked through but still firm, about 5 minutes. Drain and cool. In a medium skillet, cook the bacon until crispy. Remove it with tongs or a slotted spoon and drain on paper towels. Add the potatoes to the leftover bacon fat, and cook over medium heat until golden brown and crisp on all sides, about 7 minutes. Add the mushrooms, season with salt and pepper, and continue to cook until mushrooms are tender and lightly brown. Drain any excess fat from the pan and set it aside while you cook the eggs.

SLOW-SCRAMBLED EGGS

3 tablespoons butter

10 eggs

2 tablespoons heavy cream

Salt and pepper

Melt 1 tablespoon butter in a small, heavy-bottomed saucepan over medium-low heat. In a medium bowl, lightly beat the eggs and cream. Pour the eggs into the pan and stir with a wooden spoon or plastic spatula until they just begin to thicken, about 10 minutes.

At this point, lower the heat, add the remaining 2 tablespoons butter, season with salt and pepper, and continue to stir. Don't cheat—in order to make the eggs as creamy as possible, it's important to stir gently and continuously, and take your time. When the eggs begin to thicken, after about 5 minutes, remove the pot from the heat.

TO ASSEMBLE

4 individual brioche rolls, or 2 slices
good-quality bread, crusts
removed, sliced in half into
triangles

Potatoes, Mushrooms, and Bacon

Slow-Scrambled Eggs

Snipped fresh chives, for garnish

Warm the brioche or toast the bread lightly. Set the potato-mushroom mixture over medium heat, add the bacon, and warm thoroughly. Return the eggs to low heat and cook until they will just barely hold together and resemble a thick, creamy sauce, then spoon them over the brioche or toast. Spoon the potato mixture over or around the eggs and sprinkle with chives.

Truffles and eggs are a friendly, elegant combination and a great way to elevate this dish. If you're lucky enough to get hold of a fresh truffle, place it in a bowl with the whole eggs and cover tightly with plastic wrap. Refrigerate overnight, and the eggs will absorb the truffle aroma through their porous shells! (They absorb other smells too, which is why it's best to store them in their carton.) If you don't have a truffle, a drop or two of truffle oil at the end of cooking will do the trick.

Bahamian Conch Fritters
with Cat Island Cocktail Sauce

MAKES 24 TO 30 FRITTERS   PREP TIME: ABOUT 30 MINUTES, PLUS FRYING TIME

The summer before I started cooking professionally, a friend and I spent three months on a sailboat in the Bahamas. Hey, it was tougher than it sounds! Every day we had to catch our dinner with spears, no less. If we didn't get a fish or lobster, one thing we could always count on was finding conch. They were and are delicious, but man, are they labor-intensive, as it's hard to extract the meat from their shells. These fritters, which are easy enough to stir together on a sailboat and are served all over the Bahamas, are so delicious that we didn't (and you won't) much mind the work, especially as your conch meat will already be extracted from the shell. Serve them with ice-cold beer, plenty of hot sauce (or my Cat Island Cocktail Sauce), and a creamy Lime Mayonnaise (p. 181) that will help cool the fire. And don't be surprised if they inspire you to slip into a swimsuit and snorkel mask.

Vegetable oil, for frying (about 1 quart)

1 pound fresh or frozen conch meat, finely chopped

½ large onion, finely chopped

2 celery stalks, finely chopped

½ cup finely chopped green bell pepper

½ cup finely chopped red bell pepper

⅓ cup cornmeal

⅓ cup flour

1 egg

¼ cup buttermilk

Salt

Hot sauce

Heat 2 inches of oil in a deep skillet or fryer over medium heat until hot but not smoking, approximately 350°F.

Meanwhile, mix the conch with the onion, celery, and peppers in a medium bowl. Combine the cornmeal and flour and stir into the conch mixture. In the same bowl that you used for the flour, use a fork to mix the egg and buttermilk together, and stir into the conch-flour mixture. Season to taste with salt and hot sauce.

Working in batches and not overcrowding the pot, gently drop the batter by spoonfuls into the hot oil and cook 3–4 minutes, turning once, until golden brown and cooked through. Drain and serve immediately with Cat Island Cocktail Sauce, additional hot sauce, and/or Lime Mayonnaise (p. 181).

CAT ISLAND COCKTAIL SAUCE

1 mango, peeled, seeded, and diced

½ cup ketchup

Scotch bonnet–based hot sauce, such as Inner Beauty, as you dare

Place the diced mango and ketchup in a blender or food processor; puree until smooth. Add hot sauce to taste and pulse until smooth. You can also serve this feisty sauce with boiled Gulf shrimp, crisp-fried oysters, or scrambled eggs.

Feel free to substitute equal portions of shrimp or crayfish for the conch—the fritters will be just as tasty.

Smoked Salmon Beignets with Brandied Tomato Sauce

MAKES 24 BEIGNETS   PREP TIME: ABOUT 35 MINUTES

Here's one I stole from my friend, mentor, and sometimes tormentor from Louis XVI Restaurant, Daniel Bonnot. He taught me how to make these about twenty-five years ago. *Beignet* is essentially just a fancy French word for a fritter. In New Orleans, people have been known to subsist on beignets and coffee alone. This is not advisable. Feel free to substitute chopped crayfish tails for the smoked salmon—both versions are dangerously addictive.

2 cups flour

2 teaspoons baking powder

1½ cups soda water

½ pound smoked salmon (or crayfish tails), coarsely chopped

1 red bell pepper, diced

½ green bell pepper or poblano, diced

1 bunch scallions, chopped fine

1 garlic clove, minced

2 teaspoons grated lemon zest (about 1 medium lemon)

Salt

Hot sauce

Vegetable oil, for frying

Sift the flour and baking powder together and whisk in the soda water to make a smooth, thick paste. Stir in the salmon, peppers, scallions, garlic, and lemon zest. Add salt and hot sauce to taste. Let the batter rest 10 minutes.

Heat 1 inch of oil in a medium deep skillet over medium-high heat. Drop batter by spoonfuls into the preheated oil and cook, turning frequently, until golden brown, about 3 minutes. Drain the beignets on paper towels and serve with Brandied Tomato Sauce.

BRANDIED TOMATO SAUCE

1 cup mayonnaise, preferably
   homemade (p. 181)

2 tablespoons cream

¼ cup ketchup

1 tablespoon brandy

1 tablespoon chopped fresh tarragon
   or basil

Mix all the ingredients together in a small bowl. Serve immediately with hot beignets, or cover and chill until needed. This sauce will keep 2–3 days in the refrigerator.

Asparagus Flan
with Smoked Salmon–Potato Salad

MAKES 4 INDIVIDUAL (6-OUNCE) FLANS, OR 3 CUPS   PREP TIME: 1 HOUR

Flan is essentially custard—the creamy melding of milk and eggs in what has proved to be a delectable revelation: you can make a savory flan out of virtually any vegetable. We do several savory flans at my restaurants, including mushroom and carrot, but its delicate flavor and pale green color makes asparagus flan my hands-down favorite. A potato salad made with smoked salmon (which is great on its own for lunch or brunch) is a stylish partner, but you can easily serve this flan with toasted slices of French bread and Grana Padano (or your favorite cheese) and a simple green salad with tomatoes.

---

1 pound asparagus, trimmed of woody stem ends and coarsely chopped, reserving unchopped 1-inch tips to garnish the flans or add to the salad (see p. 40)

1 tablespoon butter, plus more for greasing ramekins

1 tablespoon finely chopped shallots

1½ cups heavy cream

1 cup milk, plus more if needed

3 egg yolks plus 1 whole egg

Salt and pepper

Pinch of freshly grated nutmeg

Blanch only the asparagus tips in a small saucepan of boiling salted water for 2–3 minutes, drain, and shock in ice water to stop the cooking process. Drain again and set aside. Melt the butter in a 2-quart saucepan over medium heat and add the shallots. Sauté for 2 minutes, until softened, then add the chopped asparagus stalks, cream, and milk and simmer gently over low heat for about 10 minutes, or until the asparagus pieces are quite tender. Remove them from the heat and cool about 10 minutes, then pour the mixture into a blender (in batches if necessary) and puree until smooth. Strain the asparagus cream through a fine sieve.

In a large mixing bowl, whisk the egg yolks and whole egg together until well mixed and just barely frothy. Slowly whisk in the asparagus cream and season with salt, pepper, and nutmeg.

Preheat the oven to 325°F.

Butter 4 individual ramekins (with sides about 2 inches high) and place them in a baking dish. Pour the asparagus mixture into the dishes, dividing equally. Carefully fill the baking dish with hot water until it comes halfway up the ramekins. Cover the baking dish with foil and bake in the water bath for about 30 minutes. Watching for steam, carefully open the foil and jiggle the pan to see if the flans are set. They should be firm around the outside but just barely set in the middle, with no bubbles. If they are still liquid in the middle, return to the oven and bake for another 5–10 minutes. Remove the flans from the oven, uncover, and set aside until ready to serve. These flans can be prepared up to 24 hours in advance, refrigerated, and gently reheated in a water bath.

This recipe will result in a pale green flan. To brighten the color, you can add ¼ cup blanched, finely chopped spinach or 2 tablespoons fresh parsley to the cream the minute before you remove it from the heat. Proceed to blend the mixture as described above, and the result will be a delightful emerald green flan.

Smoked Salmon–Potato Salad

MAKES 4 SERVINGS   PREP TIME: 30 MINUTES

2–3 medium potatoes, such as Yukon gold, peeled and diced (about 1 large cup)

Salt

1 tablespoon finely chopped shallots

2 tablespoons white wine vinegar or apple cider vinegar

6 tablespoons olive oil

3 tablespoons finely chopped celery

2 tablespoons finely chopped red onion

¼ cup Classic Croutons (p. 88)

¾ cup diced smoked salmon or gravlax

Freshly ground pepper

2 slices bacon, fried until very crisp, crumbled (about 2–3 tablespoons), optional

Asparagus tips, for garnish

Put the potatoes in a small pot, cover with cold water, add a sprinkling of salt, and bring to a boil. Reduce the heat and simmer until cooked through but still firm, about 5 minutes. Drain and cool.

Whisk the shallots, vinegar, and olive oil together in a small bowl. In a large bowl, mix the potatoes, celery, onion, croutons, and salmon. Stir in half the dressing, season with salt and pepper, toss, and add more dressing to desired taste. Add the bacon and toss again. To serve, divide the salad among four plates. Place one warm flan on each plate. Place two asparagus tips on top of each flan and add the rest to the salad.

Making Gravlax

Gravlax is surprisingly easy to make at home, and you can vary the herbs or add spices to suit your taste. Once you become comfortable with the process, you'll want to have this around for easy lunches and snacks.

1 (16-ounce) section of salmon fillet, cut from middle, skin on
1 cup kosher salt
¼ cup brown sugar
1 tablespoon coarsely ground pepper
¼ cup chopped fresh herbs (any combination of dill, tarragon, chervil, and basil)
Grated zest of 1 medium lemon (about 2 teaspoons)

Place the salmon on a plate. Use tweezers, pincers, or needle-nose pliers to remove visible bones. Mix all the remaining ingredients together and gently pack onto the fish. Wrap the fish in plastic wrap and refrigerate at least 8 hours, or up to 12 hours. Brush off the salt mixture, lightly rinse the fish, and pat dry with paper towels. Dry the salmon in the refrigerator, uncovered, overnight. To serve, cut the salmon into thin slices. Wrapped in plastic, the uncut salmon will last up to 5 days refrigerated. Slices will oxidize quicker—they should be eaten in 1 to 2 days.

Crabmeat Gratin
with Mushrooms and Artichokes

MAKES 4 TO 6 SERVINGS   PREP TIME: 40 MINUTES

You can't come to the French Quarter without being seduced by a rich, bubbling crabmeat gratin. This is my take on the traditional New Orleans dish—it's luxurious and surprisingly simple to prepare. For the most elegant presentation, serve this in individual gratin dishes as a lunch or a first course for a special meal. This gratin gets added flavor and crunch from the topping, a Spicer staple.

CHEESY BREAD CRUMB TOPPING

½ cup dry bread crumbs	2 tablespoons olive oil
2 tablespoons chopped parsley	¼ cup grated Grana Padano or
1 tablespoon butter, melted	Parmesan cheese

Combine all the ingredients in a small bowl and set aside.

Be sure to pick over the lump crabmeat (even if it's labeled as "pre-cleaned") before you begin cooking. Warming the meat is an important step, because any remaining shells will turn a bright, chalky white and be easy to see. Buying lump crabmeat is a luxury, after all, so you'll be glad you took the time to make the most of your splurge.

CRABMEAT GRATIN

1 tablespoon butter, plus more for
    buttering dishes

½ cup finely chopped onion

¼ cup finely chopped red or green
    bell pepper

¼ cup finely chopped celery

1 (14-ounce) can artichoke hearts,
    drained and chopped, or 2 fresh
    artichoke bottoms, cooked until
    tender and diced (see cleaning
    artichokes, p. 300)

1 garlic clove, minced

2 tablespoons flour

1 tablespoon sherry or brandy,
    optional

¾ cup milk

½ cup cream

Salt and pepper

Hot sauce

1 tablespoon Dijon mustard

1 teaspoon minced fresh tarragon

2 tablespoons fresh lemon juice

1 teaspoon finely grated lemon zest

1 tablespoon olive oil

¼ pound button mushrooms, thinly
    sliced

1 pound best-quality cooked
    crabmeat (lump, jumbo lump, or a
    combination of lump and claw)

¼ cup finely chopped scallions

Preheat the oven to 400°F and butter 4 individual ramekins or a 1-quart baking dish.

Melt the 1 tablespoon butter in a large skillet over medium-high heat. When it begins to bubble, add the onion, peppers, celery, artichokes, and garlic and sauté for about 3 minutes, stirring. When the vegetables have wilted and are just barely beginning to color, sprinkle in the flour and stir. Cook 2 minutes more, then whisk in the sherry and milk. Bring to a boil, whisking as it thickens. If the mixture becomes too thick (if it seizes up and pulls away from the side), add a little more milk to loosen.

After about 2 minutes, add the cream and bring the mixture back to a boil, whisking the entire time. Lower the heat and simmer for about 5 minutes more, until the mixture is smooth and any raw flour taste is gone. Season to taste with salt, pepper, and hot sauce, then stir in the mustard, tarragon, lemon juice, and lemon zest. Remove from heat and set aside.

Heat the olive oil in a medium sauté pan over medium-high heat and sauté the mushrooms until golden brown. Add the mushrooms to the cream sauce. Put the crabmeat in the mushroom sauté pan and heat until it is warmed through and the liquid has evaporated, about 2 minutes. Take one last look for shells at this point. Add scallions to the crabmeat mixture and stir, then remove from heat. Fold the crabmeat into the cream sauce. Taste and adjust seasonings—it may need more lemon juice.

Divide the mixture among ramekins or pour it into the baking dish. Sprinkle with the topping and bake for 6–8 minutes, until browned and bubbly. Serve immediately.

Oyster, Eggplant, and Tasso Gratin

MAKES 4 SERVINGS   PREP TIME: 35 MINUTES

If you're not from Crescent City, this dish might seem like an unlikely trio of ingredients, but it's my twist on a much-loved Louisiana combination. In New Orleans, we tend to serve oysters with just about anything—especially if there is beer and hot sauce involved. When I'm traveling, or asked to bring New Orleans–style food to other parts of the world, tasso is one of the things I smuggle. Tasso is another Cajun staple—cured, smoked pork (usually the shoulder), seasoned with red pepper, garlic, and various spices and herbs. Tasso is typically vacuum-packed, so it doesn't spoil easily. Since the flavor is intense, it's used more as a seasoning. In other words, 3 pounds of tasso provide the same mileage as 10 pounds of andouille—which I'm not willing to schlep. (So far I've managed to infiltrate France, Thailand, and England with tasso discreetly nestled in my luggage—and the authorities were none the wiser.)

I'm an eggplant freak, and I can eat it any way, anytime. I have yet to find an eggplant dish that I don't like—unless it's one that's undercooked. Eggplant is a great flavor carrier that stands up well to other ingredients. But you can also make this recipe by substituting sautéed spinach or fennel for the eggplant. A gratin is a nifty appetizer because it can be assembled in advance and requires very little last-minute prep.

2 tablespoons butter, plus more for
    buttering
Cheesy Bread Crumb Topping
    (p. 42)
1 pint shucked oysters with liquor
2 tablespoons flour
½ cup chicken broth or milk
½ cup cream
Salt and pepper
Hot sauce
Freshly grated nutmeg

¼ cup olive oil
1 medium to large eggplant, peeled
    and diced (about 2 cups)
1 medium onion, chopped
2 ounces finely chopped tasso (about
    3 tablespoons) (see p. 384)
1 garlic clove, minced
1 teaspoon each chopped fresh sage
    and rosemary (for rosemary you
    may substitute ¼ teaspoon dried
    rosemary)

Preheat the oven to 400°F. Butter a 2-quart baking dish or pie pan, or 4–6 individual ramekins.

Make the Cheesy Bread Crumb Topping.

Pour the oysters into a bowl and check for bits of shell. Drain them and reserve the liquid (known as oyster "liquor"). Strain the liquor through a fine sieve and set aside.

Melt the butter in a small saucepan over low heat and whisk in the flour, then add the reserved oyster liquor and broth or milk. Whisking constantly, bring the mixture to a boil. Whisk in the cream, then reduce the heat and simmer gently for about 10 minutes, stirring from time to time. Season the sauce with salt, pepper, hot sauce, and a pinch of freshly grated nutmeg. Remove it from the heat; cover to keep warm.

Heat the olive oil in a medium skillet over medium-high heat. Add the eggplant and cook for about 5 minutes, stirring as needed, until lightly browned. Add the onion, tasso, and garlic and stir in the herbs. Cook for an additional 5–7 minutes, until the eggplant is tender and cooked through. Season with salt and pepper and transfer it to a colander for 5 minutes to drain excess oil.

Divide the eggplant mixture among the prepared ramekins or spread into the baking dish. Place the oysters in one layer on top. Drizzle evenly with the sauce and sprinkle on the topping. Bake for 10 minutes, until golden brown and bubbly.

Poached Oysters with Leeks and Bacon

MAKES 4 SERVINGS   PREP TIME: 45 MINUTES

This sumptuous appetizer stars oysters in an elegant and creamy guise. The oyster mixture spills over the sides of a thick triangle of toasted, buttered bread, and the whole thing is topped off with smoky bacon and snipped chives. The flavors of this dish are great with champagne and have a holiday feel, but it's delicious anytime you can get great oysters. You could also toss the warm sauté with bow tie pasta for a decidedly rich Sunday supper.

2 strips thick-sliced bacon (preferably applewood-smoked), diced

¼ cup white wine or vermouth

1 pint shucked oysters, drained and rinsed

1 tablespoon butter, plus softened butter for spreading

¼ cup finely chopped onion

¼ cup finely chopped celery

2–3 leeks, washed and thinly sliced (about 1 cup) (see technique for cleaning leeks, p. 109)

2 tablespoons flour

¼ cup milk

½ cup cream

½ teaspoon chopped fresh thyme or sage

1 tablespoon fresh lemon juice

Salt and pepper

Hot sauce

4 thick slices (½ inch) good-quality white bread or brioche, halved into triangles

Minced scallions or snipped fresh chives, for garnish

In a large skillet, cook the bacon until crispy. Transfer it to a plate topped with paper towels, then drain the skillet of all but 1 tablespoon fat; set the skillet aside.

Heat the white wine in a medium skillet over medium-high heat. When it starts to simmer, add the oysters and poach just until the edges start to curl, about 4 minutes (reduce the heat if the simmer gets too lively). Drain the oysters in a fine colander placed over a large bowl, reserving the poaching liquid.

Reheat the skillet with bacon fat over medium-high heat and add the 1 tablespoon butter. When the foaming subsides, add the onion, celery, and leeks and cook until fragrant and softened, 3–4 minutes. Sprinkle the vegetables with flour, then whisk in the reserved oyster poaching liquid. Simmer over medium heat, continuously whisking, for 3 minutes. Add the milk, cream, and herb and bring to a boil. Reduce the heat and simmer gently until thickened and creamy, about 5 minutes. Add the lemon juice and salt, pepper, and hot sauce to taste.

When the sauce is thick enough to coat a spoon, remove it from the heat and keep warm. Toast the bread; spread with softened butter and place it on a platter or individual plates. Stir the oysters into the sauce and warm through, over low heat. To serve, spoon the oysters over the toast and sprinkle with bacon. Top with green onions or chives, if desired.

Louisiana Oysters

I've eaten oysters all over the world. When it comes to slurping them raw, from the half shell, I love oysters from the Pacific (like the Japanese varieties), because they taste briny, like the ocean. But when it comes to cooking, nothing beats Louisiana oysters. They come from the brackish waters where the salt water of the Gulf mingles with the fresh water of the bayou and rivers, so they have a milder flavor that blends better with other ingredients. Because Louisiana oysters are larger, they're less likely to overcook in a poaching pan. I may be biased, but I definitely think they're the most versatile oysters in the kitchen. For my favorite sources, see p. 384.

Pork Quesadillas with Ancho-Mango Sauce

MAKES 4 SERVINGS   PREP TIME: 15 MINUTES (NOT INCLUDING ROASTING PORK)

Loaded with onions and peppers and cheese, these substantial quesadillas have a lot of personality—and make great use of leftover Jalapeño-roast Pork (p. 269). Serve them with margaritas for an instant party, or simply add a green salad with orange segments and red onions for an easy week-night meal. The Ancho-Mango sauce keeps well for several days, and it will perk up any number of sandwiches.

1 tablespoon olive oil

1 small red onion, thinly sliced

1 poblano pepper, seeded and thinly sliced

1 cup shredded cheese, such as white cheddar, pepper Jack, or *queso blanco*

12–16 ounces Jalapeño-roast Pork (p. 269) or other cooked pork, shredded (about 1¾ cups)

16 flour tortillas

Olive oil or butter, for frying

1 ripe Hass avocado, diced and seasoned with salt and lime juice, optional

1 cup chopped cilantro, optional

Heat the olive oil in a medium skillet over medium-high heat, then add the onion and poblano. Cook, stirring, until the vegetables are wilted, 2–3 minutes. Remove from heat and cool. Place some of the cheese, onion-pepper mixture, and pork on each tortilla and fold over into a half-circle. Heat a little oil or butter in a medium skillet, add one or two quesadillas, and brown on both sides. You may want to cover the cooked quesadillas with foil and keep them in a warm oven while you finish cooking the others.

To serve, drizzle Ancho-Mango Sauce around the quesadillas (or serve it in ramekins on the side) and garnish with avocado and cilantro.

ANCHO-MANGO SAUCE

1 small dried ancho chile

1 ripe mango, peeled, seeded, and
   diced

Juice of 1 lime (about 2 tablespoons)

1 tablespoon honey

½ bunch cilantro leaves and tender
   stems, chopped (about ¼ cup)

Pinch of salt

Heat the ancho chile in a small, dry skillet over medium-high heat for a minute or two on each side, until puffed and fragrant. Place it in a small bowl of hot water for 5 minutes, then remove the stem and seeds, and tear or cut the chile into pieces. Place the chile and all the remaining ingredients in a blender and puree. If necessary, add a little water to make a smooth puree. Taste, and adjust the flavor with a little more lime or honey if you like.

Seared Scallops
with Spinach, Bacon, and Tomatoes

MAKES 4 SERVINGS   PREP TIME: 20 MINUTES

When I was little, my mom used to deep-fry tiny bay scallops and serve them with melted butter. One time I ate so many that I made myself sick. It was years before I could try another scallop! These days I like to serve large sea scallops, which are easy to sear and make for a beautiful presentation. What's more, their rich, sweet taste marries well with so many ingredients that sometimes it's hard to decide what to serve alongside. Here, I've paired them with spinach, bacon, and tomatoes for a quick one-skillet sauté that's bright and festive. The bacon can be omitted, but let's face it: everything is better with bacon, and here its rich, salty flavor is a nice foil for the sweet scallops. I recommend a nonstick pan, as the juices sometimes get a little syrupy and sticky.

2 strips thick-sliced bacon, preferably applewood-smoked, diced

¾ pound sea scallops (dry pack, not treated with preservatives), trimmed of tough opaque muscle

Salt and pepper

2 tablespoons extra-virgin olive oil

4 cups cleaned fresh spinach

1 garlic clove, minced

1 cup cherry tomatoes, halved, or 1 cup whole currant or grape tomatoes

1 tablespoon minced shallots

2 tablespoons vinegar, such as apple cider, sherry wine, or red wine

1 tablespoon butter

Preheat the oven to 200°F and place a large serving platter in the oven to warm.

Cook the bacon in a large nonstick skillet over medium heat, stirring occasionally, until brown and crisp. Using tongs or a slotted spoon, remove the bacon from the skillet and drain on paper towels. Pour the rendered fat into a small dish and set aside.

Rinse the scallops and pat dry with paper towels. Season them lightly with salt and pepper on one side. Return the skillet to the stove, over high heat. When it is smoking, pour in the olive oil, then sear the scallops, seasoned side down, for 2–3 minutes, until crusty and light brown. Using a spatula, turn and sear them on the other side for a minute, then remove the scallops from the pan and cover them with foil to keep warm.

Return the skillet to the stove, heat for 1 minute, then add the spinach and garlic and a pinch of salt; stir with tongs or a spatula. When the spinach is wilted, remove it from the pan and pour off the excess liquid. Add the tomatoes and shallots to the pan and cook for 2 minutes. Add the vinegar and bring to a boil. Whisk in the butter and 1 tablespoon of the bacon fat and taste for seasoning.

To serve, place the spinach in the middle of the warmed platter. Using tongs, arrange the scallops and tomatoes around the spinach and drizzle with the warm sauce. Garnish with the bacon.

Be sure to look for "dry pack" or "untreated" scallops. This refers to scallops that have not been dipped in preservatives, which make them absorb water and give them an unnatural, soapy flavor. Once you taste the difference, you'll never go back to the treated version.

Portobello Mushrooms Stuffed with Italian Sausage

MAKES 4 SERVINGS   PREP TIME: 45 MINUTES

When I first started cooking professionally in 1979, even getting fresh button mushrooms was exciting. These days, portobello mushrooms, and any number of other exotic varieties, are practically an everyday item. When it comes to portobellos (which, mercifully, have remained fairly inexpensive), you can buy just the caps, but I like to buy whole mushrooms so I can use the stems to "beef up" the stuffing. Any favorite stuffing recipe will work here, but this spicy Italian sausage mixture is my favorite because it provides the perfect counterbalance to the earthiness of the mushrooms.

Serve this with a simple tomato sauce, lemon butter, or just a drizzle of good balsamic vinegar. Sautéed broccoli rabe and a twirl of angel hair pasta turn it into a complete meal. Bring on the chianti!

PORTOBELLO MUSHROOMS

2 tablespoons olive oil

1 tablespoon balsamic vinegar

1 garlic clove, minced

1 sprig fresh rosemary, lightly
    chopped, or ½ teaspoon dried

4 large portobello mushrooms, stems
    removed and set aside

Salt

Preheat the oven to 400°F.

In a small bowl, whisk together the olive oil, vinegar, garlic, and rosemary. Wipe the top of the portobello caps with a damp cloth or paper towel. Using a spoon or paring knife, scrape the gills from the mushrooms (see p. 55). Using a pastry brush, brush both sides of the mushrooms with the marinade. Salt them lightly and bake, gill side up, for about 5 minutes, or just until they start to wilt. Set aside.

ITALIAN SAUSAGE STUFFING

½ pound spicy Italian sausage,
  removed from casing

2 tablespoons olive oil

1 medium yellow onion, chopped

1 red bell pepper, stemmed, seeded,
  and chopped

Reserved portobello stems, cut in
  ¼-inch dice, optional

1 medium zucchini, grated

1 egg, lightly beaten

¼ cup dry bread crumbs

½ cup fresh ricotta cheese, optional

2 tablespoons lightly chopped fresh
  parsley and/or fresh basil

Salt and pepper

¼ cup grated Parmesan or Grana
  Padano cheese

Cook the sausage in a medium skillet over medium-high heat, stirring, until no longer pink. Remove from the heat, drain, and place in a medium bowl. When it is cool, break up the sausage with your fingers. Return the pan to the heat and pour in the olive oil; swirl to coat the bottom. Add the onion, pepper, and portobello stems and cook, stirring, over medium-high heat for about 5 minutes, until wilted. Add the zucchini and stir to combine. Cook another 3–5 minutes, until the zucchini has released its liquid. Transfer the vegetables to the bowl with the sausage. Stir the mixture and let it cool for 5 minutes, then add the egg, bread crumbs, optional ricotta, and herbs, and season with salt and pepper. Mound the filling onto the portobello caps and top with grated cheese. Place them in a baking dish and bake immediately, or cover with plastic wrap and refrigerate up to several hours.

When ready to serve, bake at 400°F for 10–12 minutes (20 minutes if the mushrooms have been chilled), until the filling is heated through and the cheese is golden brown.

Cleaning Portobellos

I love portobellos, but a pet peeve of mine is the way the gills tend to bleed when they cook, making everything dark and muddy-looking. I avoid this by getting rid of the gills altogether. Hold the mushroom, gill side up, and scrape the gills off with a spoon or paring knife held parallel to the mushroom surface. It's best to do this over a bowl or the trash, as it is a messy operation. Then proceed to use the mushroom in whatever way the recipe calls for. It's an extra step, but to me it's worth it.

Indonesian Pork Satés with Spicy Peanut Sauce

MAKES 4 SERVINGS   PREP TIME: 30–40 MINUTES

My mother learned this dish when we lived in Holland in the late '50s. It was part of the *rijstafel*—an Indonesian take-out feast of many dishes—that my parents used to have delivered to the house. We used to watch wide-eyed as a flurry of delivery guys carried in dish after dish stacked in round metal containers. When we gather as a family on Christmas and other special days, we rarely have turkey or ham, but more often rice and curry or *bami goreng,* a noodle dish, with these satés as an appetizer. It is still the favorite family snack. The pork marinade is effortless to put together. While the meat absorbs the flavors, you can stir together the spicy peanut sauce. I tend to grill the satés, but my mother actually cooks these on an old waffle iron that has a smooth side, not unlike a panini grill.

PORK SATÉS

2 garlic cloves, coarsely chopped

1 teaspoon minced fresh ginger

2 tablespoons salad oil, such as peanut or canola

4 tablespoons *ketjap manis* (Indonesian sweet soy sauce; see p. 14)

1 pound lean pork loin or trimmed pork butt, cut in ½-inch cubes

Spicy Peanut Sauce

12–16 wooden skewers, soaked in water (15 minutes)

Thinly sliced radishes or cilantro sprigs, for garnish

To make the satés, mix the garlic, ginger, oil, and *ketjap manis* in a medium bowl and add the pork cubes. Stir to coat with marinade; set aside. Meanwhile, make the sauce.

To make satés, thread the pork (4–5 cubes per skewer) onto the soaked wooden skewers. Grill or broil for 2–3 minutes on each side. Serve with the warm peanut sauce and a garnish of sliced radishes or cilantro sprigs.

SPICY PEANUT SAUCE

1 cup peanut butter (we use smooth, but you can use crunchy if you like the texture)

1 garlic clove, minced

1 teaspoon *sambal oelek* (red chile paste)

4 tablespoons *ketjap manis*

1–2 cups Chicken Stock (p. 206) or water, as needed

Place the peanut butter, garlic, chile paste, and *ketjap manis* in a small pot and warm gently over low heat for about 4 minutes. Stir in the Chicken Stock or water slowly, adding a little at a time; the mixture will thicken after each addition as it warms. This sauce can be made ahead of time and kept warm or rewarmed. You will need to add more liquid when ready to serve, as the peanut butter will thicken while standing. The sauce should have a thick, creamy consistency but be loose enough to stir easily. The seasonings can be adjusted to your personal taste; we like it a little spicy.

Pork and Shrimp Pot Stickers with Chile-Soy Dipping Sauce

MAKES 36 POT STICKERS   PREP TIME: 1 HOUR

I remember being terribly impressed the first time I was served these at a friend's house in the early '80s. At that time, it was exotic and ambitious to attempt Chinese food at home. Times have changed, thanks in large part to the late Barbara Tropp, the famed chef of China Moon Café in San Francisco, whose wonderful books, like *The Modern Art of Chinese Cooking,* have made cooking authentic Asian food at home much less daunting. These crispy, flavorful little dumplings make a great starter or hors d'oeuvre if you're feeding a crowd. The filling multiplies easily, and once you get the hang of filling the dumplings, you can whip up a lot in a relatively short period of time. If you're a vegetarian, leave the pork and shrimp out and add some sautéed shiitake mushrooms instead. The tart dipping sauce is the perfect complement to the rich filling.

½ pound medium or small shrimp, peeled and chopped

½ pound ground pork

1 medium onion, grated

1 large carrot, peeled and grated

½ cup thinly sliced scallions (about ½ bunch)

1 cup thinly sliced green cabbage (¼ head)

2 garlic cloves, minced

1 tablespoon grated or minced fresh ginger

¼ cup chopped cilantro (leaves and tender stems)

2 tablespoons soy sauce

1 egg

1 teaspoon red chile paste

1 teaspoon salt

36 (1 package) round *gyoza* or wonton wrappers (widely available in the refrigerated produce or freezer section of grocery stores)

Cornstarch, for dusting

Peanut or canola oil, for frying

Water, or chicken or vegetable broth, for steaming

Mix all the filling ingredients in a large bowl. Take 1 teaspoon and bake or steam it, to taste for adjusting the seasoning. Set a large pot of lightly salted water over high heat, ready for boiling.

To make the pot stickers, lay down about 4 *gyoza* or wonton wrappers and brush the edge halfway around with cornstarch mixed with a little water. Place about a teaspoon of filling in the center of each wrapper and fold over into a half moon, being careful to keep filling away from the edge. Using your fingers, crimp to seal. As you become more adept, you can pleat one side against the other. Press each pot sticker onto the table to flatten the bottom, and place on a tray lightly dusted with cornstarch. Pot stickers can sit there until ready to cook.

When all the pot stickers have been shaped, boil them in batches in the lightly salted water for about 2 minutes, until the dough is cooked through (it will become slightly translucent). Drain and cool until ready to fry.

Heat about 1 tablespoon oil in a nonstick skillet over medium-high heat until almost smoking. Place pot stickers in the skillet in batches, to avoid crowding, and lower the heat. When they're golden brown and crispy on the bottom, carefully pour in a little hot water or broth to just cover the bottom of the pan. Watch out for steam! Cover the pan tightly and steam 3–4 minutes, until almost all the liquid is absorbed. Remove from the heat, and repeat with the remaining dumplings. Serve with Chile-Soy Dipping Sauce.

CHILE-SOY DIPPING SAUCE

½ cup soy sauce

2 tablespoons Chinese black vinegar
    or balsamic vinegar

1 teaspoon sesame oil

½ teaspoon red chile paste

1 tablespoon lime juice

2 scallions, thinly sliced

Mix all the ingredients together in a small bowl. The sauce will keep in the refrigerator for up to a week.

Shao mei is a Chinese dumpling shaped like a little sack gathered at the top. To make them, place 1 teaspoon filling in the center of the wrapper and gather the sides up around the filling, leaving the top open ½ inch to 1 inch and flattening the bottom.

Layered Crêpe Gâteau with Prosciutto, Ham, and Cheese

MAKES 4 SERVINGS   PREP TIME: 1 HOUR 30 MINUTES

This recipe is an adaptation of a dish from the Troisgros Brothers, a famous restaurant in Lyon. The "gâteau" is a stack of delicate crêpes layered with creamy béchamel sauce, Gruyère or Comté cheese, ham, and prosciutto. There are countless variations to this elegant dish. You can use plain crêpes or herbed, as I do here. I sometimes make a more "locally flavored" version by folding crayfish and spinach into the béchamel (and omitting the hams). The key is cooking the assembled gâteau until it's bubbly and brown. I like to serve this with a deeply flavored Smoked-Tomato Butter (p. 63), but this dish is great on its own. For a quick assembly, make the sauce and the crêpes a day or two in advance. Wrap the crêpes in plastic wrap and freeze until needed.

CRÊPES

¾ cup milk

2 tablespoons butter, plus extra for frying

3 eggs

1 cup flour

⅛ teaspoon salt

2 tablespoons chopped mixed fresh herbs, such as any combination of tarragon, thyme, chives, and parsley, optional

Scald the milk and add the 2 tablespoons butter, then cool to lukewarm. Place the eggs, flour, salt, and cooled milk in a blender and blend until smooth. Add the herbs and pulse a time or two to mix. Let the batter sit for 15 minutes (or overnight in the refrigerator) to relax and release air bubbles. (If you chill the batter overnight, thin it with a tablespoon or two of water before using.) Melt a small amount of butter in a small nonstick skillet or crêpe pan and when hot, pour in about 2 tablespoons of batter, swirling to coat the bottom of the pan. Cook for about 30 seconds, then flip and cook for about 5 seconds. Remove from the pan and repeat. Should make 12–16 crêpes. Wrap extra crêpes in plastic and refrigerate or freeze for another time.

BÉCHAMEL SAUCE

3 tablespoons butter, plus 1 teaspoon softened butter	1 to 1½ cups milk
	Salt and pepper
3 tablespoons flour	Freshly grated nutmeg

In a small saucepan, melt 3 tablespoons butter, whisk in the flour, and cook over low heat for 1 minute. Whisk in the milk, ½ cup at a time, making sure to cook it for a minute or so after each addition. The sauce should be as thick as thin mayo, but will thicken a bit more when it is brought to a boil.

Season to taste with salt and pepper and add a pinch of nutmeg. Simmer the sauce, whisking, over medium heat for about 5 minutes, until the raw flour taste is gone. Pour it into a container and place the 1 teaspoon softened butter on top to allow it to melt. Place a piece of plastic wrap directly on the surface of the béchamel to keep it warm, and set aside until ready to use.

TO ASSEMBLE

8 herb crêpes	4 ounces grated Comté or Gruyère cheese
Béchamel sauce (about 1 cup)	
3 ounces thinly sliced baked ham (smoked or unsmoked)	3 ounces thinly sliced prosciutto

Preheat the oven to 400°F and lightly oil or butter a baking pan. Place one crêpe on the baking pan and spread with a thin layer of béchamel. Cover with a layer of baked ham and top with another crêpe. Spread this crêpe lightly with béchamel and sprinkle with cheese. Cover with another crêpe, spread with béchamel, then cover with a thin layer of prosciutto. Repeat the process, then top with the last crêpe. Spread with more béchamel and sprinkle with cheese. For the best results, refrigerate for at least 15 minutes—the goal here is to firm the gâteau. Cut it into quarters, keeping it intact, and bake for 10–12 minutes, until cheese is melted and golden brown and the gâteau is warm all the way through. Divide the wedges among 4 plates and ladle Smoked-Tomato Butter alongside.

SMOKED-TOMATO BUTTER

Smoked tomatoes give this sauce a tremendous depth of flavor. But if you want a quicker option, fresh tomatoes will do just fine.

½ cup chopped onion

1 garlic clove, minced

2 medium or 4 roma tomatoes, seeded and smoked (see smoking technique, p. 293), finely chopped

½ cup white wine

1 sprig basil, thyme, rosemary, or tarragon

1 tablespoon extra-virgin olive oil

2 tablespoons softened butter

Salt and pepper

Place the onion, garlic, tomatoes, wine, and herbs in a small saucepan and bring to a boil. Reduce the heat and simmer, stirring, until the tomatoes break down and the mixture starts to dry up, 10–15 minutes.

Remove it from the heat, take out the herb sprig, and cool it about 5 minutes. Pour the mixture into a blender and, with the motor running, drizzle in olive oil and softened butter. Season to taste with salt and pepper. The sauce should be thick enough to hold its shape on a plate. Return it to the pan and keep warm until ready to serve.

Peppered Tuna with Asian Guacamole and Hoisin Dipping Sauce

MAKES 4 TO 6 SERVINGS   PREP TIME: 1 HOUR

Fusion cuisine gets scoffed at a lot, but it can work beautifully, as this dish, with its Latin and Asian influences, attests. From the marriage of avocado, cucumber, limes, chiles, garlic, and cilantro (known as coriander everywhere else but the Americas), Peppered Tuna with Asian Guacamole was born. The cucumber lightens up the avocado and adds a bit of crunch. Hoisin Dipping Sauce rounds out the peppery warmth with sweet spiciness. Serve four plates as a first course, or top Sesame Wonton Crisps (p. 89) with a slice of the tuna and a dollop of the guacamole and serve on a platter to make an elegant party snack.

PEPPERED TUNA

1 piece star anise

1 teaspoon Szechuan peppercorns

1 teaspoon whole black peppercorns

2 tablespoons soy sauce

3 tablespoons vegetable oil

¾ pound tuna loin, skinned, trimmed, and cut in half lengthwise

Coarsely ground sea salt or kosher salt

Asian Guacamole

Hoisin Dipping Sauce

Heat the star anise and peppercorns in a small, dry skillet over medium-high heat until you can smell the pepper when standing over the pan, about 30 seconds. Remove from the heat and cool. Grind in a spice grinder or mortar and pestle. Combine the soy sauce and 1 tablespoon oil, and brush the mixture on all sides of the tuna. Sprinkle the tuna lightly on all sides with the peppercorn mixture and salt. Let it stand for 15 minutes, or refrigerate for several hours.

To cook the tuna, heat the remaining 2 tablespoons oil in a medium skillet over medium-high heat until very hot, then sear the tuna for about 2 minutes on each side, just until rare to medium-rare (the sides will be browned, but the tuna will still feel slightly soft when pressed). Transfer it to a plate to cool.

To serve, cut the tuna into ⅛-inch-thick slices and divide it among the plates. Serve with a spoonful of guacamole and a ramekin of dipping sauce.

ASIAN GUACAMOLE

1 ripe Hass avocado, peeled and diced

1 small cucumber, peeled, seeded, diced, and squeezed in a towel to remove excess moisture

2 radishes, finely diced

½ teaspoon grated fresh ginger

¼ teaspoon sesame oil

1 teaspoon peanut or canola oil

Juice of 1 lime (about 2 tablespoons)

2 scallions, finely chopped

⅓ cup chopped cilantro

1 teaspoon wasabi paste

Salt

Red chile paste, such as *sambal oelek* (see p. 14)

Place the avocado, cucumber, radishes, ginger, sesame oil, peanut oil, lime juice, scallions, cilantro, and wasabi in a bowl, add salt and chile paste, to taste, and stir just until combined. Taste for seasoning and add more lime, salt, or chile paste as desired.

HOISIN DIPPING SAUCE

2 tablespoons soy sauce

2 tablespoons hoisin sauce

1 tablespoon honey or molasses

1 garlic clove, minced

2 tablespoons fresh lime juice

½ teaspoon grated fresh ginger

½ teaspoon chile paste, or more to taste

2 tablespoons peanut or canola oil

Combine the ingredients and whisk together or puree in a blender.

If you don't want to grind your own spices you can substitute 2 teaspoons five-spice powder for the star anise and peppercorns.

Spicy Shrimp with Tasso Cream and Green Chile Grit Cakes

MAKES 4 SERVINGS   PREP TIME: 1 HOUR

This dish combines some of the best New Orleans flavors—shrimp, tasso, creamy grits, and a bit of spice—in an elegant, satisfying presentation. This dish is so popular that Donald Link, my partner and the chef at Herbsaint, couldn't take it off the menu even if he wanted to. If you are serving this for a dinner party, make the grits the day before or in the morning, and the rest of the dish will come together quickly that night.

GREEN CHILE GRIT CAKES

Butter or olive oil, for frying

1 large or 2 small poblano peppers, roasted, peeled, and seeded

1 cup water

1 cup milk

1 teaspoon salt

½ cup stone-ground grits

2 tablespoons butter

1 cup grated white cheddar or Monterey Jack cheese

Lightly butter or oil an 8-inch square pan. Dice the roasted pepper and set aside. Heat the water, milk, and salt in a 2-quart saucepan over medium-high heat. Bring to a boil, then whisk in the grits and cook for 1 minute. Lower the heat to medium-low and cook, stirring occasionally, 30–40 minutes, until the

Stone-ground Grits

Technically, grits can be just about any coarsely ground grain, but usually they are made from corn. There's a pronounced difference in flavor between quick-cooking commercial grits and a stone-ground product. Stone-grinding corn preserves its sweet flavor and results in a coarse, satisfying texture (that takes a bit longer to cook). Stone-ground grits are available at most specialty food stores, or you can find them at www .hoppinjohns.com (see Sources, p. 384).

grits have lost their raw taste and begin to hold together and pull away from the sides of the pan. Add a little water if the grits get too thick. Stir in the butter, roasted pepper, and cheese. Pour onto the prepared pan to a thickness of about ½ inch. Press plastic wrap directly on the surface of the grits and chill thoroughly in the refrigerator, about 1 hour.

Cut the cold grits into triangles or rounds, and brown them in butter in a nonstick skillet over high heat for about 2 minutes on each side. You can heat the grits all the way through for 8–10 minutes in the skillet, or simply brown them, then transfer to a baking sheet. Heat in a hot oven for about 10 minutes when ready to serve.

TASSO CREAM

2 tablespoons butter	1 garlic clove, minced
¼ cup diced onion	2 tablespoons flour
¼ cup diced celery	½ cup Shrimp Stock (p. 229)
¼ cup diced tasso (see Sources, p. 384)	½ cup heavy cream
1 teaspoon chopped fresh thyme	½ teaspoon each salt and pepper
½ teaspoon cayenne	Lemon juice
½ teaspoon Hungarian paprika	Hot sauce

Melt 1 tablespoon butter in a large skillet over medium heat. Add the onion, celery, tasso, thyme, cayenne, paprika, and garlic and cook until vegetables are soft, 3–5 minutes. Add the remaining tablespoon butter, then sprinkle the flour over the vegetables and stir to combine. Whisk in the Shrimp Stock, bring it to a boil, then lower the heat and reduce the liquid by half. Add the cream and simmer until the sauce is thickened to a creamy consistency, about 4 minutes. Finish sauce with the salt, pepper, and the lemon juice and hot sauce, to taste. Keep it warm while you cook the shrimp.

Chef Donald says that whenever you make sauce with a roux in the base, like this one, always add your liquids in stages so that you don't make your sauce too thin. Sauce is always easier to thin out, by adding a bit more liquid, than to thicken.

SHRIMP

2 tablespoons olive oil

1 pound shrimp (16–20 count),
  peeled and deveined

Salt

Tasso Cream

Green Chile Grit Cakes

Thinly sliced scallions, for garnish

Heat the oil in a medium skillet over medium-high heat. When the oil is shimmering, add the shrimp, season with salt, and cook, stirring, for 2–3 minutes until *almost* cooked through. Pour in the tasso cream and stir to coat shrimp. Lower the heat to medium and cook about 2 more minutes. Taste and adjust seasoning.

To serve, place one portion of grits on each plate and spoon the shrimp and cream over the top. Garnish with sliced scallions.

Bayou "Chicken Wings" with Fines Herbes Butter

MAKES 4 SERVINGS   PREP TIME: ABOUT 30 MINUTES

I don't think chef Donald Link knew what a sensation he was going to cause when he changed a beloved appetizer from chicken wings to frogs' legs tossed with this irresistible herbed butter. Fines herbes is a combination of very finely chopped herbs, such as parsley, tarragon, chives, and chervil, but you can use just one or two of the herbs if you'd like. Although we use fresh Louisiana frogs' legs whenever we can, these are awfully good even with the more readily available frozen variety. The meat is delicate and tender, and doesn't really taste like chicken . . .

FINES HERBES BUTTER

½ pound (2 sticks) butter, softened

2 tablespoons minced fresh fines
    herbes

1 tablespoon hot sauce

½ teaspoon cayenne

1 garlic clove, minced

Juice of ½ medium lemon
    (1 to 2 tablespoons)

Salt and pepper

Place the butter in a bowl and stir in fines herbes, hot sauce, cayenne, garlic, and lemon juice. Season with salt and pepper. Taste, and adjust the seasoning.

FROGS' LEGS

Peanut or canola oil, for frying

8 pairs of frogs' legs, cut into
    individual legs, or 1 pound
    chicken wings, defrosted if frozen

Salt and pepper

2 cups flour

½ cup buttermilk

Fines Herbes Butter

Heat 2 inches of oil in a large, heavy-bottomed pot or deep skillet over medium-high heat.

While the oil is heating, rinse the frogs' legs and pat dry with paper towels. Combine the flour with a light sprinkling of salt and pepper in a pie tin or plate. Pour the buttermilk into a wide, shallow bowl. Coat the legs with seasoned flour, then dip in buttermilk, then coat again with flour. Shake off excess flour.

When the oil is hot (about 350°F), fry the frogs' legs in batches (to avoid overcrowding) until golden brown, 4–5 minutes (cook chicken wings a bit longer, for about 7 minutes). Use tongs to remove the legs from the oil, and drain them on paper towels for 1 minute. Place the hot legs in a large serving bowl and toss with Fines Herbes Butter. Serve immediately.

Goat Cheese Croutons
with Wild Mushrooms in Madeira Cream

MAKES 4 SERVINGS   PREP TIME: 30 MINUTES

This dish was an accidental smash hit. Like many of our best sellers, it began as a special and was created in a moment of resourcefulness when we had an overabundance of mushrooms. It quickly became a signature, and it remains one of our most popular items. To achieve the best flavor and texture, it's essential to sauté the mushrooms in a very hot pan, so they will be nicely browned and crispy.

GOAT CHEESE CROUTONS

¼ cup fresh goat cheese, softened to room temperature

1 tablespoon butter, softened

4 slices 7-Grain (or any whole-grain) bread

In a small bowl, use a fork to combine the goat cheese and butter. Lightly toast the bread. Spread equal portions of the goat cheese mixture on the toast. Trim the crusts and cut the squares in half. (The toasts will have a cleaner edge if you trim the crusts *after* spreading on the goat cheese.) Set aside.

MADEIRA CREAM

2 tablespoons shallots, finely chopped

1 cup Madeira (such as Rainwater or Sercial)

1 cup heavy cream

In a small saucepan, simmer the shallots in Madeira until the liquid is reduced to ¼ cup. Add the cream, bring to a boil, then lower the heat and simmer 5–10 minutes, until the cream thickens slightly. Set aside.

WILD MUSHROOMS

½ pound wild mushrooms (preferably a mix of oyster mushrooms, shiitakes, and/or chanterelles)
2 tablespoons butter
1 garlic clove, minced
Madeira Cream
Salt and pepper
2 teaspoons snipped fresh chives, plus extra for garnish
Goat Cheese Croutons

Turn on the broiler. Remove the tough stems from the mushrooms and discard. Slice or tear the mushrooms into pieces. Melt the butter in a large skillet over medium-high heat. When the butter is bubbling but not browned, add the mushrooms and cook until they're golden brown and crispy, 4–5 minutes. Stir in the garlic and Madeira cream. Turn the heat to high and boil for about 2 minutes, until the mushrooms have absorbed most of the cream. Season with salt and pepper and fold in the 2 teaspoons chives.

Broil the goat cheese croutons until bubbly and lightly browned. Arrange the croutons on plates and spoon the mushroom mixture over them. Garnish with chives.

Grilled Shrimp with Black Bean Cakes and Coriander Sauce

MAKES 4 SERVINGS   PREP TIME: 2 HOURS AND 30 MINUTES (INCLUDES BLACK BEAN COOKING TIME)

Over the years, we have probably sold more of this dish than any other item on the Bayona menu. And it all started when I stole the idea for the black bean cakes from my friend Bruce Auden, who at the time was chef at Charlie's 517 in Houston. (He's now chef and owner of Biga on the Banks in San Antonio.) I have no idea what his original recipe was, but the idea of black beans (which I love) in the crispy-on-the-outside-creamy-on-the-inside package was just too good to resist! I adapted a Cuban black bean recipe, added some grilled shrimp and a double-coriander sauce (using both the seeds and leaves). I'm guessing I've served over 150,000 of these babies in the last twenty years.

This dish will come together much more quickly if you prepare the black bean cakes the night or morning before you plan to serve them.

Black Bean Cakes

½ pound black beans, picked clean
    and rinsed
1 tablespoon olive or corn oil, plus
    more for frying
1 small yellow onion, finely chopped
1 small green bell or poblano pepper,
    finely chopped
1 jalapeño, chopped (if not using
    poblano)

1 garlic clove, minced
1 tablespoon honey
1 tablespoon apple cider vinegar
1 teaspoon chili powder
½ teaspoon ground cumin
Salt and pepper
Flour, for dusting cakes
Sour cream and cilantro sprigs,
    as garnish

Place the black beans in cold water to cover. Soak overnight, or for at least 1 hour. Drain, rinse, place in a large pot, and cover with fresh cold water. Bring to a boil, skim the foam, then simmer over low heat for about 1 hour. Add more water, if necessary, to keep the beans covered.

Meanwhile, heat the 1 tablespoon oil over medium-high heat in a large skillet. Add the onion, peppers, and garlic and cook for 2–3 minutes. Add the vegetables, along with the honey, vinegar, chili powder, and cumin, to the beans and continue to simmer. When the beans are quite soft and are starting to break down, season with salt and pepper. Continue to cook until the beans are creamy.

Remove the bean mixture from the heat and strain, reserving the liquid. Puree in a food processor, then transfer to a baking sheet. Spread the puree evenly and let it cool completely. Form the puree into little cakes shaped like hockey pucks (use about ½ cup per cake). The consistency is perfect if it is moist enough to gather into a ball, but not so wet that the mixture sticks to your hands.

Preheat the oven to 400°F. To finish the cakes, lightly dust them with flour. Heat a medium skillet (lightly coated with oil) over medium-high heat. Sauté the cakes just long enough to get a nice crust on each side. When ready to serve, place them on baking sheets in the oven to warm through. Garnish with a dollop of sour cream and a sprig of cilantro.

Grilled Shrimp

4 (6-inch) bamboo skewers

2 tablespoons olive oil

¼ teaspoon chili powder

¼ teaspoon ground cumin

¼ teaspoon cayenne

¼ teaspoon salt

16 medium or large headless shrimp, peeled and deveined (leaving tails intact)

Soak the skewers in hot water.

In a medium bowl, combine the olive oil and seasonings. Toss the shrimp with this marinade and refrigerate while you make the coriander sauce.

Turn on the broiler or light the grill.

Place 4 shrimp on each skewer.

Meanwhile, heat the black bean cakes.

Broil or grill the shrimp 2–3 minutes on each side, until just cooked through. Remove from the skewers, arrange on four plates, and drizzle with the warm coriander sauce. Serve with a black bean cake.

CORIANDER SAUCE

1 medium shallot, finely chopped

½ teaspoon grated orange zest

¼ cup orange juice

½ cup white wine

2 tablespoons sherry wine vinegar

½ teaspoon ground coriander

5 tablespoons butter, softened

2 tablespoons chopped cilantro

Salt and pepper

Place the shallot, orange zest and juice, wine, vinegar, and coriander in a small saucepan and bring to a simmer over medium heat. Cook until the liquid is reduced to 2 or 3 tablespoons. While it's still hot, whisk in softened butter by the spoonful until the sauce is emulsified (it will look thick and creamy). Stir in the chopped cilantro and season with salt and pepper to taste. Cover and keep warm over low heat.

Crayfish and Curried Cream Cheese Turnovers

MAKES ABOUT 16 TURNOVERS, OR 4 SERVINGS   PREP TIME: 1 HOUR

With a creamy, spicy filling that stars a beloved Louisiana ingredient, these crispy, delicate little turnovers will be a hit at any party. I love how the curry plays off the sweet crayfish and flavors of the herbs and scallions. You might double this recipe and freeze half for a future get-together (or light supper when paired with a big salad or spinach omelet). Chances are you will be craving these turnovers again soon after you make them.

CRAYFISH FILLING

1 (8-ounce) package cream cheese, softened

½ pound cooked and peeled crayfish tails, coarsely chopped

1 tablespoon chopped cilantro

2 teaspoons chopped fresh tarragon

4 scallions, minced

1 garlic clove, minced

2 teaspoons mild curry paste (such as Patak's) or curry powder

½ teaspoon red chile paste (such as *sambal oelek*)

Pinch of salt

1 tablespoon fresh lime juice

½ pound frozen phyllo, thawed

¼ pound (1 stick) butter, melted

½ cup unseasoned dry bread crumbs

Soften the cream cheese in an electric mixer. Add the crayfish, cilantro, tarragon, scallions, garlic, curry paste, chile paste, salt, and lime juice and mix well to combine. Taste for seasoning and add more chile paste or lime, as desired. Chill for at least 10 minutes or up to 8 hours.

Line a baking sheet with parchment paper. Lay 1 sheet of phyllo in front of you (keep the remaining dough covered with a damp towel), with the long side facing you. Using a pastry brush, lightly butter the phyllo, then sprinkle with bread crumbs. Repeat with 2 more sheets of dough, stacking them on top of the first sheet. When you have stacked 3 sheets, cut them into 3 even pieces. Place a large spoonful (about 2 tablespoons) of crayfish filling in a lower corner of each piece and fold, flag style, into triangle shapes. Brush the top of each turnover with butter and sprinkle with crumbs. Place on the baking sheet and refrigerate at least 30 minutes, or until ready to serve.

Preheat the oven to 400°F when you are ready to serve. Bake the turnovers for 10–12 minutes, until golden brown and crispy. Serve immediately.

Feel free to substitute shrimp or picked lump crabmeat for the crayfish.

Smoked Duck Hash in Puff Pastry with Apple Cider Sauce

MAKES 6 SERVINGS   PREP TIME: ABOUT 1 HOUR

These are little golden pyramids of puff pastry with a savory filling of smoked duck, sausage, and apple, served with a tart cider sauce. When it comes to entertaining, these packets can be made a day in advance and baked right before serving. Garnish with a scattering of pretty celery leaves.

SMOKED DUCK HASH

1 tablespoon butter

¼ cup diced onion

¼ cup diced celery

2 ounces andouille sausage (see Sources, p. 384), quartered lengthwise, then sliced ¼ inch thick

1 Granny Smith apple, peeled and diced

½ cup diced or shredded smoked duck (see Sources, p. 384)

1 tablespoon flour

1 tablespoon sherry, optional

½ cup Chicken Stock (p. 206)

½ teaspoon each chopped fresh sage and thyme, or ¼ teaspoon each dried

Salt and pepper

½ pound frozen puff pastry, thawed, cut into 4-inch squares

1 egg, beaten with 2 tablespoons milk

Apple Cider Sauce

Melt the butter in a large skillet over medium heat. When it begins to bubble, add the onion and celery and cook for 2 minutes, then add the andouille and apple. Raise the heat to medium-high and cook for 2 more minutes, then add the duck. Sprinkle the mixture with the flour and stir to coat evenly. Cook for 1 minute, then add sherry, if using, and half the chicken stock, stirring to mix. Bring to a boil, and if the mixture is too dry, add the rest of the broth. Add herbs and salt and pepper, to taste. Taste for seasoning. The mixture should be moist but not too wet. Cook for about 2 more minutes, then remove from the heat and cool.

Brush the edges of each pastry square with egg wash. Place 3 ounces (about ¼ cup) of the filling in the center of a square, and bring two opposite corners of the square to meet in the center. Then bring the other two corners to the center to form a small pyramid and pinch the four seams to seal. Brush lightly with egg and refrigerate until ready to bake.

To serve, preheat the oven to 450°F. Bake the pastry pyramids on a parchment-lined baking sheet for 10 minutes, or until golden brown. Serve on warmed plates with a drizzle of the Apple Cider Sauce.

APPLE CIDER SAUCE

1 cup apple cider or juice

1 cup Chicken Stock (p. 206)

¼ cup apple cider vinegar

1 teaspoon apple jelly, optional

1 tablespoon Calvados, optional

1 tablespoon butter

Salt

Combine the cider, stock, and vinegar in a small saucepan. Bring to a boil and reduce to ¼ cup. Whisk in the jelly and Calvados, if using, and boil for about 2 minutes, or until the mixture is slightly syrupy. Whisk in the butter, season with a little salt, and cover to keep warm (but lower the heat to stop cooking).

Salads Every Day

Croutons

Classic French Vinaigrette

Creole Buttermilk–Black Pepper Dressing

Classic N'Awlins Remoulade

Brown Butter Dressing with Chestnut Honey

Bayona House Salad with Balsamic Vinaigrette

Green Salad with Dried Figs, Blue Cheese, Walnuts, and Sherry Vinaigrette

Autumn Salad with Apples, Comté, and Hazelnuts

Bayona Caesar with Arugula

Parisienne Bistro Crudité Plate

Watermelon, Cucumber, and Feta Salad

French Braised Leeks with Dijon Vinaigrette

Cracked Wheat Salad with Green Olives and Golden Raisins

Marinated Lentil Salad with Creamy Goat Cheese and Ripe Tomatoes

Simple Orzo Salad with Black Olives and Feta

Summer Crab Salad with Carrots, Basil, and Lime

Asian Noodle Salad with Spicy Peanut Sauce

Barbecued Chicken Salad with Corn, Avocado, and Creamy Poblano Dressing

Cornmeal-crusted Oyster and Black-eyed Pea Salad with Jalapeño Dressing

Spinach and Crispy Oyster Salad with Rosemary-Dijon Dressing

Crispy Smoked Quail Salad with Bourbon-Molasses Dressing

Spicy Thai Salad with Shrimp, Pork, and Crispy Rice Noodles

When it comes to salads, sometimes I crave pungent blue cheese vinaigrette drizzled over crisp hearts of romaine. Other times I want just the simplest tumble of tender leaves splashed with oil, vinegar, and a sprinkling of salt. Once in a while I want a more substantial mix of greens, vegetables, rich meat, and even a tangle of noodles, that serves as a meal. Maybe it's a southern thing, but I also have a weakness for crisp-fried foods atop a well-dressed mélange. In other words: I love all sorts of salads, and could eat them every day. Sound familiar?

In the spirit of such whims, this chapter offers up dressings and salads for every mood and appetite. (Or you can try my dad's old favorite, the honeymoon salad—lettuce alone with no dressing!) To kick things off I offer a mix of crisp croutons to add a bit of crunch to the bowl. Then you'll find my very favorite dressings that you can toss with just about any salad you choose (though I make suggestions to stoke your inspiration). Next are salads of increasing heft and complexity. There are pretty green salads to start a meal (including signatures from my restaurants), and vibrant grain, bean, and pasta combinations that are great for lunch. When you're good and hungry you'll love the heartier creations that include meat—each partnered with a distinctive dressing that pulls the other ingredients into focus and creates an extraordinary meal.

When it comes to choosing the salad you want to prepare, think about where it will fit in the context of your meal. If the salad is a starter, you need to think about the food that will follow. If the second course is rich, you'll want to keep the salad simple, dressing nice greens with vinaigrette (as opposed to a creamy dressing). If the main course is grilled fish, you may want to have a little more indulgence up front or serve your salad right on the plate as an accompaniment to that fish or meat.

Even a simple lettuce salad can be perfectly delicious and satisfying if you remember a few simple rules. If you're beginning with a whole head of lettuce (as opposed to packaged greens), trim and discard any bruised or limp outer leaves. Use your hands to tear leaf lettuce into bite-sized pieces, or chop sturdier romaine. The tender, sweet inner hearts of the head should be prized (I don't chop them, I simply pull the small, beautiful leaves apart). When you wash the lettuce, submerge it in water (in the bowl of a salad spinner or a spotless sink). Use your fingers (or the spinner insert) to pull the leaves up and out of the water (as opposed to dumping the water back over the greens into a strainer) so the grit stays on the bottom. Next you'll need to dry the leaves in the spinner, or do it the old-fashioned way: gather greens in a clean dish towel, hold the corners (which will be encasing the greens), and windmill it around a few times. It's a good idea to step outside when you do this! There's nothing more disappointing than a salad composed of greens that haven't been thoroughly dried. Wet lettuce will leave you with a soggy salad and a diluted, tasteless dressing on the bottom of the bowl.

Americans tend to shy away from bitter greens, but these can be really appealing when mixed with sweeter lettuces. For instance, frisée, a pale (light green or even yellowish white), feathery, and slightly bitter lettuce, gives a salad added volume and color. Mix it with Boston lettuce and spinach for a result that's appealing to a wide range of eaters.

When it comes down to it, I love all varieties of lettuce. Ruffly red leaf lettuces are sweet and beautiful. For pure flavor, peppery arugula is my pick. My favorite salad mix, in fact, would be a tumble of frisée, red oak, and arugula. To dress it, I'd opt for the Classic French Vinaigrette (p. 90) and a bit of crumbled blue cheese. But that's today; tomorrow it might be just a pile of baby greens tossed with shallots, bacon, and currant tomatoes.

———————————————

Croutons

Whether they're diced, sliced, or tossed with butter, oil, herbs, cheese, or spices, croutons are a thing of beauty. Or consider a croûte: a thin toasted round of bread designed to soak up the last drops of dressing on the plate, or scoop up an unctuous spread like the Eggplant Caviar (p. 191). It's the crunch that excites your mouth and makes all the other flavors more pleasurable. What's more, croutons are a resourceful way to use day-old bread, resurrecting it into something that elevates countless other meals. The following edibles enhance any number of my salads, as well as the soups and bread spreads in the following chapters.

Classic Croutons

Slice your favorite bread (we use sourdough, semolina, potato-scallion, multigrain, brioche, and corn bread, to name a few) into cubes (¼ inch or larger, as desired). Toss the cubes in a bowl (or on a baking sheet) with just enough melted butter or olive oil (or my favorite, a combination of both) to moisten (say, 4 tablespoons for every 4 cups of bread), and minced garlic and salt, if desired. Then brown the cubes in a skillet over medium-high heat, or in the oven on a baking sheet at 350°F for about 8 minutes, until golden brown and crispy. Remember that most croutons will crisp a little more as they cool.

Crispy Rounds (Croûtes)

In France, a croûte is simply a slice of bread that has been either toasted or fried. For the crispy rounds, a baguette-style bread is ideal. We like sourdough, olive bread, ciabatta, or pumpernickel, although any type of thinly sliced bread works. We cut the bread into thin rounds or triangles and brush one side with butter or olive oil, then toast them on the grill or under the broiler until lightly golden. Depending on what you're serving them with, you can cook them like toast, so that they're still a little tender, or until crisp all the way through. The toasted, chewy variations are best served right away, while still warm, whereas thoroughly crisp croûtes will keep for several days in an airtight container or Ziploc bag. Be sure to let them cool completely before storing or they will steam and soften when stored. If you want to get a little fancy, try mixing some chopped herbs, grated cheese, or smashed raw or roasted garlic in with the butter or oil.

Seasoned Pita Crisps

¼ cup olive oil

2 tablespoons lemon juice

½ teaspoon ground cumin

½ teaspoon paprika

1 teaspoon dried dill, optional

3 rounds of white or whole wheat pita bread

Salt

Preheat the oven to 350°F. In a small bowl, whisk together the olive oil, lemon juice, and seasonings (except salt). Brush the pita rounds on both sides with the seasoned oil. Cut each round into 12 wedges. Lay the wedges on a baking sheet in a single layer. Sprinkle lightly with salt and bake for about 10 minutes, then turn wedges over and bake another 3–5 minutes. They should be darkened and crispy but not too brown. Cool completely and serve. Any leftovers will keep for several days in a Ziploc bag or airtight container.

Sesame Wonton Crisps

Fried wonton or *gyoza* wrappers, available in the frozen section of most Asian markets, make fantastic chips to scoop up savory ingredients. They are delicious served with any Asian-inspired tartare or seviche, with Asian Guacamole (p. 66), or as a garnish for just about any salad that would benefit from crunch and nutty sesame seeds.

1 (16-ounce) package wonton wrappers (about 24)

2 egg whites, beaten

Black and white sesame seeds, for garnish

Vegetable oil, for frying

Defrost the wrappers and peel them apart. Stack and cut them in half (some are round and some are square; it doesn't matter). Brush them with a little egg white and sprinkle with black and white sesame seeds. Heat 2 inches of oil to 350°F in a saucepan or wok and gently drop in the crisps, a few at a time. If they start to curl, straighten them with tongs. Turn them once, and when they are light golden brown (about 30 seconds), remove and drain them on paper towels. When the crisps are cool, place in an airtight container or Ziploc bag; they will stay crisp for several days.

Classic French Vinaigrette

MAKES ABOUT I CUP OR 6 TO 8 SERVINGS   PREP TIME: 5 MINUTES

Once you master a classic vinaigrette, the variations in flavor—and the things you can drizzle it over—are endless. What follows are my all-time favorite dressings, but feel free to alter the recipes to include your favorite vinegar, citrus juice, mustard, or herb. You'll find a range of dressing personalities to suit just about every salad under the sun.

1 tablespoon minced shallots
2 teaspoons Dijon mustard
3 tablespoons red or white wine
   vinegar

Kosher salt
Freshly ground black pepper
½ to ¾ cup olive oil

Whisk together the shallots, mustard, and vinegar in a small bowl and add salt and pepper, to taste. Whisk in the olive oil in a slow, steady stream. After you've added ½ cup, taste the mixture. It might be perfect for you, but if it still tastes a bit acidic, add the remaining ¼ cup olive oil. Taste and adjust seasonings as needed.

Variation: Smashed Blue Cheese Vinaigrette

A simple classic gets more sass from crumbled blue cheese.

There are two versions of blue cheese dressing. There's the thick, rich, mayonnaise-based dressing, which is the standard in steakhouses and on salad bars, then there's this version, which is simpler, less gloppy, and a better way to showcase the cheese. Using a fork, mash ½ cup blue cheese right into a finished batch of classic vinaigrette.

I used to use Roquefort exclusively for this dressing, but these days there are so many great domestic blue cheeses that I use any variety that catches my eye at the market. If you don't like blue cheese, you can opt for another crumbly variety of cheese, like feta. In addition to green salads, this dressing is great over chilled asparagus or a simple vegetable salad.

A few of my favorite American blue cheeses are Maytag from Iowa, Great Hill Blue from Massachusetts, and Point Reyes Blue from California.

For most salad dressings, I prefer a mix of pure olive oil and extra-virgin olive oil. For my palate, straight extra-virgin olive oil is often too strong and overpowers the other ingredients. The exception is when a simple salad, such as a plate of sliced ripe tomatoes, fresh mozzarella, and basil, cries out for the deepest green, most flavorful olive oil.

Creole Buttermilk-Black Pepper Dressing

MAKES ABOUT 1 CUP OR 6 TO 8 SERVINGS   PREP TIME: 10 MINUTES

This dressing is delicious with a ripe tomato salad, Bibb lettuce, and fried popcorn shrimp or crayfish tails.

½ cup mayonnaise (see Basic
   Mayonnaise, p. 181)
¼ cup sour cream (low-fat is okay)
1 tablespoon Creole mustard
2 tablespoons finely chopped shallot
   or onion

3 tablespoons buttermilk
1 teaspoon prepared horseradish,
   optional
¼ teaspoon salt
¼ teaspoon (or more to taste) freshly
   ground black pepper

Whisk all the ingredients together in a small bowl. If you want it a little more tart, you can add a squeeze of lemon or splash of vinegar.

Classic N'Awlins Remoulade

MAKES ABOUT 2 CUPS OR 8 TO 12 SERVINGS   PREP TIME: 15 MINUTES

There are two versions of remoulade. French remoulade means celery root remoulade, a beloved bistro slaw bound in a creamy white mustard-mayo dressing. But in New Orleans, classic remoulade is red and more of a vinaigrette, made with two traditional spices, paprika and cayenne, and balanced with plenty of celery and parsley that provide a fresh, clean crunch.

This remoulade is my favorite way to eat chilled, boiled shrimp, crab, or crayfish, but the dressing is also great on crabmeat or on a simple boiled egg, sliced in half and served atop crisp shredded lettuce.

---

2 tablespoons finely chopped onion or shallots

1 garlic clove, minced

2 tablespoons Creole mustard

1 tablespoon apple cider vinegar

1 teaspoon sweet Hungarian paprika

½ teaspoon cayenne

Juice of 1 medium lemon (about 3 tablespoons)

1 tablespoon prepared horseradish

Salt and pepper

1 cup olive oil

¼ cup finely chopped celery heart

2 tablespoons chopped fresh parsley

2 tablespoons finely chopped scallion

Whisk the onion, garlic, mustard, vinegar, paprika, cayenne, lemon juice, horseradish, and salt and pepper, to taste, together in a medium bowl. Whisk in the olive oil, then stir in the chopped celery, parsley, and scallion. This dressing will keep for 2–3 days in the refrigerator.

Brown Butter Dressing with Chestnut Honey

MAKES ABOUT ¾ CUP OR 4 TO 6 SERVINGS   PREP TIME: 5 MINUTES

I created this recipe after tasting Italian chestnut honey. It has a haunting, slightly bitter flavor that might not be for everyone. But for me it was a revelation, not unlike the first time I tasted arugula or an artichoke. Up to that point, honey was honey. But this honey smelled as earthy as a barnyard—I went running through my restaurant having people taste and smell it. In this dressing, I pair it with the rich, nutty flavor of brown butter, which mellows the honey's sharp edges.

Because of the brown butter, this dressing works best with a warm salad. Try it with diced roasted butternut squash; thick slices of grilled onion alongside roasted chicken; or a lightly wilted spinach salad with bacon, apples, and chopped hazelnuts.

---

2 tablespoons butter	1 teaspoon chestnut honey
1 tablespoon finely chopped shallots	½ cup olive oil
2 tablespoons apple cider vinegar	Salt

Melt the butter in a small saucepan. Swirl the pan over medium heat until the foam subsides and turns a nutty brown color. Remove from heat; cool. Place the shallots, vinegar, and honey in a medium mixing bowl and whisk to dissolve honey. Whisk in the brown butter and olive oil, and season with salt.

Bayona House Salad with Balsamic Vinaigrette

MAKES 4 SERVINGS   PREP TIME: 15 MINUTES

Chances are that this irresistible green salad, one of the simplest recipes in this book, will fit into your dinner repertoire several times a week. At Bayona we use a mix of lolo rosso, red oak, frisée, Boston or Bibb, red leaf, watercress, and radicchio lettuces. The dressing, which gets a sweet-tart kick from two types of vinegar, mustard, and honey, really makes this salad sing. A small portion of an assertive cheese, like Grana Padano or crumbled blue cheese, will add an appealing sharpness.

A mix of assorted greens (2–3 cups per person), cleaned and dried

Balsamic Vinaigrette, as needed (approximately 2 tablespoons per portion)

Grana Padano or blue cheese, such as Great Hill Blue or Roquefort, as desired

Toss the desired amount of greens with just enough dressing to lightly coat each leaf. Top with shaved Grana Padano or crumbled blue cheese, as desired.

BALSAMIC VINAIGRETTE
MAKES 1 CUP, OR ENOUGH FOR ABOUT 8 FIRST-COURSE SALADS

2 tablespoons balsamic vinegar

2 tablespoons apple cider vinegar

1 tablespoon plus 1 teaspoon Dijon mustard

1 tablespoon honey

¾ cup olive oil

1 tablespoon fresh lemon juice

Salt and pepper

Whisk together the vinegars, mustard, and honey in a small bowl, then gradually whisk in the olive oil. Taste the dressing and finish by adding lemon juice, and salt and pepper, to taste.

Green Salad with Dried Figs, Blue Cheese, Walnuts, and Sherry Vinaigrette

MAKES 4 TO 6 SERVINGS   PREP TIME: 30 MINUTES

This irresistible combination of pungent and sweet flavors—figs, blue cheese, walnuts, and deeply flavored sherry vinaigrette—explains why this house salad flies out the door at Herbsaint.

4 large handfuls salad greens—such as red leaf, spinach, arugula, frisée, or premixed mesclun

4 generous tablespoons chopped dried figs (we use Calmyrna and Black Mission figs, plumped in warm water and drained)

3 tablespoons chopped toasted walnuts (see Toasting Nuts, p. 99)

½ cup Sherry Vinaigrette

4 tablespoons crumbled Valdeon (Spanish blue cheese), or your favorite blue cheese

Place the salad greens, figs, walnuts, and dressing in a bowl and toss. Divide among plates and crumble the blue cheese on top of each salad.

SHERRY VINAIGRETTE
MAKES ¾ CUP OR 4 TO 6 SERVINGS

1 medium shallot, finely minced

2 tablespoons sherry wine vinegar

1 tablespoon fig preserves, or 1 tablespoon honey

2 teaspoons chopped capers

1 teaspoon Dijon mustard

½ cup olive oil

Salt and pepper

Whisk together the shallot, vinegar, preserves, capers, and mustard in a small bowl. Whisk in the olive oil until the dressing is emulsified. Taste for balance, and add a little more olive oil, if you like. Season with salt and pepper.

Autumn Salad with Apples, Comté, and Hazelnuts

MAKES 4 SERVINGS   PREP TIME: 25 MINUTES

This is a crisp and pleasing salad that gives you a chance to show off the subtle, clean-tasting apples you can find in the fall and winter, such as Macoun, Braeburn, or Gala (though it's great with tart Granny Smith apples any time of year). It gets a mellow richness from Comté, a high-quality Swiss-style cheese that's made in France, and the nuttiness of the cheese is echoed by the hazelnuts. (Walnuts would be a fine substitute, however.) I frequently use apple cider for the basis of sauces and dressings, because it's lightly fruity but still fairly neutral, so it blends well with lots of different things. When cooked down or reduced, cider gets almost syrupy, which gives body as well as flavor to the dressing.

8 cups mixed greens, cleaned

1 medium apple (Granny Smith or other firm, tart-sweet variety), peeled and thinly sliced into matchsticks

2–3 ounces Comté cheese, cut in matchsticks

¼ cup sliced celery hearts

1 cup Cider Dressing

Salt

¼ cup chopped toasted hazelnuts

In a large bowl, use your hands or two wooden spoons to toss together the lettuce, apple, cheese, and celery hearts. Drizzle in enough dressing to lightly coat the salad; reserve remaining dressing. Season the salad with a little salt, if necessary, and divide among four plates. Sprinkle salad with hazelnuts and drizzle with equal portions of the remaining Cider Dressing.

I've suggested that you peel the apple because many varieties have an unpleasantly thick, waxy skin. However, if you have a great farmers' market apple with a beautiful, thin skin, you don't have to peel it. In other words, it's your call.

CIDER DRESSING

1 cup apple cider or juice

2 tablespoons apple cider vinegar

1 tablespoon finely chopped shallots

1 teaspoon Dijon mustard

½ cup pure olive oil or a mild
    vegetable oil

1 teaspoon hazelnut oil, optional

Salt and pepper

Place the cider and vinegar in a small saucepan and bring to a boil. Lower the heat and simmer until reduced to 3 tablespoons of liquid. Pour it into a small bowl and add the shallots and mustard. Whisk to combine, then slowly whisk in the olive oil and the hazelnut oil, if using. Season to taste with salt and pepper.

Toasting Nuts

Place the nuts on a baking tray and roast in a 325°F oven for 5–7 minutes, until they turn one shade darker and become fragrant. Watch them closely and be careful not to burn them! If it's necessary to remove the skin, as is often the case with hazelnuts, place the warm nuts in a dish towel and rub together (the skin will come off in flakes) until clean.

Bayona Caesar with Arugula

MAKES 4 SALADS, WITH DRESSING TO SPARE FOR THE NEXT FEW DAYS   PREP TIME: 30 MINUTES

Caesar salads may be ubiquitous on menus of all stripes, but a truly memorable one can be hard to find. Our version is unique because it pairs the usual romaine with arugula, which adds a peppery bite. I omit the anchovies from the dressing in favor of tossing them with the salad because I like the texture and the intense bites of salty flavor. Feel free to make this salad more substantial (and savory) with the addition of grilled chicken, shrimp, or even fried oysters. Adding a raw egg yolk to the dressing is optional, but it will create a richer, more stable body.

---

1 head romaine lettuce, leaves cut in half lengthwise and then into bite-sized pieces

1 bunch arugula, washed and stemmed (tear into pieces if leaves are large)

4 anchovy fillets, finely chopped

½ cup Classic Croutons (p. 88)

Shaved Grana Padano or Parmesan cheese, as desired

½ recipe Bayona Caesar Dressing (about ¾ cup)

Toss together the romaine, arugula, anchovies, croutons, cheese, and dressing. Top with more cheese, if desired.

BAYONA CAESAR DRESSING

MAKES 1½ CUPS, ENOUGH FOR ABOUT 8 SALADS

1 raw or coddled egg yolk, optional

2 tablespoons Dijon mustard

¼ cup red wine vinegar

2 tablespoons fresh lemon juice

1 teaspoon finely grated lemon zest

1 teaspoon Worcestershire sauce

½ teaspoon Tabasco sauce

2 tablespoons minced shallots

3 garlic cloves, minced

1 cup pure olive oil

¼ cup extra-virgin olive oil

Salt and pepper

Whisk together everything but the olive oils and salt and pepper in a medium bowl. Slowly whisk in the oils, until the dressing is emulsified and creamy. If it gets too thick while you're adding the oils, whisk in a teaspoon of water, then continue adding oil. Season to taste with salt and pepper.

Alternatively, you can puree the dressing ingredients in a blender.

If you would prefer to have the anchovies pureed in the dressing (as opposed to chopped in the salad), simply add the 4 fillets listed with the salad ingredients to the blender instead (or whisk them into the dressing).

Grana Padano vs. Parmigiano-Reggiano

If I could use Parmigiano-Reggiano, my favorite aged cheese, all the time, I would. It's the best all-around eating, and my choice for a cheese plate. But it's also expensive! Its cousin, Grana Padano (grana is Italian for "grain," referring to its granular texture), is a similar cheese prepared in the same way, and it's an excellent substitute. Grana Padano is the work-horse in my kitchen. I use it in bread crumbs, on salads, and as a garnish for soups. It's less complex than Reggiano, but it still has a good sharpness and a great texture.

Parisienne Bistro Crudité Plate

MAKES 4 SERVINGS   PREP TIME: 1 HOUR 15 MINUTES

My initial exposure to French cuisine was during my first trip to Europe. It was long before I would eat in any three-star restaurants, and that exposure—the best I could have asked for—came from sitting in cafés. I was a wide-eyed twenty-three-year-old (and I was told by a waiter not to practice my high school French on him). I remember beautiful, colorful plates of vegetables going past me. I soon learned it was the classic French presentation of crudités, an assortment of three or four salads served together. It was fresh, affordable, and very appetizing, and it was served all over the city. Once in a while I'll run this as a special in my restaurant; then I'll forget about it until I crave it again. Any one of these salads can stand on its own, but if you put them all together they make for an extraordinary meal. Marinated Lentil Salad with Creamy Goat Cheese and Ripe Tomatoes (p. 113) would be a welcome addition to the mix.

Roasted Red or Golden Beet Salad

When I was a kid, I used to think that beets tasted just like the dirt they were grown in. Happily, I am older, wiser, less fussy, and can appreciate the sweet earthiness of these beautiful vegetables—and I do find that dressings made with a little fruit vinegar bring out the sweet and temper the earthiness. A bright, tangy goat cheese is such a perfect match that it's become ubiquitous on bistro menus.

ROASTED BEETS

1 bunch baby beets (6 or 7), or   Olive oil, as needed
   1 bunch regular beets (3 or 4)   Dressing

Preheat the oven to 350°F.

For baby beets, slice the tops off ½ inch above the stem and place on a baking pan. Toss beets with just enough olive oil to evenly coat; add a little water to the bottom of the pan. Cover and bake for about 25 minutes, then test the beets by inserting a paring knife into the center of one. The knife should slip out easily when you pick it up. If not, continue to cook for 5–10 more minutes. Cool, then rub the skins off with a paper towel.

For larger beets, slice off the tops ½ inch above the stem and roast on a baking pan in the oven without covering and without water for about 40 minutes. Test doneness in the same manner. When they are cool enough to handle, peel with a sharp paring knife.

For a richer salad, toss the beets with your favorite creamy horseradish or blue cheese dressing. If the beet stems and leaves are pretty, don't discard them. Instead chop them up, wash them, and sauté with garlic and olive oil as an iron-rich green vegetable.

Place sliced or diced beets in a bowl and toss to coat with dressing. Let marinate for 10 minutes. Serve the beets simply dressed or with sliced red onion, arugula or spinach, and crumbled goat cheese or shaved ricotta salata for a more substantial salad.

DRESSING FOR RED BEETS

1 medium shallot, finely chopped

1 teaspoon raspberry vinegar

1 teaspoon red wine vinegar

3 tablespoons olive oil

Salt and pepper, to taste

Whisk all ingredients together in a small bowl.

DRESSING FOR GOLDEN BEETS

1 medium shallot, finely chopped

2 teaspoons apple cider vinegar or pear vinegar

3 tablespoons olive oil, pure or extra-virgin

Salt and pepper, to taste

Whisk all the ingredients together in a small bowl.

Celery Root Remoulade

½ cup Basic Mayonnaise (p. 181)

1 heaping tablespoon Dijon mustard

2 cups grated or matchsticked celery root (see p. 105)

Salt and pepper

In a large mixing bowl, whisk together the mayonnaise and mustard.

There are generally two ways to prepare celery root for remoulade. Some people like it grated (in a food processor or by hand) and tossed raw with the dressing. But you can also use a Japanese mandolin to slice the celery root into matchsticks, and then blanch them. The grated way is good raw, because I think it gets a little moister. The blanched matchsticks are appealing because the cooking process brings out the flavor more. If you choose to blanch the root, cover the matchsticks with acidulated water (water with the juice of

1 lemon and a pinch of salt) as you do your slicing, to avoid discoloration. When you're done slicing, place the matchsticks and the water over high heat, bring to a boil, then drain. Rinse them briefly with cold water, then dry thoroughly. When cool, toss the celery root with the dressing and season with salt and pepper.

Grated Carrots with Lemon and Walnut Oil

Just in case you've been wondering what to do with that walnut oil that someone gave you for Christmas . . .

2½ cups (about 1 pound) grated
   carrots
3 tablespoons fresh lemon juice

2 tablespoons walnut oil
Salt, to taste

Toss the carrots, lemon juice, and walnut oil together in a bowl. Season with salt. Taste, adding more lemon juice or salt as needed.

Celery Root

Celery root, also known as celeriac, is an unusual vegetable. It's not actually the root of celery stalks, but a bulb of a special variety of celery cultivated specifically for its root. You want to buy one that feels pretty dense and heavy. If it's too light, chances are it's dried out. They're typically best in the fall and spring. By early summer they tend to get dehydrated and cottony.

To peel celery root, trim the rough peel away with a paring knife (it's too tough and roughly textured to do with a peeler).

Cucumber-Onion Salad

If you're making this salad ahead of time, you'll want to lightly salt the cucumbers, let them sit in a colander to drain for 10 minutes, drain, then pat dry with a paper towel. If you're going to serve this salad right away, you can skip that step.

1 medium or 2 small cucumbers, peeled

½ small sweet onion, such as Vidalia, Walla Walla, or Texas 1015

¼ cup sour cream or plain yogurt (low-fat is fine, but don't use nonfat)

Dill sprigs, snipped

White wine vinegar, to taste

Salt and pepper

Split the cucumbers in half and use a melon baller or teaspoon to scoop out the seeds. Thinly slice cucumber and place in a medium bowl with the onion, sour cream, dill, and vinegar. Use a rubber spatula to combine well. Season with salt and pepper. Taste and add salt or vinegar, as needed.

All these salads can be prepped several hours in advance. In the spirit of Paris bistros, serve with a crusty baguette and a chilled glass of Provençale rosé.

Watermelon, Cucumber, and Feta Salad

MAKES 4 SERVINGS   PREP TIME: 15 MINUTES

This refreshing summer salad—a play of sweet and salty flavors—was inspired by some friends of mine reminiscing about the food they ate on a trip to Israel, where the pairing of fresh melon and feta cheese is fairly common. I was never one to sprinkle salt on my watermelon, but somehow with the addition of cucumber and citrus dressing, the contrast is incredibly refreshing.

2 cups seeded and diced ripe red or yellow watermelon (or a combination of both)

2 cups seeded and diced cucumber

1 bunch arugula or 2 cups spinach, washed and dried

1 small red onion, cut in half and thinly sliced

Citrus Dressing

¼ cup crumbled feta cheese

Toss the watermelon, cucumber, arugula, onion, and Citrus Dressing together in a large salad bowl. Divide the salad evenly among four plates. Top the salads with equal portions of the crumbled cheese.

CITRUS DRESSING

MAKES ABOUT ½ CUP, ENOUGH FOR 1 BATCH OF SALAD

1 tablespoon fresh lemon juice

2 tablespoons fresh lime juice

2 teaspoons honey

⅓ cup olive oil

1 tablespoon chopped fresh mint

Pinch of cayenne

Salt

In a small bowl, whisk together the lemon and lime juices with the honey, then add the olive oil, mint, cayenne, and salt, to taste.

French Braised Leeks with Dijon Vinaigrette

MAKES 4 SERVINGS   PREP TIME: 15–20 MINUTES FOR STOVETOP, 20–30 MINUTES IN THE OVEN

I have always loved leeks, but now they have a particularly romantic context in my life. The first time I met my (then future) husband, Chip, he cooked chicken with leeks, a dish that knocked me out. (I guess I should mention that he worked as a professional chef in New Orleans for ten years.) He blanched the leeks, so they were bright green and pliable, then wrapped them around a stuffed chicken breast. It was the most beautiful, seductive presentation. Since then, every time I cook with leeks I think of that dish—and him.

Leeks have an interesting, subtle flavor that suggests asparagus or salsify (a root vegetable). A lot of Americans don't know how to use them, and they tend to be pricey. But this simple bistro presentation shows that they are worth the splurge. This is the most basic French preparation for leeks, and one of the most delicious. It's also the recipe that sold me on them forever.

---

1 bunch leeks (5 small or 3 large)
1 tablespoon butter, softened
¼ cup white wine
½ cup Chicken Stock (p. 206)
    or water

Salt and pepper
Dijon Vinaigrette

Cut the root end off the leeks, as well as the dark green stem end, leaving just the white and light green portion. Split them lengthwise and remove the outer two layers. Wash thoroughly under running water, being careful to rinse between layers to remove any grit. Shake off the excess water.

Rub the bottom of a large, heavy-bottomed skillet with the softened butter, then lay the leeks, cut side down, in the pan. They should fit snugly in one layer across the pan. Pour the wine and Chicken Stock over the leeks, sprinkle with salt and a little pepper, then cover with waxed paper or parchment (which will keep the tops of the leeks moist), and bring the liquid to a boil.

Reduce the heat, cover the pan, and simmer over low heat for about 15 minutes. Use a small spatula or tongs to turn the leeks once, halfway through the cooking process. When cooked, the leeks should be completely tender and not stringy. Turn them over once more, so the outer layers are facing up. To test doneness, I usually just peel off one or two outer layers, the last to get cooked, and sample them (if they are the least bit tough, cook for another 5 minutes).

Remove pan from the heat and cool. If there are more than 2 tablespoons of juices left in the pan, remove the leeks to a serving platter and reduce the juices to 2 tablespoons. Reserve juices for the Dijon vinaigrette.

Pour the dressing over the leeks and let sit for at least 10 minutes. These leeks are wonderful served warm or cold, but I like them best at room temperature.

DIJON VINAIGRETTE

1 medium shallot, minced	Reserved leek pan juices
1 tablespoon Dijon mustard	½ cup olive oil
2 tablespoons wine or apple cider vinegar	Salt and pepper

Whisk together the shallot, mustard, vinegar, and pan juices in a small bowl. Slowly whisk in the olive oil, then season with salt and pepper.

Oven-braised Leeks

Alternatively, you can braise the leeks in a 350°F oven for 20–30 minutes in a buttered gratin dish (which, when cooled slightly and served atop a trivet, can go right to the table as a rustic-looking serving dish). Oven braising is actually easier: cooked in this manner, the leeks do not need to be turned. Simply prepare the leeks as described on p. 109 (placing them cut side down), and don't forget to cover them with parchment.

Cracked Wheat Salad
with Green Olives and Golden Raisins

4 TO 6 SERVINGS   PREP TIME: 1 HOUR

Wheat berries are whole wheat kernels that become appealingly chewy when cooked, and bulgur, a Middle Eastern staple, is crushed dried wheat kernels (best known as the basis for tabbouleh). Together they make a nutritious and satisfying salad (the grains are hearty and filling) that can stand alone as a meal or work as a side dish with grilled lamb chops or crispy seared fish. I've called for celery hearts because I love their sweetness, but regular stalks of celery work just fine.

½ cup wheat berries

Salt

1½ cups bulgur

Finely grated zest of 4 lemons (about 2 tablespoons plus 2 teaspoons)

Grated zest of 2 medium oranges (4–5 tablespoons)

Juice of 2 lemons (about 6 tablespoons)

Juice of 2 oranges (about ⅔ cup)

¼ cup extra-virgin olive oil

1 tablespoon kosher salt

½ teaspoon crushed red pepper, optional

3 tablespoons chopped fresh parsley

2 tablespoons chopped fresh mint

2 tablespoons chopped cilantro

½ cup green olives, pitted and roughly chopped

½ cup golden raisins, plumped and roughly chopped

¾ cup thinly sliced celery hearts

Place the wheat berries, a sprinkling of salt, and enough water to cover them by 2 inches in a 2-quart saucepan. Bring to a boil, reduce the heat, and simmer until the wheat berries are tender but not mushy, about 45 minutes. Drain and set aside. Meanwhile, place the bulgur in a large bowl and cover with 1½ cups of steaming hot water. Let it sit about 15 minutes, stirring occasionally, until the water is absorbed and the bulgur is soft. (I always taste it;

the bulgur shouldn't have any crunch or hard edges.) Add the cooked wheat berries to the bulgur.

Whisk together the citrus zests, juices, olive oil, kosher salt, and crushed red pepper in a small bowl. Add the dressing to the grains and toss well. Add the parsley, mint, cilantro, olives, raisins, and celery hearts, and use a rubber spatula to combine enough to moisten all ingredients. Taste again for seasonings, adding additional salt, citrus juice, or olive oil as needed.

I always chop golden raisins. I like the taste, but it's a quirk of mine that I don't like to bite into a whole raisin. By all means leave them whole if you like. If you're not a cilantro lover, leave it out or substitute some fresh basil.

Marinated Lentil Salad with Creamy Goat Cheese and Ripe Tomatoes

MAKES 4 TO 6 SERVINGS   PREP TIME: 40 MINUTES

I used to think that lentils were bland in a brown rice (good-for-you-but-boring) sort of way. But the luscious combination of ingredients in this salad changed all that. Loretta Keller, a former sous chef who is now an acclaimed chef in San Francisco, gave me this recipe. The lentils and dressing are great on their own, but they're even better paired with goat cheese, with its creamy texture and tangy flavor, and ripe garden tomatoes. This salad makes a quick and easy lunch, especially with a loaf of crusty sourdough bread or some crostini (thin slices of toasted bread rubbed with garlic, sprinkled with salt, and drizzled with olive oil).

½ pound brown lentils

¼ medium yellow onion, stuck with
   2 cloves

1 bay leaf

½ small red onion, finely chopped

3 tablespoons balsamic vinegar

¼ cup extra-virgin olive oil, plus extra
   for drizzling

Salt

1 garlic clove, minced

¼ teaspoon ground cumin

2 tablespoons chopped fresh mint
   and/or basil

Pepper

½ cup fresh goat cheese, such as
   Capriole or other good-quality
   domestic chèvre, blended with
   1 tablespoon heavy cream or
   half-and-half

Sliced ripe tomatoes, as desired

Mint or basil sprigs, for garnish

Place the lentils in a 2-quart saucepan with the yellow onion and bay leaf and cover with about 4 cups of cold water. Bring to a boil, then reduce the heat and simmer until lentils are tender but not mushy, 15–20 minutes.

Remove the lentils from the heat and pour into a colander. Run warm water over them to rinse off the sludge. Shake off any excess water, then turn the lentils into a bowl, and immediately add the red onion, vinegar, olive oil, and some salt. Stir gently with a spatula, then add the garlic, cumin, and mint. Season with salt and pepper. Marinate for 10 minutes, then taste again and adjust the acidity (adding more oil or vinegar as desired) and salt and pepper.

Place about ½ cup dressed lentils on each plate, then add a spoonful or two of goat cheese and some sliced tomatoes. Drizzle the tomatoes with olive oil, and season with salt and a grind of black pepper. A mint or basil sprig in the center makes a pretty garnish.

Lentils of Late

When I first learned this recipe, about eighteen years ago, common brown lentils were pretty much the only ones on the market. They're still the cheapest and the most readily available. But these days there are several other delicious options, including black beluga (so named because they resemble caviar) and Puy lentils (also known as French green lentils). Both varieties have a deep, earthy flavor and hold their shape well in salads. Use your favorite and simply adjust the simmering time as necessary until the lentils are tender but not mushy.

Simple Orzo Salad with Black Olives and Feta

MAKES 8 SERVINGS   PREP TIME: 25 MINUTES

These days the phrase "pasta salad" registers as a bit of a throwback. But as long as I've been making this salad, people have raved about it and asked for the recipe. Orzo is a small rice-shaped pasta. It's easy to overcook, so watch it closely and taste it toward the end of the cooking time. I actually prefer orzo imported from Greece—it's a bit more toothsome than Italian varieties. Serve this salad as a meal on its own, or alongside grilled fish, lamb chops, or roast chicken.

1 pound orzo pasta

½ cup sun-dried tomatoes, plumped in water and minced, or diced fresh tomato

½ cup pitted Greek olives, sliced lengthwise

½ cup crumbled feta cheese

½ cup artichoke hearts or quartered artichoke bottoms

½ cup sliced celery (preferably the smaller, lighter green inner hearts)

1 roasted red bell pepper (see roasting technique, p. 122), peeled, seeded, and diced

1 small red onion, diced

2 tablespoons chopped fresh basil or oregano

2 tablespoons chopped fresh Italian parsley

1 tablespoon fresh lemon juice

3 tablespoons balsamic vinegar

6 tablespoons extra-virgin olive oil

Salt and pepper

Bring a large pot of salted water to a boil. Add orzo and boil until al dente, or just tender, according to package directions. Drain; rinse the pasta briefly with fresh water. Toss the still-warm pasta with all the other ingredients and season with salt and pepper. Taste, and add more lemon juice or seasonings, if needed.

Summer Crab Salad with Carrots, Basil, and Lime

MAKES 8 SERVINGS   PREP TIME: 30 MINUTES

All along the Gulf Coast, crab is plentiful and almost cheap during the summer. It has a luxurious flavor, but it's still light, and in this ceviche-like salad the lime and basil enhance the warm-weather flavors. The salty capers are a good foil for the sweetness of the crab and carrots. Serve this refreshing combination on lettuce leaves, as described below, or in a parfait or martini glass, garnished with a wedge of lime and some tortilla chips.

½ cup finely diced carrots

Juice of 2 limes (about 4 tablespoons)

1 teaspoon finely grated lime zest

2 medium shallots, minced

1 tablespoon white wine vinegar

⅓ cup good-quality olive oil

Salt and pepper

Hot sauce

3 tablespoons coarsely chopped fresh
   basil

2–3 tablespoons minced scallions

1 pound jumbo lump crabmeat
   (Blue or Dungeness), well
   picked for shells

2 tablespoons coarsely chopped
   capers

1 head Bibb lettuce, cleaned and
   dried

1 avocado (preferably Hass), sliced or
   diced

Basil sprigs, as garnish

Bring a small saucepan of water to a boil. Add the diced carrots and simmer 2–3 minutes; drain and shock in ice water. Remove the carrots from ice water and set aside.

Place the lime juice and zest, shallots, and vinegar in a small bowl and whisk in the olive oil. Season to taste with salt, pepper, and hot sauce. In

I prefer the texture of finely diced carrots in this salad. However, they need to be blanched, then shocked in ice water, before you use them, to ensure that the texture is not too dramatically different from that of the other ingredients in the salad. Raw carrots with too much crunch would take away from the elegance of this salad.

another bowl, mix the basil, scallions, crabmeat, capers, and carrots, and then fold in the lime vinaigrette. Taste for seasonings, adding hot sauce, lime juice, or salt as needed.

To serve, arrange a few lettuce leaves on each of the salad plates. Top the lettuce with equal portions of the crab salad and avocado slices, and garnish with basil sprigs.

Blanching

Blanching preserves a vegetable's color and enhances its flavor. It can also be used to loosen skins, as with tomatoes and peaches, to make for easier peeling. To blanch a vegetable, plunge it into lightly salted boiling water for a few minutes, drain, and put it into ice water, to "shock" the vegetable (i.e., stop the cooking).

Asian Noodle Salad with Spicy Peanut Sauce

MAKES 6 TO 8 SERVINGS   PREP TIME: 20 MINUTES

This salad was a customer favorite at Spice Inc. It's best with buckwheat noodles, but it can also be made with somen (wheat) noodles or even spaghetti. This is a great salad to eat all summer long.

NOODLES

1 (12-ounce) package buckwheat (soba) noodles

Salt

Spicy Peanut Sauce

2 tablespoons thinly sliced scallions

2 tablespoons chopped cilantro

Cook the noodles in boiling salted water for about 5 minutes, until cooked through but still firm. Drain well and place in a large bowl.

Toss the Spicy Peanut Sauce with the noodles and garnish with the scallion and cilantro.

SPICY PEANUT SAUCE

MAKES ABOUT 1½ CUPS,
ENOUGH FOR 1 BATCH OF NOODLES WITH A LITTLE LEFT OVER

2 tablespoons *ketjap manis* (Indonesian sweet soy sauce; see p. 14)

2 tablespoons fresh lime juice

1 tablespoon rice wine vinegar

1 tablespoon honey

½ cup lightly toasted peanuts

2 garlic cloves

½ teaspoon minced or grated fresh ginger

1 teaspoon *sambal oelek* or other red chile paste

¼ cup chopped cilantro

¼ cup thinly sliced scallions

½ teaspoon sesame oil

½ cup peanut or canola oil

Salt

Place all the ingredients (reserving 2 tablespoons cilantro and 2 tablespoons sliced scallions) except the peanut oil and salt in a blender or the bowl of a food processor and puree. Stop the motor and use a spoon or spatula to lift and incorporate the bottom of the mixture. With the motor running, slowly pour in the peanut oil. The sauce should be thick and creamy, like honey. Add a little water if it is too thick. The final sauce should be about the consistency of thin mayonnaise. Taste, and adjust seasoning for spiciness or salt.

For a bit more texture, add some chopped peanuts to the finished sauce.

Barbecued Chicken Salad with Corn, Avocado, and Creamy Poblano Dressing

MAKES 4 SERVINGS   PREP TIME: 30 MINUTES

I have never been able to do the cold-pizza-for-breakfast thing, but there are some foods I just love eating cold the day after—fried or barbecued chicken, for instance. Happily, my local grocery store does rotisserie chicken, either plain or barbecue, and on weeknights when homework is taking forever, I am grateful for this easy main course salad that the kids will actually dig into. For my husband and me, it's all about the creamy, spicy poblano dressing. But for the kids it's strictly ranch—no cilantro, please! For a more substantial meal, serve this with corn bread or, better yet, jalapeño corn bread (add chopped pickled jalapeños to your favorite recipe).

1½ to 2 cups diced barbecued chicken meat, from leftovers or a store-bought roasted chicken
1 ripe avocado, diced
½ cup frozen corn kernels, thawed, or 2 ears corn, grilled in the husk (see sidebar, p. 122), then shucked and cut from the cob

¼ cup thinly sliced celery or celery hearts
3 scallions, thinly sliced
1 head Bibb lettuce, broken into leaves, washed, and dried
Creamy Poblano Dressing (or quick ranch dressing)

Toss all the ingredients except dressing in a salad bowl, then toss in the dressing or serve it on the side.

Feel free to also add red peppers, tomatoes, and cotija (an aged Mexican cheese) or any crumbly white cheese to the salad. This salad is also delicious with corn bread croutons. (Day-old corn bread actually works best, because it will be drier. If you use fresh, you can dry it out in a 350°F oven for a few minutes.) Cut the corn bread into cubes, toss them with a little melted butter, and toast in a 350°F oven until golden brown and crisp. Let them cool, and toss with the salad.

CREAMY POBLANO DRESSING

Taste a portion of the poblano. Some are spicier than others, so adjust the amount accordingly. If it's really spicy you might want to add more mayo.

1 poblano, roasted and peeled
   (see below)
2 tablespoons fresh lime juice
2 tablespoons chopped scallion
   greens

1 garlic clove
1 cup Mayonnaise (p. 181)
2 tablespoons sour cream or
   buttermilk

Place all the ingredients in a blender and puree until smooth. Adjust seasonings as necessary.

Grilling Corn

Grilled corn has a sweet, smoky flavor that's great on its own (eaten off the cob with butter and a squirt of lime) and in salads. You'll want to grill the corn in its husk, because this preserves moisture and imparts a distinctive sweet and "corny" flavor. Simply soak the ears in cold water for about 20 minutes. Place them directly on a medium-low grill or over pale gray coals, and cover. Grill for about 20 minutes, turning the cobs every 5 minutes to ensure even cooking. As with any cooked corn, you'll know it's done when the kernels are tender and release a milky liquid when pierced. Peel away the husk and silk and serve as you wish.

Roasting Peppers and Chiles

To roast fresh poblanos or other peppers or chiles, place them directly on the grill over a low flame on a gas range, or on a baking sheet under a broiler, and char until evenly blackened, turning as necessary. Transfer peppers to a bowl and cover with a hand towel for about 5 minutes to steam the peppers (this will make their skins easier to remove). Alternatively, you can steam the peppers in a sealed plastic bag. Use your paring knife and/or your fingers to remove the stem, seeds, and skin from the peppers and use the smoky flesh as directed in the recipe.

Cornmeal-crusted Oyster and Black-eyed Pea Salad with Jalapeño Dressing

MAKES 4 SERVINGS   PREP TIME: 45 MINUTES

This is another dish that Ashley taught me. It's too good not to share. Cornmeal-coated oysters are crisp-fried and placed atop a salad of black-eyed peas, scallions, and red peppers. A chiffonade of spinach and celery root adds additional flavor and crunch (but it's the killer sweet, hot Jalapeño Dressing that steals the show). Feel free to add a few more hand-fuls of greens to make this a more substantial salad. This is a great lunch salad with a fat wedge of corn bread and a cold beer.

CORNMEAL COATING

1 cup cornmeal

1 teaspoon chopped fresh thyme

¼ teaspoon salt

½ teaspoon black pepper

¼ teaspoon cayenne

2 teaspoons minced fresh parsley

Mix all the ingredients in a small bowl or pie pan. Adjust the seasoning to your own taste, adding more cayenne or herbs as desired.

SALAD

1 (14-ounce) can black-eyed peas, drained and rinsed, or 1 cup dried, cooked as directed below

½ onion stuck with 2 cloves, optional

Bay leaf, optional

1 red bell pepper, stemmed, seeded, and diced

4 scallions, finely sliced

Jalapeño Dressing

1 small celery root

2 tablespoons fresh lemon juice

Pinch of salt

Canola or peanut oil, for frying

1 pint (about 24) shucked oysters

1 cup Cornmeal Coating

10 ounces fresh spinach, cleaned and sliced into a chiffonade

If using dried peas, place them in a small pot with about 3 cups of water, half an onion stuck with 2 cloves, and a bay leaf. Bring to a boil, then reduce the heat and simmer until the peas are tender but not mushy, about 30 minutes. Drain and rinse. If you're using canned peas, drain and rinse. Combine peas with the bell pepper and scallions in a small bowl. Pour ½ cup Jalapeño Dressing over this mixture and marinate for at least 5 minutes (or up to 30) at room temperature, or up to 4 hours in the refrigerator.

Use a chef's knife to trim away the rough skin and slice the celery root into fine julienne strips. Place a small saucepan with the celery root, lemon juice, salt, and water to cover over medium-high heat. Bring to a boil, drain, and set aside to cool. Meanwhile, prepare the Cornmeal Coating.

Heat 2 inches of frying oil in a medium saucepan or deep skillet over medium-high heat. Pour the shucked oysters into a colander and rinse, checking for shells. Pat them dry with paper towels. Dredge the oysters in the coating and place on a plate. When the oil is hot (about 350°F), fry the oysters (in batches to avoid overcrowding) until golden and crisp, about 2 minutes. Use a slotted spoon to remove them from the oil; drain on paper towels.

To serve, toss the celery root and spinach and place in a small mound on the center of each plate. Spoon black-eyed peas around the salad, and top with the fried oysters. Drizzle plate with any leftover dressing.

JALAPEÑO DRESSING

MAKES ABOUT I CUP

5 garlic cloves
1 heaping tablespoon chopped
    pickled jalapeños, plus 1 or 2
    whole pickled jalapeños, minced
1 tablespoon Dijon mustard
¼ teaspoon salt

¼ teaspoon hot sauce
¼ teaspoon Worcestershire sauce
1 tablespoon sugar
¼ cup apple cider vinegar
½ cup olive oil
1 shallot, finely minced

Combine the garlic, 1 tablespoon jalapeños, and mustard in a blender or food processor and pulse to puree. Add the salt, hot sauce, Worcestershire sauce, sugar, and vinegar and puree until smooth. With the blender running, add the olive oil in a slow, steady stream. Transfer the mixture to a small bowl and stir in the minced shallot and remaining jalapeños.

Spinach and Crispy Oyster Salad with Rosemary-Dijon Dressing

MAKES 4 SERVINGS   PREP TIME: 50 MINUTES

This irresistible salad became a signature at Savoir Faire. I coat the oysters with bread crumbs flavored with sage, rosemary, and parsley—and strongly encourage you to use all three. The smell alone will have your mouth watering. Fried in this coating, the oysters take on a rich flavor that suggests stuffing. Placed atop a fresh spinach salad, the dish becomes a playful twist on Oysters Rockefeller (raw oysters on the half shell, topped with a spinach–bread crumb mixture and baked). The Rosemary-Dijon Dressing (which should be made first so the salad will come together easily at the end) is one you'll make again and again—it's delicious on just about any mix of greens.

1 pint (about 24) shucked oysters

2 cups dry bread crumbs

4 tablespoons chopped fresh herbs (such as sage, rosemary, and parsley), or 2 tablespoons mixed dried herbs

1 cup egg whites (from about 8 large eggs), lightly beaten

6 cups spinach, stemmed, washed, and dried

4 large or 8 small button mushrooms, sliced

Olive or vegetable oil, for frying

Rosemary-Dijon Dressing

4 scallions, thinly sliced, as garnish

Rinse and drain the oysters, then dry them thoroughly on paper towels. On a plate or pie tin, combine the bread crumbs and herbs. Dip the oysters in frothy egg whites and then in herbed bread crumbs. Press the oysters in the crumbs to ensure an even coating. Lay the oysters on a tray in one layer and set aside or refrigerate (uncovered) until ready to cook. Prepare the spinach and divide among four plates. Arrange mushroom slices around the spinach. Heat 1 inch of olive oil in a medium skillet over medium-high heat. Add the oysters and cook until evenly golden brown, about 4 minutes. Divide oysters evenly among the four plates. Drizzle with the dressing and sprinkle with scallions. Serve immediately.

ROSEMARY-DIJON DRESSING

MAKES ABOUT I CUP,
ENOUGH FOR 4 SERVINGS PLUS A LITTLE LEFT OVER

2 tablespoons finely chopped shallots

¼ cup red wine vinegar

1 tablespoon Dijon mustard

1 teaspoon fresh lemon juice

¾ cup olive oil

1 tablespoon chopped fresh rosemary

Salt and pepper

Hot sauce

Whisk together the shallots, vinegar, mustard, and lemon juice in a small bowl. Slowly whisk in the olive oil until the dressing is creamy and emulsified. Stir in the rosemary and season with salt, pepper, and hot sauce. Taste and adjust seasonings, adding more oil if the dressing is too sharp.

For this dish, I suggest panfrying in olive oil because I love the flavor, but you can use any neutral vegetable oil, such as canola or peanut. Either way, you should use enough oil to completely cover the bottom of the pan, and make sure it gets good and hot (but not smoking). To reduce spattering when frying, see that your oysters are dry before dipping them into the egg white and bread crumbs. You might also invest in a spatter screen, which is inexpensive and works well. If your mushrooms aren't nice enough to use raw, you can sauté them.

Crispy Smoked Quail Salad with Bourbon-Molasses Dressing

MAKES 4 SERVINGS   PREP TIME: 2 HOURS 30 MINUTES (INCLUDES MARINATING AND SMOKING TIME)

This rich and smoky salad has become, hands down, the most popular dish on the menu at Bayona. I think it's owing to the combination of textures and flavors, and the way they all mingle together and complement one another. There are several components to this salad, and that's why it's so satisfying. The good news is that many of these steps can be done in advance.

The trickiest technique is cold-smoking the quail, which infuses it with natural smoky flavor without cooking it. That means when we fry the batter-dipped bird at the last minute, the result is both crispy and juicy. At the restaurant we make a stock with the smoked quail wings and use it to enrich the dressing, but this is not necessary. If pears are not in season, apples make a good substitute.

QUAIL

1 tablespoon honey

1 tablespoon *ketjap manis* (see p. 14)

3 tablespoons canola oil

4 quail, partially deboned (about 5 ounces total)

Whisk together the honey, *ketjap manis,* and oil in a medium bowl. Nestle the quail in the marinade, ensuring that each inside cavity is moistened, and refrigerate for at least 1 hour. Drain the quail and cold-smoke (see p. 128) for about 15 minutes. The quail should not cook in the process.

BOURBON-MOLASSES DRESSING
MAKES ABOUT ¾ CUP OR 4 TO 6 SERVINGS

1 tablespoon molasses

2 tablespoons apple cider vinegar

1 tablespoon walnut vinegar (or 1 teaspoon walnut oil)

1 shallot, finely chopped

½ cup pure olive oil

Salt and pepper

2 teaspoons bourbon

Note: Walnut vinegar can be hard to find, but it imparts a wonderfully nutty flavor. Look for it in specialty food stores, or on the Internet.

Whisk together the molasses, vinegars, and shallot in a small bowl. Whisk in the olive oil, season with salt and pepper, and stir in the bourbon.

RICE FLOUR BATTER

½ cup rice flour	¼ teaspoon salt
⅓ to ½ cup cold water	

Whisk the ingredients together in a small bowl and set aside. The batter should be the consistency of whipping cream in order to lightly coat the quail.

TO ASSEMBLE

Peanut or vegetable oil, for frying	Bourbon-Molasses Dressing
Marinated, smoked quail	¼ cup chopped celery hearts and
Rice Flour Batter	tender leaves
1 ripe pear, cut into quarters, then	2 tablespoons chopped Pickled Red
each quarter into 4 wedges	Onions (p. 196)
4 cups young spinach or other salad	2 tablespoons Cajun-spiced Pecans
greens, cleaned	(p. 22)

Heat 2½ inches of the frying oil in a deep skillet (large enough to hold the quail in a single layer) to about 350°F. Dip the quail in the batter. Lift them out of the batter and hold over the container, letting the excess drip off. Fry the quail for about 4 minutes, turning once. Drain them on paper towels, cool slightly, and cut into quarters (2 legs and 2 breasts).

    Place 4 pear wedges on each of four plates. Toss the greens with a few spoonfuls of dressing and the celery hearts and pickled onions, and divide among the plates. Top the salads with the quail and sprinkle with spiced pecans. Drizzle with more dressing, if desired.

Cold Smoking

Cold smoking allows you to cool the smoke before it reaches the food (so the food absorbs flavor without cooking). To cold-smoke, open the vents on both the bottom of the grill and the lid. Remove the lid and top rack from the grill, and center a disposable roasting pan on the coals. Place 1½ cups of sawdust in the pan. Fill the drip pan between the grill and the hot coals with an aluminum or metal tub of ice. Cover the grill and smoke for 15 minutes.

Spicy Thai Salad with Shrimp, Pork, and Crispy Rice Noodles

MAKES 4 SERVINGS   **PREP TIME: 1 HOUR**

In 1995, I was lucky enough to be invited as a guest chef at the Oriental Hotel in Bangkok. I brought my sous chef and pastry chef with me, and for two weeks we toured the temples and markets of the city, seeing (and eating) many unusual and beautiful things. I vividly remember the profusion of flowers and the tasty and sometimes strange street food (such as the edible insect cart, which we avoided), and the gradual change from barely tolerating hot chiles to actually craving them on a daily basis. When I returned, my sous chef, Ronald Carr, helped me develop this dish to showcase the new flavors that I'd fallen for.

This substantial salad could be served for lunch, dinner, or as a first course before something light, such as grilled fish. To lighten up the salad, you can add an extra handful of shredded cabbage or even more of the crispy noodles (keep in mind that the salad will be a bit drier if you do this). Small or medium shrimp work just fine in this recipe, and they're less expensive than larger varieties.

THAI BASE

½ cup fish sauce

⅓ cup *ketjap manis* (see Spicer Pantry, p. 14)

½ cup lime juice

½ cup rice wine vinegar

1 cup sugar

1 tablespoon *sambal oelek* (red chile paste)

Whisk everything together and taste. Adjust for acidity, sweetness, and heat; set aside.

The recipe for the Thai base makes more than you'll need in this salad, but the base will keep in the refrigerator for several weeks. It's great to have on hand to flavor other dishes; you can basically use it anywhere you'd use soy sauce. Splash it into stir-fried broccoli, shrimp, eggplant, or noodles. It's delicious with pork dishes as well.

CRISPY RICE NOODLES

Vegetable oil, for frying

2 ounces dried rice noodles

Heat 2 inches of the oil in a wok or large, deep skillet to 375°F, or just below the smoking point. Fry the noodles in two batches; they will cook and expand almost instantly (and the shape of the wok has room for the noodles to puff). Remove them with a slotted spoon or basket, and drain on paper towels.

SALAD

2 cups shredded napa cabbage

1 carrot, grated

4 scallions, sliced on the bias

½ cup chopped fresh herbs (any
   combination of mint, basil, Thai
   basil, and cilantro)

½ teaspoon very thinly sliced kaffir
   lime leaves

Assemble the ingredients in a large bowl; set aside.

SHRIMP AND PORK MIXTURE

2 tablespoons peanut or canola oil

½ cup thinly sliced shallots
   (4–5 shallots)

4 garlic cloves, minced

1 or 2 stalks lemongrass, minced
   (2 tablespoons)

2 tablespoons grated fresh
   ginger

4 ounces shrimp, finely chopped
   (about ½ cup)

4 ounces lean pork, finely chopped
   (about ½ cup)

½ cup Thai Base

Salt, optional

Salad

Crispy Rice Noodles

In a medium nonstick skillet, heat the peanut oil and sauté the shallots and garlic until golden, stirring constantly so as not to burn the garlic. Add the lemongrass and ginger and stir for 1–2 minutes. Stir in the shrimp and pork and cook, breaking up lumps with a spoon, for about 3 minutes. Add the Thai Base and stir to incorporate. Allow the mixture to simmer and thicken for about 2 minutes. Taste for seasoning, adding salt if necessary, and remove from the heat.

TO ASSEMBLE

Shrimp and Pork Mixture

Salad

Crispy Rice Noodles

Thai Base

Toss the warm shrimp and pork mixture with the salad ingredients until well combined. Add the noodles and toss again; serve immediately on a large platter or individual plates. Garnish with additional chopped herbs and a drizzle of the Thai Base, if desired.

All That Simmers,
and Sandwiches with Soul

Cream of Garlic Soup

Cream of Celery Soup

Indonesian Peanut-Celery Soup

Farmer's Market Chicken and Vegetable Soup

Elegant Oyster and Artichoke Soup

Mexican Green Gazpacho with Shellfish

Herbsaint Shrimp and Tomato Bisque

Smoked Duck and Andouille Gumbo

Gumbo z'Herbes (Green Gumbo with Oysters)

Jalapeño-roast Pork on Ciabatta with Pickled Cabbage and Creole Mustard

Prosciutto-wrapped Tuna Muffuletta

Roast Turkey with Blue Cream Cheese on Multigrain Bread

Crayfish Croque Monsieur

Danish Roast Beef Sandwich with Crispy Onions

Shrimp Salad with Fennel and Herbed Cream Cheese on Brioche

Grilled Andouille Po'boy "Creolaise"

Hibachi Souvlaki with Cucumber-Yogurt Sauce

Smoked Duck "PBJ" with Cashew Butter, Pepper Jelly, and Apple-Celery Salad

I am always amazed at how instantly the smell of split pea soup takes me back to the summer of '69, and a cabin in the chilly Wisconsin woods that I shared with my three girlfriends on our first road trip after high school graduation. None of us knew much about cooking, but we managed to track down some onions and smoked ham, and we ate split pea soup for about three days straight! Every single time I make it, that memory comes roaring back, and I stand there over the simmering pot in a delicious daze, reliving all the adventures we had.

Having been in charge of "soup du jour" for twenty-something years, I have since made soup out of just about anything in the kitchen (from meager vegetable scraps to leftover lamb and duck). Needless to say, I've learned a thing or two about concocting the richest stocks, the tastiest garnishes, and the very best flavor combinations.

Soups can be complex, exotic, delicate, substantial, and exciting. From a simple and elegant Cream of Celery Soup (p. 141) to a hardy Farmer's Market Chicken and Vegetable Soup (p. 143) or sausage-laden gumbo, soups serve any number of needs in a meal: the perfect introduction, the satisfying main dish, the soul-soothing meal-for-one, or the focal point for a group celebration.

Over the years I've also constructed sandwiches for just about every occasion, from Jazz Fest to lunch for noshers at Spice Inc. to casual alfresco dinners on the patio with friends. Let's face it, the old soup-and-sandwich combo still works when you need a substantial lunch or light dinner. There's an art to pairing soup and sandwiches. Just like matching wine with food, sometimes the perfect marriage is about contrast; other times it's simply about complementing flavors. Shrimp and Tomato Bisque (p. 149) and Prosciutto-wrapped Tuna

Muffuletta (p. 155), for instance, make a dynamic Crescent City combo. Soothing Cream of Celery Soup (p. 141) nestles easily alongside Roast Turkey with Blue Cream Cheese on Multigrain Bread (p. 157).

I have recently become something of a sandwich expert, now that I am packing one up for my husband to take to work each day. My collection of pickles, relishes, salsas, chutneys, mustards, and butters (see Spicer Pantry, p. 9) is really paying off here. According to Chip, they help me transform the ordinary into the extraordinary.

———————————————

Cream of Garlic Soup

MAKES 8 SERVINGS   PREP TIME: 1 HOUR

The secret to this soup, a luscious puree of caramelized garlic and onions thickened with French bread, is patience. I originally developed it at Savoir Faire. At the time I had a boyfriend who frequently traveled to Mexico. He would rave about *sopa de ajo*—a broth flavored with garlic and egg—and it sounded so earthy and scrumptious that I decided to try to make it. My approach to recipe development typically involves looking up several versions of a dish, then taking what I like from each of those recipes. That's exactly how this soup was created. I trained with French chefs, so a puree leapt to mind. Then I read that in Latin countries soups are often thickened with bread. One version relied on fish stock, but I thought chicken stock would be more universally appealing. So I stirred all my ideas together, my mentor Daniel gave it his enthusiastic blessing, and my first true culinary creation was born.

When we initially started making this soup, my dishwashers had to peel 10 pounds of garlic at a time. Thankfully, these days at Bayona, we buy peeled garlic by the gallon. In order to develop the proper deep, rich flavor, it's essential to take your time cooking the garlic. You need to stir the mixture a lot over low heat and wait until the onions and garlic get very dark and caramelized. I love garnishing this soup with tiny croutons that provide a crunchy contrast to the silky body.

---

2 tablespoons butter

2 tablespoons olive oil

6 cups peeled and sliced onions (about 2 pounds)

2 cups peeled but not chopped garlic cloves

1 tablespoon chopped fresh thyme, or 1 teaspoon dried

7 cups Chicken Stock, preferably homemade (p. 206)

1 Bouquet Garni (p. 145) made with parsley stems, thyme sprigs, and bay leaf

3 cups stale French bread, torn into ½-inch pieces

1 cup half-and-half or heavy cream

Salt and pepper

Heat the butter and oil in a heavy-bottomed 2-quart saucepan or Dutch oven over medium-low heat. Add the onions and garlic and cook, stirring frequently, until they turn a deep golden brown, 30–40 minutes. Add the thyme, 6 cups Chicken Stock, and Bouquet Garni and bring to a boil. Stir in the bread cubes and let simmer for 10 minutes, until the bread is soft. Remove the soup from heat and cool for 10 minutes.

Remove the Bouquet Garni and puree the soup in a blender (in batches, if necessary), until completely smooth. Return the soup to the pot and heat to the desired temperature. Whisk in more Chicken Stock if the mixture is too thick. Add half-and-half or cream until the soup reaches the texture of a classic cream soup. Season to taste with salt and pepper.

If the bottom of the pot gets sticky while you're cooking the onions and garlic, add a little water and stir to dissolve.

Cream of Celery Soup

I belong to the growing cult who believe that celery is an underappreciated vegetable. Used raw, it has a juicy, nutty crispness that stands on its own with just a couple of other ingredients. When cooked, the flavor becomes deeper and richer, as it does in this soup. Don't be fooled by the deceptively simple sound of this soup. This celadon puree is elegant and comforting, and can serve as the basis for more complex variations, such as adding leeks, asparagus, broccoli, or poached shredded chicken. Judicious seasoning is important, as salt will really round out the flavors. Croutons made from multigrain bread are the perfect garnish.

---

3 tablespoons butter

2 medium onions, coarsely chopped

1 bunch celery, washed and chopped (leaves removed)

1 medium potato, peeled and diced (about 1 cup)

2 tablespoons flour

Salt and pepper

4 cups Chicken Stock (p. 206) or Vegetable Stock (p. 204)

½ cup heavy cream

Snipped fresh chives, for garnish

Classic Croutons (p. 88), made with multigrain bread, for garnish

Microcelery, or cutting celery, for garnish

Melt the butter in a 2-quart pot over medium heat and add the onions, celery, and potato, and stir. Cover the pot, reduce the heat to low, and let the vegetables steam for about 10 minutes, stirring once. Remove the cover and stir in the flour. Add a little salt and pepper, then whisk in the Chicken Stock, 1 cup at a time. Bring to a boil, whisking, then reduce the heat and simmer for about 15 minutes, until the vegetables are completely tender. Remove the mixture from the heat, let it cool, then puree it in a blender (in batches, if necessary) and return it to the pot. Bring to a boil, whisk in the cream, adjust the seasonings and consistency (adding stock or a little water if the soup is too thick), and serve hot in warmed bowls, garnished with snipped chives and multigrain croutons or add cutting celery, as shown.

Indonesian Peanut-Celery Soup

MAKES 6 TO 8 SERVINGS   PREP TIME: 35 MINUTES

This recipe came about much like the Reese's Peanut Butter Cup commercial—"You got chocolate on my peanut butter," etc. One day a long time ago, I had some peanut sauce left over from making pork satés, and I was in the process of putting together a cream of celery soup. I started thinking about how people have been known to eat celery sticks with peanut butter, so I swirled the rich sauce into the delicate soup. With a little extra garlic, chile paste, and soy sauce, the result was pretty darn tasty—and I've been making it ever since.

2 tablespoons cooking oil, such as
   peanut or canola
1 medium onion, chopped
1 bunch celery, trimmed and chopped
2 garlic cloves, minced
4–5 cups Chicken Stock (p. 206) or
   Vegetable Stock (p. 204) or water

1 cup creamy peanut butter
¼ cup *ketjap manis* (p. 14)
1 teaspoon *sambal oelek* (or other red
   chile paste)
¼ cup chopped dry-roasted peanuts

Heat the oil in a 2-quart pot over medium heat and add the onion, celery, and garlic and cook, stirring, for about 5 minutes, until the vegetables have softened. Reduce the heat to low, cover the pot, and let them steam for about 10 minutes, stirring once. Add the Chicken Stock and whisk in the peanut butter, a little at a time. Bring to a boil, whisking, and add the *ketjap manis* and *sambal oelek*, and a little more stock or water if the soup is too thick. Simmer about 10 minutes, then let it cool. Working in batches if necessary, puree the soup in a blender and return it to the pot. Heat the soup to the desired temperature, adjusting the seasonings (add more chile paste, if desired) and consistency (add more stock or water, if needed). Garnish with roasted peanuts and serve.

Farmer's Market Chicken and Vegetable Soup

MAKES 8 SERVINGS   PREP TIME: 1 HOUR

The Crescent City Farmer's Market has had a huge impact on the quality of cooking and eating in New Orleans, and on my own life as well. Over the years it has grown from one location where you could get only bell peppers and tomatoes, one day a week, to four bustling locations (open four days a week) where you can buy anything from Creole cream cheese to colorful varieties of eggplant and Swiss chard, lemongrass, Thai basil, soft-shell crabs, tamales, hibiscus flowers, sweet potato pies, and mayhaw jelly! Happily, post-Katrina, the farmers are back, and this vital part of the community is still up and running.

My only complaint is that I can't just run in and grab what I need in a hurry. When I go, I spend at least an hour perusing produce, catching up with farmers, and socializing with all the other shoppers and chefs I know. The market is a modern-day village green. Of course, this is also what I love about it. If you're lucky enough to have a real farmer's market in your area (they're sprouting up everywhere), be sure to seek it out. It's bound to have the makings for this soothing and delicious chicken and vegetable soup, among other satisfying meals. Feel free to substitute local seasonal vegetables for any of the ones listed here.

---

2 tablespoons butter

1 medium onion, chopped

2 celery stalks, split lengthwise and sliced in ¼-inch slices

1 carrot, split lengthwise and sliced in ¼-inch slices

2 leeks, split lengthwise, washed, and sliced

6 cups skimmed Chicken Stock (p. 206)

1–2 cups fresh tomato puree made by blending and straining chopped ripe tomatoes or canned or boxed chopped tomatoes, optional

Bouquet Garni (p. 145)

Salt and pepper

1 yellow squash, cut lengthwise into quarters and sliced ¼ inch thick

¼ pound blanched green beans, cut in ½-inch pieces

2 cups chopped escarole, chard, or kale, optional

1 cup cooked noodles or diced boiled potatoes, optional

The meat from 2 poached boneless chicken breast halves, diced or shredded (about 2 cups), optional

1 tablespoon chopped mixed fresh herbs, such as tarragon, chives, basil, and/or dill

2 teaspoons grated lemon zest

Melt the butter in a large pot over medium-high heat. Add the onion, celery, carrot, and leeks and sweat for 10–15 minutes. Add the stock and tomato puree and bring to a boil. Reduce the heat, add the Bouquet Garni, and simmer for 10 more minutes, then season with salt and pepper. About 10 minutes before serving add the squash, green beans, and greens, if using. Continue to cook and in 5 minutes add the noodles or potatoes, chicken, herbs, and lemon zest and cook 5 more minutes. Check and adjust the seasonings, then ladle into warmed soup bowls and serve.

Poaching Chicken Breasts

To poach chicken breasts, bring 2 cups of strained Chicken Stock (p. 206) to a simmer in a medium skillet. Add 2 boneless, skinless chicken breasts that have been seasoned with salt and pepper, and a sprig of tarragon and/or thyme, if desired, and gently simmer for 15 minutes, turning once. Allow the chicken to cool and shred or dice the meat, and add the remaining broth to the soup pot.

Soup Variations

Feel free to vary the vegetables in this soup to fit the season or the personality of your particular market. To give the chicken soup an Asian flavor, for instance, replace the cloves with star anise and add cilantro stems to the Bouquet Garni. Then add Asian greens like bok choy, gai lan (Chinese broccoli), Japanese eggplant, and dried or fresh mushrooms. For an autumn-inspired soup, replace the green beans and summer squash with root vegetables (parsnips, turnips, and rutabaga), butternut squash, and/or cabbage.

Bouquet Garni

Having trained with French chefs, I find a bouquet garni—a pretty little bundle of fresh herbs—an indispensable seasoning for adding depth and an herbaceous perfume to stocks, soups, and sauces. Plus I always feel just a little more French when I cinch one up.

To assemble one, take 1 bunch of parsley stems, stripped of leaves (or most of them), 2 small bay leaves or 1 medium, and a generous sprig of fresh thyme. Lay the parsley stems down and spread them a little, then place the bay leaf and thyme in the center and surround with the parsley stems. Cut a 15-inch piece of kitchen twine and pick up the bundle in your left hand. Holding the string about 3 inches from the end between the thumb and index finger of your left hand, use your right hand to wrap the string twice around one end of the bundle, then bring the string down to the other end, wrapping around twice, then back to the middle and around once, meeting the 3-inch piece and tying a secure knot. Some folks like to leave a long piece to tie the bouquet onto the pot handle (making it easier to remove later), but I usually just trim it short. In a nod to French perfectionism, I also trim the ends of the herbs so they're nice and neat. And be sure to tie it snugly. If the bundle is not tied tightly, it can disintegrate when the parsley stems cook and become limp.

Elegant Oyster and Artichoke Soup

This silky concoction makes an elegant starter, or a light supper if paired with the Parisienne Bistro Crudité Plate (p. 102) or the Bayona House Salad with Balsamic Vinaigrette (p. 95) and a warm baguette. Oysters and artichokes are another favorite New Orleans combination. For your convenience I've called for canned artichoke hearts, but if you're feeling expansive (and industrious), use fresh artichoke hearts. Your efforts will be rewarded.

3 tablespoons olive oil or butter

1 medium onion, finely chopped

2 celery stalks, finely chopped

1 (12-ounce) can artichoke hearts, rinsed and chopped, or an equal amount of fresh hearts

1 garlic clove, minced

3 tablespoons flour

½ cup dry white wine

2 cups milk

1 pint oysters, drained (reserve the liquid) and coarsely chopped

1 cup heavy cream

4 scallions, minced

Salt and pepper

Hot sauce

Fresh lemon juice, as desired

Classic Croutons (p. 88), optional

In a 2-quart saucepan, heat the olive oil over medium-high heat until it starts to sizzle. Add the onion, celery, artichoke hearts, and garlic and stir. Sauté for 5 minutes, then sprinkle with the flour and stir. Slowly whisk in the white wine, milk, and the oyster liquid. Bring to a boil, stirring or whisking, then add the cream, reduce heat, and simmer for about 10 minutes. Stir in the oysters, scallions, and a little salt and simmer about 5 more minutes. Season to taste with salt, pepper, and hot sauce. Add a squeeze of lemon and garnish with croutons.

Mexican Green Gazpacho with Shellfish

MAKES 4 SERVINGS   PREP TIME: 45 MINUTES

I remember a time when gazpacho became very trendy and was on every menu. I decided to come up with a different version—even with a different color. It was José Andrés of Jaleo in Washington, D.C., who made the best Spanish gazpacho I ever tasted, so I borrowed his technique of frying the bread in olive oil. The toasted flavor and richness of the fried bread helps mellow the acidity and round out the flavors of the other ingredients. The shellfish garnish is not necessary but makes the dish a little more elegant and sumptuous.

---

6 tablespoons olive oil, plus extra for frying and for crab

1 large onion, diced

2 poblano peppers, stemmed, seeded, and diced

½ pound tomatillos, husked, rinsed, and diced

1 slice of bread, white or wheat, diced or torn into pieces

1 garlic clove, minced

2 cucumbers, peeled, seeded, and diced (reserve 2 tablespoons for garnish)

1 bunch scallions, trimmed and minced (reserve 1 for garnish)

1 bunch cilantro, washed and roughly chopped (reserve a few nice sprigs for garnish)

1 jalapeño, seeded and minced

½ teaspoon ground cumin

Juice of 3 limes (about 6 tablespoons), plus extra for crab

Salt and pepper

Hot sauce

Vegetable oil, for frying

2 corn tortillas, cut into strips

¼ pound lump crabmeat, well picked

12 large cooked shrimp, peeled and deveined

1 small ripe avocado, peeled and sliced or diced

½ small ripe mango, peeled and diced, or 2 or 3 radishes, grated or diced

Heat 2 tablespoons olive oil in a medium skillet over medium-high heat. Add the onion, poblanos, and tomatillos. Cook for about 10 minutes, until the peppers are softened and the tomatillos begin to break down. Remove the skillet from heat and let it cool for a bit, then transfer the vegetables to a blender and puree until smooth.

Wipe out the skillet and heat the remaining 4 tablespoons olive oil until shimmering. Fry the pieces of bread until golden. Turn off the heat, stir in the garlic, then add the bread mixture to the blender. Add the cucumbers, scallions, cilantro, jalapeño, cumin, and half the lime juice and blend until smooth.

Season the puree with a little salt, pepper, and hot sauce, and taste. Balance the seasoning, adding more lime or even cucumber if the flavor is too strong. Pour the soup into a container and chill thoroughly.

Heat 1½ inches of the vegetable oil in a medium skillet until hot but not smoking. Add the tortilla strips and fry until crisp and golden. Remove with a slotted spoon and drain on paper towels.

When ready to serve, moisten the crabmeat with a little olive oil and lime juice. Place about 1 cup of gazpacho in the bottom of four soup plates or bowls. Place 3 shrimp and equal portions of the crabmeat in the center of each bowl. Sprinkle with avocado, mango, and cucumber, and top with crispy tortilla strips, scallions, and cilantro sprigs.

Sometimes poblanos are really spicy, sometimes they are not. Depends on what they're grown near, etc. You can usually smell when you cut into them. Or cut a small sliver. If it's way fiery, decrease the amount you use in this dish.

Herbsaint Shrimp and Tomato Bisque

MAKES 10 TO 12 SERVINGS   PREP TIME: ABOUT 50 MINUTES

One of the richest, creamiest soups around, bisque is traditionally a puree of seafood, rice, and cream. This luscious version is New Orleans's eating at its finest. The elegant flavors call for little more than an equally impressive white wine to serve alongside this dish. The aromatic vegetables, tomatoes, tarragon, and liqueur make this recipe particularly distinctive.

2 tablespoons butter or olive oil

2 medium onions, chopped

4 celery stalks, chopped

2 medium carrots, chopped

1 bunch scallions, chopped

3 garlic cloves, minced

½ pound small shrimp (40–50 count), peeled

2 cups tomato dice with juice, or 1 (14-ounce) can

1 tablespoon tomato paste

4 cups Shrimp Stock (p. 229)

1 bay leaf

½ cup raw rice, or 1 cup cooked rice

2 tablespoons chopped fresh tarragon

1 cup heavy cream

2 tablespoons brandy

1 teaspoon Herbsaint or Pernod

Salt

Hot sauce (preferably Crystal or Louisiana brand)

Chopped scallions or snipped fresh chives, for garnish

Heat the butter in a heavy-bottomed pot over medium-high heat. Add onions, celery, carrots, and scallions and cook, stirring, for about 10 minutes, then add the garlic and shrimp and cook 3 more minutes. Add the tomato dice, tomato paste, shrimp stock, 4 cups water, and bay leaf and stir. Bring it to a boil, then lower the heat and simmer for about 10 minutes. Stir in the rice and tarragon and cook another 20 minutes, until rice is completely soft. Let it cool for about 10 minutes. Carefully puree in a blender, in batches if necessary, and strain through a fine sieve into another pot. Whisk in the cream, brandy, and Herbsaint and taste for seasoning. Add salt and hot sauce and adjust consistency as desired with water, stock, or more cream. Serve hot, garnished with scallions or chives.

You might want to reserve a few whole shrimp for garnish (or simply sauté a few extra). This recipe makes a lot, but it freezes well.

Smoked Duck and Andouille Gumbo

MAKES 8 SERVINGS   PREP TIME: 3 HOURS (INCLUDES DUCK ROASTING TIME)

Although I was not born in New Orleans—we moved here when I was six—I most definitely consider it my hometown. Even post-hurricanes, I am eternally grateful to my dad for deciding to make this simmering, sumptuous, gumbo-of-a-city our permanent home when he retired from the navy. What a happy circumstance for a food lover like me!

Speaking of gumbo, I could eat it every day of the week. And you can't claim to be a cook in Louisiana without having your own version of its most famous dish. While I have to say that Donald Link, the chef at Herbsaint, makes the best gumbo I have ever eaten, I've learned to make a pretty mean version myself. Here is one of the most basic. Feel free to substitute an equal amount of roasted chicken for the duck.

---

4 duck legs, or 1 whole duck

Salt and pepper

½ cup vegetable oil or rendered duck fat, plus extra for cooking okra

½ cup flour

2 medium onions, chopped

2 bell peppers, chopped

3 celery stalks, chopped

½ pound andouille sausage, halved lengthwise and sliced

4–5 garlic cloves, minced

6 cups rich Chicken Stock (p. 206)

2 cups sliced okra, fresh or frozen

½ cup plus 2 tablespoons chopped scallions

1 teaspoon chopped fresh thyme

1 teaspoon filé powder, optional

1 tablespoon Worcestershire sauce

Bouquet Garni (p. 145)

Hot sauce

Cooked white rice, optional

Preheat the oven to 350°F. Place the duck in a roasting pan and season with salt and pepper. Roast the legs for about 1 hour (the whole duck for about 2 hours), until tender. If desired, save the rendered fat to make the roux. Let the duck cool and pick the meat off the bones.

Heat the ½ cup oil (or duck fat) in a large, heavy-bottomed Dutch oven or cast-iron pot over medium-high heat until almost smoking. Add the flour and whisk constantly until the roux turns a deep brown resembling the color of peanut butter (or even a little darker, for a richer flavor), 10–12 minutes. Add the onions, peppers, and celery, reduce the heat to medium, and cook, stirring, for 5 minutes. Stir in the sausage and cook 3 more minutes. Then add the garlic and whisk in the stock, 1 cup at a time. Bring to a boil, reduce the heat, and simmer for 15 minutes.

Heat 2 tablespoons vegetable oil in a small skillet over medium-high heat. When the oil is hot but not smoking, sear the okra and add to the pot, along with ½ cup scallions. Add the thyme, optional filé powder, Worcestershire sauce, Bouquet Garni, hot sauce to taste, the reserved duck meat, and a little salt. Simmer over low heat, stirring from time to time, for at least 1 hour. Skim off any fat from the top. Season with salt, pepper, and hot sauce and serve hot, with or without rice. Garnish with the reserved scallions.

To enrich your chicken broth or intensify a store-bought one, pour it into a pot, add the picked duck or chicken bones, and simmer for 15 minutes. You may need to add a little water to make sure you end up with 6 cups.

The right cookware is essential for gumbo—don't even think about using a thin, flimsy pot.

Filé Powder

An essential ingredient in Creole cooking, filé powder (see Sources, p. 384) is a spice made from cured sassafras leaves. The Choctaw Indians from the southern Louisiana bayou taught the Cajuns to use the spice, which has an earthy, woodsy flavor.

Gumbo z'Herbes (Green Gumbo with Oysters)

MAKES 8 TO 10 SERVINGS   PREP TIME: 2 HOURS

This fabulous, herbaceous gumbo used to be primarily a meatless Lenten dish, served on Good Friday. It is a pretty rare find on menus these days, but if you should come across it, give it a try. It is a thinner, soupier gumbo than most, and you'll be surprised how much flavor the greens impart to the broth. When I made it the first time, I thought of how wonderful oysters would taste with the herbs, so I decided to top it off with a few fried ones. You could still serve it during Lent, but don't reserve this delicious gumbo for once a year.

½ cup cooking oil (or bacon fat), plus more for frying oysters

½ cup flour

2 medium onions, chopped

2 green bell peppers, chopped

½ bunch celery, chopped

2 medium turnips, peeled and chopped

1 cup plus ½ cup chopped scallions

2 garlic cloves, minced

6 cups total of 2 or more of the following (washed thoroughly and coarsely chopped): turnip greens, mustard greens, collard greens, spinach, kale, escarole, or chard

1 tablespoon chopped fresh thyme leaves, or 1 teaspoon dried

1 teaspoon filé powder

2 quarts Chicken Stock (p. 206)

1 pint oysters (strain and reserve the liquor)

1 tablespoon Worcestershire sauce

Bouquet Garni (p. 145) made with parsley stems, bay leaf, and thyme

Salt and pepper

Hot sauce

Cornmeal, for dusting

Cooked white rice, optional

Heat ½ cup oil in a large, heavy-bottomed pot over medium-high heat until almost smoking. Carefully whisk in the flour. Continue whisking until the roux is the color of peanut butter, or a little darker. Add the onions, bell peppers, celery, turnips, 1 cup scallions, and garlic, and cook, stirring to coat vegetables with roux, for 5 minutes. Add the greens, stir, and cook for about 10 minutes, or until they are wilted; add the thyme and filé powder. Stir in the chicken stock, 2 cups at a time, bringing the mixture to a boil after each addition. Whisk in the oyster liquor and Worcestershire sauce. Bring the gumbo to a boil, then reduce the heat to a simmer. Add the Bouquet Garni and cook over medium-low heat for about 1 hour, adding more chicken stock or water if the mixture gets too thick. Season to taste with salt, pepper, and hot sauce.

Heat ½ inch of the vegetable oil in a medium skillet to about 350°F. Dust raw oysters with cornmeal and shallow-fry very quickly, until golden. Season with salt and pepper.

To serve the gumbo, ladle generous portions into bowls and garnish each bowl with 3 oysters, the remaining scallions, and hot rice, if desired.

Jalapeño-roast Pork on Ciabatta with Pickled Cabbage and Creole Mustard

MAKES 8 SERVINGS   PREP TIME: 30 MINUTES (NOT INCLUDING PORK COOKING TIME)

On its own, Jalapeño-roast Pork (p. 269) makes for an incredible meal. But these sandwiches, made from the leftover pork, are so delicious that you may end up roasting the shoulder just to make them. We served the sandwiches at Spice Inc. for two years. I originally learned this recipe from my partner Regina Keever, but the recipe has since been taken over by Jane Ruppel, our beloved office manager and resident party monster, who prepares it for virtually every Bayona get-together, by request. The meat can be used in countless ways and is simply irresistible. The pickled cabbage, spicy Creole mustard, and pickles cut the richness of the pork.

PICKLED CABBAGE

2 cups apple cider or cane vinegar

2 tablespoons salt

½ cup sugar

4 cups finely shredded green cabbage

2 cups finely sliced white or yellow onions

1 teaspoon freshly ground black pepper

Place the vinegar, salt, and sugar in a small saucepan and bring to a boil. Place the cabbage and onions in a large bowl. Pour the hot vinegar mixture into the bowl, add pepper, and toss. Let stand for 15 minutes, then toss again, taste, and adjust seasoning. Add more vinegar, salt, or sugar accordingly. Place in a glass or plastic container and set aside.

TO ASSEMBLE

24 ounces shredded Jalapeño-roast Pork (p. 269) or other cooked pork (about 3 cups)

8 ciabatta rolls, or 2 loaves ciabatta, each cut into 4 equal squares

Mayonnaise (p. 181)

Creole mustard

Pickles

Pickled cabbage

Place about 3 ounces of warmed shredded meat on bread or rolls with a little mayonnaise, mustard, and sliced pickles, and top with pickled cabbage.

Prosciutto-wrapped Tuna Muffuletta

MAKES 4 SANDWICHES   PREP TIME: 40 MINUTES

The fragrant, filling, dripping-with-oil muffuletta is New Orleans's beloved version of a hero or hoagie. The sandwich originated at Central Grocery in 1906, and people still line up out the door to buy them there. In a traditional muffuletta, a sesame seed–speckled round loaf of crusty Italian bread is stuffed with slices of provolone, salami, mortadella, and a pungent olive salad (which ranks alongside hot sauce and beignet mix as the best souvenirs from the Quarter). A muffuletta is a cousin to one of the great street foods of Nice, the niçoise-salad-on-a-roll known as *pan bagnat*. The sandwich, which literally translates as "bathed bread," is so named because the crusty bread is "bathed" in the rich oils from olives and tuna. With this preparation in mind, I created a tuna-driven version of the classic New Orleans sandwich. I think it's a happy combination.

PROSCIUTTO-WRAPPED TUNA

1 teaspoon fennel seeds, toasted and
    crushed
1 teaspoon lemon zest
½ teaspoon crushed red pepper flakes
1 garlic clove, minced
3 tablespoons olive oil

1 pound fresh tuna loin, cut into
    4 pieces approximately ½ inch
    thick
Sea salt
4 long, thin slices prosciutto (about
    1 ounce each)

Using a small bowl, mix the fennel seeds, lemon zest, red pepper, garlic, and 2 tablespoons olive oil. Brush the mixture onto both sides of the tuna. Season lightly with salt and wrap each piece of tuna with 1 piece of prosciutto. Refrigerate for at least ½ hour or up to 8 hours. When you're ready to assemble the sandwiches, heat the remaining 1 tablespoon olive oil in a medium skillet over high heat. Sear the fillets about 1 minute on each side (just enough to crisp the prosciutto). Ideally, the tuna should still be reddish pink in the middle. You can also grill the tuna 2–3 minutes on each side if you prefer.

OLIVE SALAD

If you buy it, you'll need about 1½ cups prepared olive salad (see Sources, p. 384). Or you can make your own as follows.

1 cup pitted kalamata olives, slivered lengthwise

½ cup chopped pimiento-stuffed green olives

1 cup chopped mixed pickled Italian vegetables (giardiniera)

8 pepperoncini, stemmed and chopped

2 tablespoons capers

2 teaspoons minced garlic

2 tablespoons chopped Italian parsley

½ cup chopped celery hearts

2 tablespoons red wine vinegar

½ cup extra-virgin olive oil

Mix all the ingredients together in a large bowl and let marinate in the refrigerator for at least 1 hour. Olive salad keeps beautifully—it will last in the refrigerator for up to three weeks.

TO ASSEMBLE

6 ounces provolone cheese, thinly sliced

4 ciabatta rolls, or 1 loaf ciabatta or Italian seeded round, quartered

4 fillets of seared Prosciutto-wrapped Tuna

1 to 1½ cups olive salad

1 bunch arugula, cleaned and dried (about 2 cups)

Preheat the oven to 350°F. Lay equal portions of the provolone on one half of each roll. Top with the seared tuna, olive salad, and arugula, and place the other half of bread on top. Warm in the oven if you like, until the cheese starts to melt. (If warming, add arugula after the sandwich comes out of the oven.)

Leftover olive salad makes a great instant Italian salad with romaine, arugula, cheese, and tomatoes. It's also wonderful with crabmeat, grilled eggplant, and artichokes. I always have some in my fridge and use it to fancy up a simple salami sandwich for my husband's lunch box. Stock up at Central Grocery on your next trip to New Orleans!

Roast Turkey with Blue Cream Cheese on Multigrain Bread

MAKES 2 SANDWICHES   PREP TIME: 15 MINUTES

For the spread on this sandwich, we mix the cream cheese with a full-flavored blue, but you could mix in Major Grey's chutney instead for a tasty alternative. I like to roast a whole bone-in turkey breast and serve it one night for dinner, then use the rest for sandwiches or salad. However, any good-quality precooked sliced turkey breast will work. I would eat this with a bowl of Cream of Celery Soup (p. 141) for an easy, comforting weeknight dinner.

½ cup cream cheese (or low-fat cream cheese), softened

¼ cup blue cheese (any variety)

8 slices multigrain or 7-grain bread

1 pound turkey breast, sliced

In the bowl of an electric mixer, use the paddle attachment to whip the cream cheese and blue cheese until fluffy and completely blended. (Alternatively, you can do this in a small bowl with a wooden spoon by hand.) Slather blue cream on 4 slices of the bread, and top with sliced turkey and the remaining bread slice. Feel free to add lettuce, tomatoes, or sliced cucumbers, if you like.

Crayfish Croque Monsieur

MAKES 4 TO 6 SANDWICHES   PREP TIME: 45 MINUTES

Crayfish and The New Orleans Jazz and Heritage Festival seem to go hand in hand. So when it was time to do my annual cooking demo at the Fest, I created this recipe, which is a play on the beloved French bar sandwich made with ham and cheese. I've always loved the crispy richness of batter-dipped sandwiches. This version, stuffed with a piquant crayfish salad, steals the show from diner varieties. The creamy crayfish sauce isn't necessary, but it's certainly delicious. If you feel guilty about the richness of this recipe, you can use light mayonnaise.

CRAYFISH FILLING

2 tablespoons butter

2 celery stalks, diced

½ medium onion, diced

½ pound crayfish tails

½ cup Mayonnaise (p. 181)

½ cup chopped scallions

¼ cup grated pepper Jack cheese

½ teaspoon ground cumin

½ teaspoon paprika

Salt and pepper

Hot sauce

Melt the butter in a large nonstick skillet over medium-high heat, then add the celery and onion and cook, stirring, until translucent. Drain the crayfish and add to skillet and cook, stirring constantly, just to warm through. Using a slotted spoon, transfer the mixture to a medium bowl and cool. Reduce the juices left in the pan to 1 teaspoon and add to crayfish mixture. When cool, mix with the mayonnaise, scallions, and cheese. Add salt, pepper, and hot sauce to taste.

BUTTERMILK BATTER

1 cup buttermilk

½ cup milk

2 eggs

½ teaspoon salt

Pinch of nutmeg

Whisk all the ingredients together in a medium bowl.

CREAMY CRAYFISH SAUCE

MAKES ENOUGH FOR 4 SANDWICHES

2 tablespoons butter	4 scallions, thinly sliced
4 ounces crayfish tails	2 tablespoons chopped fresh parsley
1 garlic clove, minced	Salt and pepper
½ cup heavy cream	1 tablespoon fresh lemon juice

Melt the butter in a small nonstick saucepan over medium heat. Add the crayfish and garlic, and sauté 2–3 minutes, until warmed through. Add the cream and scallions, and bring to a boil. Cook for 1 minute, and when cream is slightly thickened, add parsley and salt and pepper, to taste. Stir in the lemon juice and cook 1 more minute.

TO ASSEMBLE

8 slices firm white bread (such as *pain de mie* or Pepperidge Farm)	Butter, for frying
	Buttermilk Batter
Crayfish Filling	Creamy Crayfish Sauce

Trim the crusts from the bread. Top 4 slices with approximately ½ cup filling each, and cover with the remaining 4 slices, pressing gently. Melt 1 tablespoon butter in a medium skillet over medium-high heat. Using tongs or your fingers, dip 2 sandwiches into buttermilk batter, one at a time (hold each over the bowl so excess batter can drip off), then fry in hot butter on both sides until crisp and golden. Repeat with remaining 2 sandwiches, adding more butter to the skillet if necessary. Pour the crayfish sauce over the hot sandwiches. Serve with dill pickles and potato chips.

Danish Roast Beef Sandwich with Crispy Onions

MAKES 4 SANDWICHES   PREP TIME: 30 MINUTES

What's not to like about a roast beef sandwich? In true Danish tradition, this one is served open-faced, but it's the added golden brown crispy-fried onions that make this sandwich unusually delicious (and require a knife and fork to eat). It's been a favorite of mine since I was a kid, and I still love it when my mom makes her smorgasbord luncheon, because this sandwich is always on the menu.

---

4 slices good-quality bread of your choice

4 to 6 tablespoons Mayonnaise (p. 181)

½ pound medium-rare roast beef, thinly sliced

Salt and pepper

Crispy Onions

Spread the bread (toasted or not, as you prefer) with Mayonnaise, top with roast beef, and season with salt and pepper. Pile the onions on top of the beef and serve.

CRISPY ONIONS

2 yellow onions, halved and very thinly sliced (2 cups)

2 cups oil, for frying

Salt

In a wok or a tall pasta pot, heat the oil over medium heat until it is just hot enough to sizzle a piece of onion (about 350°F is ideal). Then *carefully* add all the onions to the pot and stir with tongs or a slotted spoon. This will create a lot of steam, so use caution. The onions will settle down pretty quickly to a simmer, and you will want to stir them every couple of minutes so that they brown evenly.

While the onions are cooking, lay some paper towels on a plate or baking sheet so that you're ready when the onions are. When they start to turn evenly golden brown, stir them and cook about 1 more minute, then remove them to the paper towels and press to get as much oil as possible out of them. If they don't crisp up pretty quickly, you may need to return them to the oil to cook another minute or two. It's also important to know that they will darken about one shade when they come out of the oil, so don't let them get too brown before you remove them.

After draining and pressing them, loosen them up with your fingers and then lightly salt them. This all sounds a little complicated, but it's just a question of doing it once and knowing what to look for. That said, you can do a test batch with just a few slivers if that will make you more comfortable.

For a bit more flavor, add a little horseradish to the Mayonnaise.

Shrimp Salad with Fennel and Herbed Cream Cheese on Brioche

MAKES 4 ROLLS   PREP TIME: 25 MINUTES

While vacationing in Cape Cod recently, Chip and I took it upon ourselves to sample lobster rolls from one end of the Cape to the other. We loved the classic filling of seafood bound in rich mayo, but I immediately started thinking about how herbs and a hint of lemon would make the salad even better. Down here in New Orleans, we don't have the luxury of leftover lobster very often, but we are lucky enough to have delicious boiled shrimp pretty much all year round. I also thought the spiffy salad deserved something more than the ubiquitous hot dog bun favored up north. A soft, rich bread like brioche is perfect. This is my spin on a venerable New England tradition.

¼ cup thinly sliced fennel

2 teaspoons olive oil

Pinch of salt

Herbed Cream Cheese

8 slices brioche or good-quality bread, or 4 soft rolls

½ pound boiled shrimp, peeled and chopped

¼ cup chopped or sliced celery hearts

In a small bowl, toss the fennel with the olive oil and salt. Spread a little herbed cream cheese on each slice of brioche. Divide the shrimp, celery, and fennel equally among the sandwiches, gently close, and serve.

HERBED CREAM CHEESE

2 tablespoons cream cheese, or light cream cheese, softened

¼ cup Mayonnaise (p. 181), or light mayonnaise

½ teaspoon grated lemon zest, and a squeeze of lemon juice

1 teaspoon each chopped fresh tarragon, dill and/or parsley, and chervil

1 tablespoon finely chopped scallion

Salt and pepper

Hot sauce

Using a fork, mash the cream cheese in a small bowl and whisk or stir in Mayonnaise. Mix thoroughly, then add lemon zest and juice, herbs, and scallion, and taste. Season with salt, pepper, and hot sauce.

Grilled Andouille Po'boy "Creolaise"

MAKES 2 SANDWICHES   PREP TIME: 15 MINUTES

More often than not, lunchtime in New Orleans means lining up for a "po'boy" (our version of a hero sandwich), a bag of Zapp's, and a cold Barq's root beer. The best versions of the sandwich are made on light, crackly Leidenheimer loaves (made at the city's most famous bakery) and piled with fried oysters and shrimp. But don't overlook a spicy sausage filling, and while you're at it, try my "special sauce." If they can make "Dijonaise," I can make "Creolaise." Creole mustard is whole-grain mustard with a little horseradish added to it, and is it good! It's made to go with sausage of any kind, but especially with hot, crusty andouille, right off the grill. Use the closest thing you can find to the light, crispy New Orleans–style French bread, add your favorite pickles, and chow down.

½ pound andouille sausage, split lengthwise into 2 even pieces

¼ cup Mayonnaise (p. 181)

2 tablespoons Creole mustard or whole-grain mustard

Hot sauce, optional

2 (6-inch) pieces New Orleans–style French bread, split in half lengthwise

Pickles, such as sweet-hot bread-and-butter pickles, pepperoncini, or jalapeño dills

½ small onion, red or white, thinly sliced, optional

Grill or broil the sausage until hot and slightly crusty. In a small bowl, combine the Mayonnaise, mustard, and hot sauce, to taste, if using. Spread a little of this "Creolaise" on both top and bottom slices of bread. Place the sausage on the bottom slice, add the pickles and onion, and top with the other slice of bread.

Hibachi Souvlaki with Cucumber-Yogurt Sauce

MAKES 4 SANDWICHES   PREP TIME: 30 MINUTES

The first apartment I rented in New Orleans was a summer sublet with a tiny balcony, just big enough for a hibachi grill. This sandwich, a beloved Greek specialty, was one I loved to make when I had friends over. We'd drink a bottle of chilled retsina and dream of being in a café looking up at the Acropolis. If you don't feel like firing up a grill, these skewers can be cooked in a grill pan or under the broiler. You can also make skewers of diced chicken (breast or thigh meat). Just grill a few minutes less, so the leaner meat doesn't dry out.

LAMB SKEWERS

3 tablespoons olive oil

2 garlic cloves, minced

¼ teaspoon ground cumin

¼ teaspoon crushed red pepper flakes

1 teaspoon chopped fresh rosemary

1 pound boneless lamb leg, cut in ½-inch dice

4 wooden skewers, soaked in water

Salt

Mix the oil, garlic, cumin, red pepper, and rosemary in a medium bowl. Add the lamb and use your fingers to turn the dice in the seasonings until they're evenly coated. Marinate in the refrigerator for at least 15 minutes, or up to 8 hours. When ready to cook, divide the lamb in 4 even portions and place on the 4 skewers. Salt lightly. Grill over hot coals or broil, turning to cook evenly, about 5 minutes for medium-rare.

CUCUMBER-YOGURT SAUCE

1 cup plain yogurt (preferably Middle
 Eastern style or whole milk)

1 medium cucumber, peeled, seeded,
 grated, and squeezed between
 hands to remove excess liquid

½ teaspoon minced garlic

1 tablespoon chopped fresh mint

1 tablespoon olive oil

Salt and pepper

Combine the yogurt, cucumber, garlic, mint, and olive oil in a medium bowl and season with salt and pepper; refrigerate until needed.

TO ASSEMBLE

Lamb skewers

4 pieces pita bread

1 small onion, sliced or diced

1 tomato, diced

Cucumber-Yogurt Sauce

When lamb is cooked, throw pita bread on the grill to warm and soften. Place one skewer on each piece of bread and remove skewer from meat. Top with onions, tomatoes, and the Cucumber-Yogurt Sauce.

Back in the '90s, I used to buy pita bread at the grocery store. Now I am lucky enough to get it freshly baked just about every day from my friends at Mona's, a Middle Eastern bakery and restaurant. Pita from a local bakery will always be more delicious than what you can buy in the grocery store, so consider seeking out a Middle Eastern bakery if there's one in your area.

Middle Eastern–style yogurts are thicker and sweeter, but in a more natural way, than other commercial yogurts. You can find them at well-stocked ethnic or Middle Eastern groceries.

Smoked Duck "PBJ" with Cashew Butter, Pepper Jelly, and Apple-Celery Salad

MAKES 4 SERVINGS   PREP TIME: 50 MINUTES

This is one of the all-time most popular dishes we have ever created at Bayona. It was the brainchild of another former sous chef, Scott Freer. He had the original idea (duck and peanuts, who knew?), and we tweaked the various components until one day, after tasting the latest version, everyone just stood there silently, grinning in a Duck PBJ reverie. The cashew peanut butter can be made well in advance, as can the grilled onions. However, for super-crisp freshness, the Apple-Celery Salad is best when thrown together right before serving.

2 teaspoons softened butter

8 slices multigrain bread

¾ cup cashew butter, at room temperature

¾ cup hot pepper jelly (sold in most southern supermarkets and specialty food stores)

¾ pound smoked duck, shredded (see Sources, p. 384)

Grilled Red Onions

Salt and pepper

Spread softened butter on both sides of each slice of bread. Grill on each side 1 minute or until toasted, but not too dark. Spread 4 slices of bread with cashew butter and the remaining 4 with pepper jelly. Warm the duck meat and onions in a 400°F oven for about 5 minutes. Divide the meat and onions among the 4 sandwiches. Season with salt and pepper. Put the sandwiches together and slice in half. Serve with Apple-Celery salad.

CASHEW BUTTER

1 cup chopped cashews

½ cup chopped peanuts

3 tablespoons honey

1 tablespoon molasses

Salt

4 tablespoons (½ stick) softened
butter

Roast the cashews and peanuts for about 7 minutes at 350°F; cool completely. In a food processor, puree the nuts, honey, molasses, and a pinch of salt. Then add the softened butter and puree. Add a splash of warm water, if necessary, to thin the mixture to a spreadable, creamy texture. Keep in mind that cashew butter will be soft while it is warm and will stiffen up as it chills—it should be at room temperature when spreading it on the sandwiches.

GRILLED RED ONIONS

1 large or 2 small red onions, sliced in
   ¼-inch-thick rings

2 tablespoons olive oil

Salt and pepper

Toss the onions with the olive oil, and a little salt and pepper. Grill, broil, or roast for about 5 minutes, until wilted.

Apple-Celery Salad

MAKES ABOUT 2 CUPS

1 Granny Smith apple

2 celery heart ribs

1 shallot, minced

1 tablespoon olive oil and
   1 tablespoon walnut oil, optional,
   or 2 tablespoons olive oil

1 tablespoon apple cider vinegar

Salt

Peel, core, and thinly slice the apple. Slice the celery hearts thinly on the diagonal. In a medium bowl, toss the apple and celery with the shallot, olive oil, vinegar, and salt, to taste.

Sensational Sauces and Creamy Bread Spreads

White Bean Hummus

Green Olive Tapenade

Herbed Goat Cheese with Garlic Confit

Smoked Salmon Spread with Lemon and Herbs

Skordalia (Greek Garlic-Almond Sauce)

Moroccan *Charmoula* Marinade and Sauce

The Best *Chimichurri* Sauce

Citrus Chili Glaze

Fast and Foolproof Lemon-Tahini Sauce

Basic Mayonnaise

Lavender Honey Aïoli

My Kind of Tartar Sauce

Roasted Red Pepper Rouille

Pumpkin Seed Pesto

Sun-dried Tomato–Pistachio Pesto

Green Pea or Fava Bean Puree

Fava Bean Pesto with Mint and Anchovy

Butternut Squash Puree

Luscious Cauliflower Cream

Eggplant Caviar and Black Olive Tapenade

Garlic Confit

Preserved Lemon

Pickled Jalapeños

Pickled Red Onions

We all need a little inspiration now and then. On those evenings when you're unsure how to perk up a lamb chop, grilled tuna steak, chicken breast, or basic burger, turn to this chapter. These sunny, spicy, and boldly flavored sauces, glazes, spreads, dips, and condiments have a lot of sass. Like any smart accessory, they lend personality and sparkle to the things that we cook most often.

A quick puree can also provide a starting point for improvisational meals and antipasto platters. Green Olive Tapenade (p. 173) or Smoked Salmon Spread with Lemon and Herbs (p. 175), for example, creates instant sandwiches or crostini toppings. With a container of White Bean Hummus (p. 172) or Fava Bean Pesto with Mint and Anchovy (p. 188) in the fridge, I have the makings of a savory snack (when friends stop by for a glass of wine) or easy dinner (add hot boiled noodles) at my fingertips. Best of all, most of these recipes can be made in a matter of minutes—giving you time to muse about how you'll dress up the next night's meal . . .

White Bean Hummus

MAKES ABOUT 4 CUPS   PREP TIME: 20 MINUTES (NOT INCLUDING GARLIC POACHING TIME)

In this hummus recipe, I use white Italian beans instead of chickpeas for a Mediterranean twist on the Middle Eastern classic. Luscious Garlic Confit (p. 193) infuses the dip with a sweet, rich flavor. This creamy, healthful puree is delicious with crudités, Seasoned Pita Crisps (p. 89), blue corn tortilla chips, or on a sandwich with grilled vegetables and (of course) hot sauce. White Bean Hummus can also partner with a few other items to create a beautiful antipasto platter. Just add, for example, roasted red pepper strips, marinated olives, and a few tablespoons of roasted garlic cloves. Don't be surprised if this becomes one of your new (snacking and entertaining) staples.

½ cup (about ¼ recipe) Garlic Confit (p. 193)

1 garlic clove

1 teaspoon salt

¼ teaspoon crushed red pepper flakes (more or less, as desired)

2 (15-ounce) cans cannellini or other white beans, drained and rinsed

½ cup tahini

¼ cup water

1 tablespoon sherry wine vinegar

2–4 tablespoons fresh lemon juice

¼ cup extra-virgin olive oil, plus 1 or 2 tablespoons oil from Garlic Confit

Prepare Garlic Confit.

Place the garlic clove, salt, and red pepper in the bowl of a food processor and process to a rough paste. Add the beans and pulse briefly. Add the Garlic Confit, tahini, water, vinegar, lemon juice, olive oil, and confit oil and process until smooth. Taste, and add more salt, lemon, or vinegar as desired.

For a pretty presentation, garnish this hummus with a sprig of fresh thyme or rosemary (which will echo the flavors in the confit), another drizzle of extra-virgin olive oil, and a sprinkling of red pepper.

Green Olive Tapenade

Another quick-to-assemble mixture of bold, pungent flavors that enhances grilled fish, toasted ciabatta, or warm pasta tossed with thin strips of salami. For a more herbaceous taste, add a handful of chopped fresh basil or parsley. You might also blend in a few lightly toasted almonds for a more pesto-like consistency.

2 cups pitted cracked green olives

2 tablespoons capers

1 teaspoon fennel seeds, toasted (see below) and crushed in a mortar

Zest and juice of 1 orange

½ teaspoon crushed red pepper flakes

1 tablespoon sherry vinegar

½ cup olive oil

¼ cup extra-virgin olive oil

Place the olives, capers, fennel seeds, zest, juice, red pepper, and vinegar in the bowl of a food processor and pulse until combined. With the machine running, slowly incorporate both the olive oils, until a smooth paste is formed. Taste, and adjust seasonings. Stored in a sealed container in the refrigerator, tapenade will last up to 2 weeks.

If you don't have a mortar and pestle, simply place the fennel seeds on the cutting board, moisten with a few drops of olive oil, and coarsely chop with a chef's knife.

Toasting Seeds and Spices

To toast fennel seeds, any herb in seed form, or seeds such as pumpkin seeds, heat them in a small, dry skillet over medium heat until they become fragrant and darken slightly.

Herbed Goat Cheese with Garlic Confit

MAKES ABOUT 2 CUPS   PREP TIME: 10 MINUTES, NOT INCLUDING GARLIC CONFIT

This silky puree is just one more way to enjoy fresh goat cheese, which is a favorite of mine. It can be served with toasted bread and sun-dried tomatoes for a quick hors d'oeuvre, or paired with a salad of fresh greens for an appealing first course. It's also irresistible slathered on a turkey or grilled portobello sandwich. This puree is similar to the garlic goat cheese filling for my Eggplant Roulades (p. 303), but the addition of fresh basil, herbes de Provence, and chives gives it a style all its own.

---

1 cup (about ½ recipe) Garlic Confit (p. 193)

1 teaspoon oil from Garlic Confit

1 cup fresh goat cheese

2 tablespoons chopped fresh basil

½ teaspoon herbes de Provence, optional

1 tablespoon snipped fresh chives

Salt and pepper

Prepare Garlic Confit.

Soften the goat cheese in a small bowl by stirring it with a wooden spoon. Add the garlic confit and garlic oil, along with the cheese, basil, herbes de Provence, if using, chives, and salt and pepper, to taste, and stir until combined. Set aside for about ½ hour at room temperature (or longer, in the refrigerator) to allow the flavors to blend.

Smoked Salmon Spread with Lemon and Herbs

MAKES 2 CUPS   PREP TIME: ABOUT 30 MINUTES

Here's a great way to use a small amount of smoked salmon to good advantage. Fresh herbs and lemon brighten the taste, and the cream cheese acts as a medium to carry the rich flavors. I love to serve this spread on toasted pumpernickel bread, atop tiny baked fingerling or new potatoes as an hors d'oueuvre, or as an open-faced sandwich with thin cucumber slices and watercress.

8 ounces cream cheese, softened at
   room temperature
¼ cup sour cream
1 teaspoon grated lemon zest
1–2 tablespoons fresh lemon juice
2 tablespoons snipped fresh chives

1 tablespoon minced fresh dill or
   tarragon, or both
2 ounces smoked salmon, finely diced
   (about ¼ cup)
Salt and pepper
Hot sauce

Use a wooden spoon or spatula to blend cream cheese with the sour cream, lemon zest and juice, herbs, and salmon. Alternatively, place the cream cheese in a food processor and process for 1 minute to soften, then add the remaining ingredients and puree. Season to taste with salt, pepper, and hot sauce. This spread is best if prepared at least an hour before serving, to let the flavors meld.

Skordalia (Greek Garlic-Almond Sauce)

MAKES 2 CUPS   PREP TIME: 5 MINUTES

Adapted from The Royal Oak Restaurant and Pub

I fell in love with this creamy sauce when I first tasted it back in 1970 at the Royal Oak Pub in New Orleans, owned by Mr. and Mrs. John Newsham. They used to serve it with fried eggplant, and it is one of those texture and flavor combinations that I will never forget: the crisp eggplant nestled into the nutty, garlicky puree (as thick and luscious as buttercream). Later, when I became a chef, the Newshams were big supporters of my career and even shared with me two of their family recipes, including this one, after Mr. Newsham passed away. I will always be grateful to them for the many food memories, and for their kindness.

---

3 slices bread (preferably a rustic white bread), soaked in 1 cup ice water, then squeezed dry

3 tablespoons red wine vinegar

¼ cup garlic cloves

Juice of 2 lemons (about 6 tablespoons)

1 teaspoon salt

⅔ cup blanched almonds

¾ cup olive oil

Place the bread, vinegar, garlic, and lemon juice in a food processor and pulse to mix thoroughly. Add the salt and almonds and blend. With the motor running, drizzle in the olive oil (the final mixture will be creamy and smooth). Taste and adjust the flavor to your liking with more lemon juice or olive oil.

This sauce will keep in the refrigerator for about a week. In addition to fried eggplant, this sauce is delicious with Seasoned Pita Crisps (p. 89) and Roasted Red or Golden Beet Salad (p. 102).

Moroccan Charmoula Marinade and Sauce

MAKES I½ CUPS   PREP TIME: 15 MINUTES

There are many different versions and interpretations of this exotic mixture, which can be used as a marinade, a sauce, or, with a little more olive oil, a vinaigrette. Use a portion of it to marinate fish or chicken, then grill, and toss the remaining mixture with thinly sliced Vidalia onions and sweet red peppers for a quick summer supper.

½ cup coarsely chopped cilantro

½ cup coarsely chopped fresh parsley
   leaves

½ yellow onion, coarsely chopped

2 peeled garlic cloves

¼ cup fresh lemon juice

1 teaspoon paprika

¼ teaspoon saffron threads, steeped
   in 2 tablespoons warm water

½ teaspoon grated fresh ginger

½ teaspoon salt

½ teaspoon ground cumin

½ teaspoon cayenne

½ cup olive oil

Place all the ingredients in a food processor or blender and pulse to blend. Taste for seasoning and adjust to your liking.

The Best Chimichurri Sauce

MAKES 1 TO 1½ CUPS   PREP TIME: ABOUT 20 MINUTES

Green and pungent, this is my favorite version of the famed Argentinean sauce. For a more traditional version, substitute fresh oregano for the cilantro, and red wine vinegar for the lime juice. Serve it with fat, juicy rib eyes, grilled chicken breasts, or tuna steaks.

¼ cup coarsely chopped garlic

1 bunch scallions, trimmed, split lengthwise, and chopped

4–5 jalapeños, seeded and finely diced

1 bunch Italian parsley, stemmed and finely chopped

1 bunch cilantro (leaves and tender stems), finely chopped

Juice of 3 limes (about ½ cup)

¼ to ½ cup extra-virgin olive oil

Salt and pepper

Combine everything except the olive oil, salt, and pepper in a medium bowl and stir to combine. Add the olive oil to desired consistency. Season to taste with salt and pepper.

Citrus Chili Glaze

This is a vibrant, sweet, and spicy sauce that is yummy on seared scallops, roast chicken breasts, and grilled fish fillets. It's easy to make and keeps well in the refrigerator for up to a few weeks. Feel free to throw in some minced garlic if you love it the way I do. The cilantro is optional, but the fresh green fragrance and color is an appealing touch.

Zest, segments, and juice of 2 oranges
   or tangerines

Juice of 2 limes (3–4 tablespoons)

4 tablespoons sugar

2 tablespoons soy sauce

1 teaspoon grated fresh ginger

2 teaspoons cornstarch

½ cup sweet chili sauce (available in a
   bottle at most Asian markets)

1 tablespoon chopped cilantro,
   optional

Use a zester to zest the oranges or tangerines; set the zest aside. To make the segments, use a sharp knife to cut a generous slice off the top and bottom of the oranges, exposing the juicy insides. Working from top to bottom with a small, sharp knife (I like a 4-inch blade), cut the peel off in strips, going deeper than usual so that the outer membrane of the fruit is removed. Work your way all around the fruit, curving your cuts with the shape of the fruit, until the orange flesh is fully exposed. Discard the skin and membrane. Pick up the fruit in one hand and, working over a bowl, turn the fruit on its side and with the knife in the other hand, slice in between the membranes that separate the sections, releasing a completely peeled segment into the bowl, which will also catch the juice. Drain the juice into a small saucepan and reserve the segments. Add the zest, lime juice, sugar, soy sauce, and ginger to the saucepan. Bring the mixture to a boil, then lower the heat and simmer for 5 minutes. Mix the cornstarch with 1 teaspoon water and whisk into the hot mixture. Bring it to a boil, then lower the heat and simmer until thickened, about 3 more minutes. Stir in the sweet chili sauce and cool. Stir in the reserved segments and cilantro.

Fast and Foolproof Lemon-Tahini Sauce

MAKES I CUP   PREP TIME: IO MINUTES

This incredibly simple, delicious sauce is great with Hibachi Souvlaki (p. 164), Turkish Stuffed Eggplant with Spicy Lamb and Rice (p. 280), and good ol' falafel sandwiches. Double the batch for parties and back-yard barbecues (it's great on lamb burgers and grilled merguez sausage, too). It keeps well in the refrigerator for a couple of weeks.

⅓ cup tahini

2 garlic cloves, minced

Juice of 2 lemons (about
    6 tablespoons)

¼ cup olive oil

Salt

Place the tahini, garlic, lemon juice, and ¼ cup of water in a blender and blend for about 1 minute. With the motor running, drizzle in the olive oil. Add salt to taste and adjust the consistency with a little more water, if necessary.

Basic Mayonnaise

MAKES ABOUT 2 CUPS   PREP TIME: 15 MINUTES

Whether you are slathering it on a turkey sandwich or making egg or chicken salad, you can't beat homemade mayo. Using one whole egg in addition to the yolks helps the mixture whip into a lighter texture and prevents the mayonnaise from being overly "eggy" tasting. For a lime, lemon, or orange variation, add a tablespoon of the appropriate zest and 2–3 tablespoons of juice, then decrease the amount of vinegar so the mixture is not too acidic. Lime mayonnaise is delicious with Bahamian Conch Fritters (p. 34).

2 egg yolks, plus 1 whole egg
½ teaspoon salt
1 heaping tablespoon Dijon mustard
Juice of 1 lemon (2–3 tablespoons)
1 tablespoon red wine or cider
   vinegar

1½ to 2 cups pure olive oil, or a
   combination of olive oil and
   canola oil
Hot sauce

Place the egg yolks and egg in the bowl of a food processor or blender. Add the salt to the eggs, to help them "cook" a bit so they will better absorb the oil. Add the mustard, lemon juice, and vinegar and process for 15 seconds. Slowly drizzle in the olive oil, stopping about halfway and adding about 1 teaspoon of water. Continue drizzling some or all of the remaining olive oil, to the desired consistency—the more you add, the tighter it will be. Add the hot sauce, to taste, and taste for seasoning. Scrape the mayonnaise into a lidded container and store in the refrigerator for up to 3 days.

We've all been groomed to use extra-virgin olive oil for everything, but I mostly avoid using it for mayos and even some vinaigrettes because the flavor is too intense and overpowering. If you have a great "splurge" extra-virgin olive oil that you want to show off here, use it to replace a couple of tablespoons of the pure oil. You can do the same with a nut or seed oil.

Lavender Honey Aïoli

MAKES I CUP   PREP TIME: 15 MINUTES

This unusual aïoli is good on any kind of grilled meat, especially lamb, and the tasty little chickens known as *poussins*. You might also serve it with roasted artichoke quarters. For this recipe you can steep your own lavender honey, as described below, or simply buy a good-quality lavender honey from Provence.

Aïoli

1 egg yolk

1 teaspoon Dijon mustard

1 garlic clove, minced

½ teaspoon lightly chopped fresh rosemary

1 teaspoon red wine vinegar

2 teaspoons Lavender Honey

½ cup olive oil

¼ cup extra-virgin olive oil

Salt and pepper

1–2 tablespoons fresh lemon juice

Whisk together the egg yolk, mustard, garlic, rosemary, vinegar, and honey in a small bowl. Slowly whisk in the regular olive oil, then the extra-virgin olive oil. The aïoli should have the consistency of a creamy mayonnaise. Add a pinch of salt and pepper, and a squeeze of lemon or a little more vinegar, if necessary. The aïoli is best made a few hours ahead so the flavors can bloom and mellow, and best if used within a day or two.

Lavender Honey

Lavender stems and flowers

1 cup honey

Place the lavender and honey in a small saucepan and warm for just a few minutes over medium heat (or heat on low in a microwave for about 1 minute). Remove from the heat and let steep for about an hour, then strain (rewarm it a little to make it easier to pour). Store the honey in a bottle or jar with a tight-fitting lid. You will need only a little for the aïoli, but it will keep and is good on biscuits and swirled into hot tea.

For a mellower flavor, feel free to substitute for the raw garlic an equal amount of Garlic Confit (p. 193), plus a teaspoon or two of its garlicky oil.

My Kind of Tartar Sauce

At Bayona, we like to jazz up tartar sauce with all kinds of extra goodies, such as preserved lemon and pepperoncini, in addition to the usual ingredients (capers, pickles, etc.). It's just the thing with sautéed cornmeal-crusted trout or fried oysters and some vinegary slaw.

---

1 cup Mayonnaise, preferably
    homemade (p. 181)

1 teaspoon lemon juice

1 tablespoon drained, chopped capers

1 tablespoon sweet pickle relish

1 tablespoon thinly sliced scallions

2 teaspoons chopped cornichons

2 teaspoons chopped pepperoncini, or
    fresh or pickled jalapeños

1 teaspoon chopped Preserved
    Lemon (p. 194)

Hot sauce, to taste

Combine all the ingredients in a small bowl. Taste, and adjust to your liking with more Mayonnaise or more "stuff."

Roasted Red Pepper Rouille

MAKES ABOUT I CUP   PREP TIME: 25 MINUTES

This spicy mayo, a variation on the classic condiment from the south of France (traditionally flavored with saffron), is the perfect garnish for my Gulf Coast Bouillabaisse (p. 220). But it's also delicious on just about any grilled fish or bowl of steamed mussels, or a crab omelet. When you serve it with a soup or stew, be sure to include plenty of toasted bread rounds to sop it up.

1 roasted red bell pepper, peeled, seeded, and chopped (see roasting technique, p. 122)

1 egg yolk

½ teaspoon crushed red pepper flakes

2 garlic cloves, crushed and coarsely chopped

1 teaspoon red wine vinegar

¾ cup pure olive oil plus 2 tablespoons extra-virgin olive oil

1 teaspoon fresh lemon juice

Salt

Red chile paste (such as harissa or *sambal oelek*)

Place the red pepper, egg yolk, crushed red pepper, garlic, and vinegar in the bowl of a food processor. Pulse for 15 seconds, then, with the motor running, add the olive oils in a slow, steady stream. Add the lemon juice, salt, and chile paste, adjusting quantities to taste (the rouille should be slightly spicy). Mix to combine.

Pumpkin Seed Pesto

This unique southwestern-inspired pesto is made with *pepitas,* which are the green pumpkin seeds that have been shelled from their white hulls. This pesto is particularly great with grilled shrimp, butternut squash ravioli, or pork chops; blended with avocado as a dip for tortilla chips; smeared on a black bean quesadilla; or tossed with penne, chorizo, and roasted red peppers. That should keep you busy for a while!

1 cup olive oil

3 garlic cloves, sliced

½ cup green shelled pumpkin seeds,
  or *pepitas*

¼ cup crumbled feta or cotija cheese

1 bunch cilantro, coarsely chopped
  (both the leaves and tender stems)

½ cup coarsely chopped fresh basil or
  parsley leaves, tightly packed

1 tablespoon cider vinegar

Salt

Crushed red pepper flakes

Warm ½ cup olive oil over low heat in a small skillet and add the sliced garlic. Raise the heat to medium and sauté until garlic is lightly tanned and aromatic. Remove garlic from oil with a slotted spoon and drain on paper towels. Add pumpkin seeds to the oil and raise heat to medium-high, stirring. Cook for about 2 minutes, until seeds start to crackle and pop (be careful!) and are lightly browned. Remove seeds from oil with a slotted spoon and drain on paper towels. Reserve the oil. When the garlic and pumpkin seeds have cooled, transfer to the bowl of a food processor, and add the cheese and herbs. Pulse 3 or 4 times, until well mixed. Add vinegar and the reserved garlic oil. With the motor running, slowly pour in remaining olive oil until mixture reaches desired consistency. Season to taste with salt and red pepper.

Sun-dried Tomato-Pistachio Pesto

MAKES 2 CUPS   PREP TIME: 20 MINUTES

This pretty, rich-tasting pesto enhances simple grilled fish or meats (try it with grilled chicken thighs). You might also consider serving it on an antipasto platter rolled up in strips of grilled eggplant, or tossed with small balls of fresh mozzarella called *bocconcini,* or "little mouthfuls."

½ cup sun-dried tomatoes (not marinated)

½ cup shelled pistachios

1 cup tightly packed fresh basil leaves

2 garlic cloves

1–2 tablespoons balsamic vinegar

3 tablespoons Parmesan cheese

½–¾ cup olive oil

¼ cup extra-virgin olive oil

Salt

Crushed red pepper flakes

Preheat the oven to 350°F.

Place the tomatoes in a small bowl and cover with hot water. Plump them for about 5 minutes, then drain and chop. Meanwhile, toast the pistachios in the oven for 5–6 minutes, until fragrant and slightly darkened. Cool, then place them in a clean dish towel and rub off as much of the skin as possible.

Place the tomatoes, pistachios, basil, and garlic in a food processor and pulse to mix. Add 1 tablespoon vinegar and the cheese. With the motor running, drizzle in about half of each olive oil. Taste, and add salt and red pepper to taste, then the remaining olive oils and the other tablespoon of vinegar, if desired.

Green Pea or Fava Bean Puree

MAKES 1½ CUPS   PREP TIME: ABOUT 30 MINUTES

This is a good way to make the most of a small amount of peas (or favas). Serve alongside some wild mushrooms sautéed with a little dice of bacon for an easy springtime starter. By the way, if, in a following life, I could come back as any vegetable, I think I would be a fava bean, so I could slumber inside that velvety soft pod. Just a thought.

---

2 tablespoons butter

1 small yellow or white onion, finely
  chopped

1 cup Vegetable Stock (p. 204) or
  water

1 sprig tarragon

¼ teaspoon salt

1 cup shelled, blanched English peas,
  or blanched, peeled fresh fava
  beans (for blanching technique,
  see p. 118)

Melt the butter in a small saucepan over medium-high heat. Add the onion and cook, stirring, until soft, about 7 minutes. Add the Vegetable Stock, tarragon, and salt, and simmer until onion is very tender, another 10 minutes. Add the peas or favas and cook about 3 more minutes. Cool slightly, discard tarragon, and puree in a blender to create a creamy consistency. Taste and adjust seasonings.

As with the other vegetable purees, this can be thinned to sauce consistency with a little stock, water, or cream.

Fava Bean Pesto with Mint and Anchovy

MAKES ABOUT 2 CUPS   PREP TIME: ABOUT 45 MINUTES

This unusual pesto variation, adapted from a recipe by Colman Andrews in his book *Flavors of the Riviera,* cries out for grilled or roasted lamb, but you will discover many other ways to use it. In fact, it's perfectly delicious on simple grilled bread with a glass of white wine or rosé.

Salt

2 pounds fresh fava beans, in pods

2 garlic cloves, minced

1 cup packed fresh mint leaves

1 cup packed fresh basil leaves

3–4 anchovy fillets, rinsed with cold water

⅔ cup extra-virgin olive oil

¼ cup pecorino or Parmesan cheese

Fill a medium saucepan with water, add a little salt, and bring to a boil over medium-high heat. While the water is heating, shell the fava beans. Blanch the beans for a minute or two in the boiling water, drain, then shock them in ice water. Peel the skins and set the beans aside. Crush the garlic, mint, and basil with ¼ teaspoon salt, using a mortar and pestle, then work in the anchovy fillets. Add about 2 tablespoons olive oil, then the fava beans, adding a third at a time. Add 2 more tablespoons olive oil, then the cheese, and finish with the oil. Season to taste. Alternatively, you can blend all the ingredients in a food processor, adding the oil last in a slow, steady stream while the motor is running.

Butternut Squash Puree

MAKES 2½ CUPS   PREP TIME: 1 HOUR

This puree is delicious with Mediterranean Roasted Shrimp with Crispy Risotto Cakes (p. 215), venison, or any other grilled or roasted meat or fish.

---

1 medium butternut squash
Salt and pepper
2 tablespoons butter
¼ cup heavy cream

1 tablespoon honey
Pinch of nutmeg
Chicken Stock (p. 206) or Shrimp
    Stock (p. 229), as needed

Preheat the oven to 400°F.

Cut the squash in half, but don't remove the seeds. Season with salt and pepper, and place cut side down in a baking pan. Pour enough water in the pan to come ¼ inch up the squash. Bake for 30–45 minutes, until squash is tender when pierced with a paring knife. Let it cool, then use a spoon to remove the seeds and spoon the flesh out of the shell. Puree the squash in a food processor. Place the puree in a saucepan with the butter, cream, honey, and nutmeg, and cook over low heat. Adjust to the desired consistency with warm stock or water, and season with additional salt and pepper, if desired.

For a lighter result, this puree can be made without the butter or cream.

Luscious Cauliflower Cream

MAKES 2 CUPS   PREP TIME: 20 MINUTES

I serve this unexpected puree (cauliflower as sauce, who knew?) with seared or grilled scallops, beef, or salmon. Simply place the warm fish or meat atop a pool of the cream.

1 tablespoon butter

1 tablespoon olive oil

1 small onion, chopped

1 small head cauliflower (about 1 pound), stemmed and coarsely chopped

2 cups Vegetable Stock (p. 204) or Chicken Stock (p. 206), or water

Salt

½ cup cream

Freshly ground pepper

Heat the butter and olive oil in a small saucepan over medium heat. Add the onion and sauté for 5 minutes, then add the cauliflower and stir. Cook for 5 more minutes, then add the stock or water and bring to a boil. Lower the heat, add a pinch of salt, and simmer uncovered for 10 minutes, until the cauliflower is tender and the liquid is reduced by half. Add the cream and simmer 2 more minutes. Allow the mixture to cool slightly, pour into a blender, and blend until you have a creamy, smooth puree. Taste, and adjust seasoning with additional salt and pepper.

Eggplant Caviar and Black Olive Tapenade

MAKES 4 TO 6 SERVINGS   PREP TIME: ABOUT 25 MINUTES FOR EACH SPREAD

When I first opened Bayona I never had time to eat, so I survived that first year on these two delicious dips. I'd duck into the pantry and dip crispy croutons into the smoky eggplant puree or the pungent olive spread (or both), and the flavors sustained me through my shift. I still crave them.

Eggplant caviar comes from many parts of the Mediterranean, including France, Italy, Turkey, and the Middle East. It's flavored simply, with fresh tomato, garlic, lemon juice, and olive oil. The secret to developing a deep, smoky flavor is to char the skin until it's black and rather scary looking.

The tapenade, or olive puree, is a pretty classic combination from the south of France. I give the black olives, capers, and anchovies a quick rinse to lessen the impact of their saltiness.

Both dips provide a great base from which to build a plate. You can add hummus, feta cheese, various crunchy vegetables, and a drizzle of extra-virgin olive oil to create a fantastic antipasto platter.

Eggplant Caviar

1 large eggplant (about 1–1½ pounds)

½ small red onion, finely chopped

1 garlic clove, minced

1 ripe tomato, peeled, seeded, and diced

2–3 tablespoons extra-virgin olive oil

1 tablespoon fresh lemon juice

1 tablespoon chopped fresh parsley

2 tablespoons chopped fresh basil (about 2 stems' worth), optional

Salt and pepper

Prick the eggplant several times with a fork (this is important—the first time I made this dish I didn't do it, and the eggplant exploded). On a grill, or in a cast-iron skillet set over high heat or under a broiler, roast the eggplant on all sides until the skin blackens, the juices turn syrupy, and the pulp feels completely soft. This takes 15–20 minutes in a skillet or under the broiler; you'll want to turn the eggplant every 4–5 minutes.

When the eggplant is cool enough to handle, peel off and discard the skin (it will flake off in pieces). Slice the eggplant in half, scrape out the pulp, and roughly chop the flesh. Add the onion, garlic, tomato, olive oil, lemon juice, parsley, and basil and season with salt and pepper; stir until smooth. You may add more olive oil or lemon juice to taste.

Black Olive Tapenade

½ pound kalamata olives, pitted and
    rinsed with cold water
4 anchovy fillets, rinsed
3 tablespoons capers, rinsed

1 tablespoon Dijon mustard
1 tablespoon water
¼ cup olive oil

Put everything except the olive oil into a food processor and pulse until coarsely chopped. With the machine running, drizzle in the olive oil. The mixture should have a little texture, not be quite completely smooth. You shouldn't need to add salt, as the ingredients are very salty.

Garlic Confit

I call this recipe "confit" because, like the French method for preserving meat, it involves slow-cooking the garlic cloves in oil and other liquids. Poaching garlic on the stovetop is an alternative to roasting garlic in the oven. I actually prefer poaching because there is less waste—when the cooking process is complete, you are left with the whole cloves as opposed to squeezing sticky partial cloves out of a softened bulb.

As with roasting, this method replaces the sharp heat of raw garlic with a flavor that's deep and sweet. I usually poach at least two bulbs so I have plenty on hand for antipasto platters, White Bean Hummus (p. 172), pastas, vinaigrettes, or even for slathering on a piece of toast for a snack.

---

2 garlic bulbs, stemmed and peeled
    (about 28 cloves)
½ cup dry white wine
1 cup good-quality olive oil

Salt
Freshly ground black pepper
2 stems of fresh thyme, or 1 sprig of
    fresh rosemary

Place the garlic cloves, wine, ¼ cup water, and olive oil in a small skillet and season with a pinch of salt and a grind of black pepper. Add the herbs, tucking them into the liquid to moisten, and bring to a simmer over low heat. Simmer until the water and wine have evaporated and the cloves have softened and turned a deep golden color, 30–40 minutes. When it's done to your liking, drain the garlic, reserving the oil. If not using right away, pour into a jar and refrigerate for up to 2 weeks.

Preserved Lemon

MAKES I CUP   PREP TIME: IO MINUTES TO ASSEMBLE, 2 WEEKS TO CURE

Pungent and concentrated in flavor, preserved lemons are popular in Moroccan and Middle Eastern cooking. To use them, pull the lemon flesh away from the rind and discard. Give the rind a brief rinse in cold water, then dice or chop and add to a dish at the end of cooking. I use preserved lemons in my Artichoke Dolmades with Lemon Sauce (p. 20). They also add a distinct flavor to couscous and cracked wheat salads. You'll want to use them sparingly (a tablespoon or two is typically enough) so they don't overpower other flavors. This recipe doubles or triples easily.

8 lemons   2 cups kosher salt

Cut 6 of the lemons lengthwise into quarters and juice the other 2.

Pour ¼ cup salt into a jar with a tight-fitting lid, then place a third of the lemon quarters on the salt. Cover lemons with another ¼ cup salt. Repeat with remaining lemon quarters and salt, ending with salt, then pour the lemon juice over the top.

Put the lid on the jar and place it on a shelf at room temperature for 10 days to 2 weeks, shaking or turning the jar upside down once a day. This ensures that all the lemons will be immersed in brine. After 10 days, take out one lemon quarter and pull the pulp away from the rind. If the rind is completely saturated with the brine (there will be no white left under the pulp), then refrigerate the jar. If it is still a little white and chalky looking, shake the jar again and leave on the shelf a few more days.

Add a tablespoon or two of the chopped rind to recipes as needed. Preserved lemon will keep for several weeks in the refrigerator.

Pickled Jalapeños

MAKES ABOUT 1 PINT   PREP TIME: 20 MINUTES

These are great on quesadillas, black beans, and in Cornmeal-crusted Oyster and Black-eyed Pea Salad with Jalapeño Dressing (p. 123).

12 fresh jalapeños, split lengthwise
   and seeded
1 cup red wine vinegar

¾ cup sugar
1 tablespoon salt

Place the jalapeños in a large bowl or glass container or jar. Bring the vinegar, sugar, and salt to a boil in a small saucepan over medium-high heat. Simmer the liquid over low heat for 20–30 minutes, then pour over the jalapeños; marinate them for 15–20 minutes. Cool the liquid completely, and refrigerate until needed.

From peppers to onions to other vegetables (like okra and green beans), pickled vegetables are essential condiments in my pantry. I love how the acidic bite of vinegar and the slight sweetness of honey or sugar intensify and transform the main ingredient, giving it more tang and personality than it had in its fresh form. I use chopped or sliced pickled vegetables in countless sandwiches and salads. I also like to skewer them whole for cocktails like Bloody Marys.

Pickled Red Onions

MAKES ABOUT 1 CUP   PREP TIME: 15 MINUTES

These sweet, sour, and slightly spicy onion slices add zest and color to just about any salad or sandwich. They are also a great accompaniment to a roasted meat, paté, or terrine, and they're delicious piled atop quesadillas!

½ cup sugar

½ teaspoon salt

¾ cup red wine vinegar

1 jalapeño, split lengthwise (remove most of the seeds)

1 large red onion, sliced very thin

Bring the sugar, salt, and vinegar to a boil in a small saucepan. Meanwhile, place the jalapeño and onion in a glass or stainless steel bowl. Pour the hot vinegar mixture over the vegetables. Stir to mix, then let them sit until cool. Pour all the liquid back into the saucepan and bring it to a boil. Reduce it by about half, until almost syrupy. Let the liquid cool completely, then stir it into the onions and jalapeños. Place the mixture in a jar or container and store in the refrigerator. These onions keep indefinitely.

From Brackish Waters
to the Deep Blue Sea

Vegetable Stock

Fish Fumet

My Favorite Chicken Stock

Cornmeal-crusted Catfish with Silky Red Bean Sauce

Pecan-crusted Fish with Citrus Meunière

Grouper Baked in Grape Leaves

Seared Scallops with Corn Cream and *Maque Choux*

Mediterranean Roasted Shrimp with Crispy Risotto Cakes

Big City Salmon with Martini Sauce

Gulf Coast Bouillabaisse

Speedy Shrimp with Tomatoes, Feta Cheese, and Basil

Sautéed Snapper with Grapefruit-Basil Butter

Shrimp or Crayfish Clemenceau

Southern Shrimp Stew

Seared Yellowfin Tuna with Walnut Red Pepper Sauce

Salmon with Choucroute and Gewürztraminer Sauce

Down here in Louisiana, living so close to the Gulf of Mexico, we are just plain spoiled when it comes to fish and shellfish. Whenever I get jealous of those California folks with their perfect produce and organic meat purveyors, I think, yeah, but how many crayfish boils do they have every year? And just when those crayfish shells are getting too hard and too small, the blue crabs start coming in strong. And then, in the middle of January when things are looking bleak, a few dozen plump, salty oysters on the half shell (with a cold beer or a glass of champagne) add a bit of sparkle and romance to your day. Not to mention sweet white shrimp; shiny, colorful, and bright-eyed pompano; mahi mahi; red snapper . . . you get the picture.

Most of the recipes in this chapter can be reproduced with regional alternatives, such as Dungeness crab or blue point oysters, and for fish varieties of similar body type and flavor. And, of course, fish like tuna are found on more than one coast.

If you can, find a fish market or check out various grocery store seafood departments to see whose product looks the best on a regular basis. The proliferation of high-quality, upscale food stores around the country means your chances of finding a wide variety of fish and shellfish are getting better all the time.

When it comes to selecting fish, you'll want to look for bright convex eyes (never sunken and dull), red gills, and firm flesh. But since you can't touch the fish yourself, you will want to try to develop a rapport with the person working the counter. That's really the best way to find out what's fresh and what's tired. And remember, fresh is not always best—some of those wonderful flash-frozen and "frozen at sea," or "FAS," products, such as Pacific wild salmon and halibut, are going to be better than a so-called fresh product that's traveled days to get to your area, and then sat on ice for a few more. Try to find out when new product comes in, and be prepared to change your dinner plans if what you're looking for isn't available or at its best. The more you cook, the more flexible you will become and the less you will be tied to preparing certain recipes and specific types of fish.

It helps to remember that the search is all part of the fun.

Keep in mind that fresh fish is a gift and a delicacy we can't take for granted. The choices we make now will have a profound effect on the choices our children and grandchildren may have in the future. For more information on which fish and shellfish are being harvested or farmed in a sustainable way, check out the Web sites of the Seafood Choices Alliance (www.seafoodchoices.com) and the Monterey Bay Aquarium (www.mbayaq.org).

Whether you're craving some Gulf Coast Bouillabaisse (p. 220) with Roasted Red Pepper Rouille (p. 184) (perfect for a dinner party), or Shrimp Clemenceau (p. 226) for a taste of New Orleans, pour yourself a glass of wine (white or red—both are fine with fish), and let's make dinner.

Vegetable Stock

MAKES I QUART   PREP TIME: 30 MINUTES

What a great way to use up some of those veggies that are beginning to look a little tired in the fridge. Start with a few fresh ingredients and be creative with your trimmings. Use this stock for a bit more flavor when making soups, moistening bread stuffing, deglazing a roasting or sauté pan, or stirring up a risotto.

1 tablespoon canola or olive oil
1 large onion, quartered
1 medium to large carrot, peeled and
    cut into large chunks
2 celery stalks, trimmed and chopped
Any of the following: leek trimmings,
    fennel bulb or trimmings,
    mushroom stems, corn cobs,
    tomato pieces

1 bay leaf
Fresh herbs, such as parsley stems,
    thyme, basil, or tarragon
¼ teaspoon salt

Heat the oil in a 1-gallon pot over medium heat, then add the onion, carrot, and celery and cook for about 5 minutes. Add any of the other suggested vegetables and continue cooking gently for another 5 minutes. Add the bay leaf, herbs, and salt, then cover with about 6 cups of cold water. Bring to a boil, then lower the heat and simmer for 20–30 minutes. Turn off the heat and let it steep for a few more minutes. Strain and cool. It will keep, refrigerated, up to 3 days, or frozen for up to 2 months.

Stay away from strongly flavored vegetables like asparagus, broccoli, cauliflower, and bell peppers, or mushy bland ones, like zucchini. Corn cobs freeze well, so think of saving them next time you trim fresh kernels from the cob.

Fish Fumet

"Fumet" is the French term for an aromatic broth (typically fish or vegetable, though it can also refer to a meat stock) that is simmered down to concentrate the flavors. Making your own fish stock is easier than you think and adds irreplaceable flavor to recipes, such as Gulf Coast Bouillabaisse (p. 220) and Southern Shrimp Stew (p. 228). Whatever you don't use can be frozen in small plastic containers (for up to 2 months), so you can pull it out for quick seafood pasta, risotto, or poaching liquid for a fresh fillet.

2 pounds bones from white fish, such as trout, snapper, flounder, or bass
2 teaspoons olive oil
1 cup chopped onion
½ cup chopped celery
1 cup diced leek (thoroughly washed) and/or fennel trimmings (bulb and feathery tops)

1 cup mushroom trimmings, or 6 button mushrooms
2 cups dry white wine
Bouquet Garni (p. 145) made with bay leaf, thyme, tarragon, parsley stems
¼ teaspoon whole black peppercorns
¼ teaspoon salt

Rinse the fish bones under running water to make sure they are free of blood and guts. Heat the olive oil and vegetables in a large pot over medium heat for about 7 minutes, stirring, until softened but not browned, then lay the fish bones on top, cover the pot, and reduce the heat to low. Sweat the bones for about 5 minutes, uncover the pot, and pour the wine over the bones. Add water to come about halfway up the pot (about 2 quarts), then add the Bouquet Garni, peppercorns, and salt. Bring to a boil slowly, then lower the heat and let it simmer for about 20 minutes. Remove the broth from the heat, let it steep about 5 minutes, then strain it through a fine strainer. Let it cool, then put it in small containers and freeze what you don't use.

An alternative to fish fumet is the strained juice from mussels steamed in white wine with herbs. Or feel free to add a few mussels to the pot with your fish bones for a really rich and tasty fumet.

My Favorite Chicken Stock

MAKES 6 CUPS   PREP TIME: 1 HOUR 15 MINUTES

3 pounds chicken parts, such as
   necks, backs, and carcasses (cut
   into smaller pieces)
1 medium onion, coarsely chopped
1 small carrot
2 celery stalks
1 leek or leek trimmings, optional

Bouquet Garni (p. 145) made with
   parsley stems, bay leaf, thyme,
   and/or tarragon sprigs
4–5 whole cloves
¼ teaspoon whole black peppercorns
3 garlic cloves, optional
Pinch of salt

Rinse the chicken pieces with cold water. Place them in a pot just large enough to hold the pieces comfortably, and cover with water by about 1 inch (about 2 quarts). Bring to a boil over medium-high heat. Lower the heat and skim the scum off the surface. Add all the remaining ingredients and return to a boil. Lower the heat; simmer gently for about 1 hour. Turn off the heat and let steep for about 5 minutes, then strain. If using the stock immediately, skim off the fat. If not, let the stock cool, then refrigerate it with the fat on top. Skim off the solidified fat before using.

Cornmeal-crusted Catfish
with Silky Red Bean Sauce

MAKES 4 SERVINGS   PREP TIME: 50 MINUTES (IF COOKING DRIED BEANS)

One day while cooking a pot of red beans, I noticed that the juice had a beautiful, silky sheen. It occurred to me that the beans might make a good sauce if pureed really smoothly with their cooking liquid. An idea was born—really: that's all it takes! I played around with seasonings and decided I liked the warm hint of cinnamon married with the spicy flavors of poblano and chipotle. Adding fresh lime juice at the end of the process brightens up the earthiness of the puree. The light coating of cornmeal gives the fish a nice crunch to contrast with the creamy sauce (which, incidentally, is wonderful with grilled fish of any kind—trout, redfish, or snapper are particularly good). A side of Green Rice (p. 309) is a perfect accompaniment.

4 fillets of catfish, 5 or 6 ounces each
Salt
½ cup cornmeal
½ cup flour
½ teaspoon each of ground cumin
    and coriander

2 tablespoons cooking oil or clarified
    butter
Silky Red Bean Sauce
Lime wedges, cilantro, scallions, or a
    fresh tomato-corn salsa, as garnish

Season the fish lightly with salt. Mix the cornmeal and flour with the spices and coat the fish on both sides. Heat the oil in a large skillet until very hot but not smoking. Fry the fillets, two at a time, until golden brown on both sides. Pour warm red bean sauce onto a plate and top with sautéed fish. Garnish with lime wedges, cilantro, and scallions, or a fresh tomato-corn salsa.

SILKY RED BEAN SAUCE

½ pound red beans, soaked overnight
    or "quick soaked," or
    1 (15½-ounce) can red beans,
    drained
Bouquet Garni (p. 145) made with
    bay leaf, cilantro stems, and
    1-inch piece of cinnamon stick
2 tablespoons olive oil
1 small onion, chopped
1 small poblano pepper, stemmed,
    seeded, and chopped

2 garlic cloves, minced
1 cup tomato puree, made from fresh
    or canned tomatoes
1 chipotle chile canned in adobo
    sauce, split lengthwise and seeded
1 teaspoon chile powder
Salt and pepper
½ bunch cilantro, cleaned and
    roughly chopped
Juice of ½ lime (about 2 tablespoons)

Place the soaked beans in a medium saucepan with 1 quart of cold water and the Bouquet Garni. Bring to a boil, then reduce the heat and simmer until the beans are tender but not mushy, about 1 hour. After the beans have simmered for 30 minutes, heat the olive oil in a large skillet over medium heat. Add the onion and poblano and cook, stirring, for about 5 minutes. Add the garlic and cook for 2 more minutes, then transfer the vegetables to the saucepan with beans and stir in the tomato puree, chipotle, and chile powder. (If using canned beans, rinse them and place in a medium saucepan with 1 cup of water and the sautéed ingredients, chipotle, chile powder, and tomato puree). If your beans start looking dry (they should be submerged and moist throughout the simmering), add a little more water. Cook for about 15 more minutes, and when the beans and vegetables are very soft, season to taste with salt and pepper. Drain them, reserving the liquid, and cool. Place the beans in a blender with the cilantro, lime juice, and a cup of the cooking liquid. Puree them, adding more liquid as necessary to make a smooth, viscous sauce (the consistency of pancake batter). You may need to do this in two batches. Pour the sauce into a pot and keep warm until ready to use. If necessary, you can add a little water.

Pecan-crusted Fish with Citrus Meunière

MAKES 4 SERVINGS   PREP TIME: 40 MINUTES

One of my first memories of New Orleans was gathering the pecans off the ground at the naval base where my father was stationed, then sitting around a table with my family at night, watching *Adventures in Paradise* and shelling the seemingly bottomless pile. We had nutpicks, silver utensils with curved sharp tips, for digging out the tiny pieces of shell trapped in the crevices of each nut meat—talk about tedious! But I was always proud to have the cleanest and choicest halves to offer up for my mom's approval.

I was surprised when I went to France to cook at the jazz festival in Nice and learned that I had to bring my own pecans to make pecan pie (the nuts are not indigenous there)! It followed, then, that I would use local nuts to create this New Orleans rendition of the more classic Trout Amandine.

---

4 fillets of snapper, redfish, drum, or trout (about 6 ounces each)

Salt and pepper

½ cup pecan pieces

½ cup flour

½ teaspoon dried thyme, or 1 teaspoon fresh

1 teaspoon chopped orange zest

½ teaspoon cayenne

1 egg

½ cup milk or buttermilk

3 tablespoons oil or clarified butter

Citrus Meunière

Season the fish with salt and pepper. Place the pecans, flour, thyme, orange zest, and cayenne in a food processor and pulse until well blended but not powdery. Transfer the pecan mixture to a plate. In a shallow bowl or pie plate, whisk together the egg and milk. Dip the fish into the egg mixture, then into the pecan mixture. Press to coat the fillets.

Heat the oil in a large skillet over medium-high heat, and when hot but not smoking, add the fish. Reduce the heat to medium or medium-low and cook for 4–5 minutes on each side. Remove to a platter or plates and keep warm while you make the sauce.

Spoon finished sauce over fish. Serve immediately.

CITRUS MEUNIÈRE

3 tablespoons butter

1 tablespoon each orange juice and
  lemon juice

1 teaspoon chopped fresh parsley

Salt and pepper

Hot sauce

Melt the butter in a pan and let it foam and turn golden brown. Swirl the pan
to see the milk solids on the bottom. When it is nice and brown, pour in the
juices and swirl the pan to mix. Add the parsley, season with salt, pepper, and
a few drops of hot sauce, and swirl.

Grouper Baked in Grape Leaves

MAKES 4 SERVINGS   PREP TIME: ABOUT 45 MINUTES

There is something particularly irresistible about food that's wrapped up like a parcel in an edible casing—especially when there's a little something inside that you're not expecting. For me, the subtle, slightly briny flavor of grape leaves represents the best of the Mediterranean. In this dish, there's an appealing exchange between the fish, grape leaves, and couscous that results in a moist, aromatic, and savory package enhanced by a tangy olive vinaigrette and roasted red pepper garnish. The feta cheese is a tasty addition and a pretty garnish, but it's not necessary. When it comes to choosing fish, a thick, super-fresh fillet of mahi mahi, grouper, amberjack, or snapper would be ideal.

COUSCOUS AND RED PEPPER GARNISH

½ cup couscous

2 red bell peppers

Grated zest of 2 lemons and 1 orange

1 tablespoon chopped cilantro

1 tablespoon chopped fresh mint

1 tablespoon chopped fresh parsley

2 scallions, thinly sliced

1 garlic clove, minced

1 tablespoon olive oil

Salt and pepper

Preheat the oven to 375°F.

Place the couscous in a large bowl and pour ½ cup boiling water over it. Cover and set aside for about 5 minutes. Then stir the grains, breaking up any lumps with your fingers. Char the peppers (see roasting peppers, p. 122) and peel, seed, and cut them into large triangles. Set them aside for garnish, and finely chop any scrap pieces that are left. Add the scraps to the couscous with the lemon and orange zest, cilantro, mint, parsley, scallions, garlic, and olive oil. Season to taste with salt and pepper.

GROUPER

1 (16-ounce) jar grape leaves
4 (5-ounce) fillets of grouper, cut
   ¾ inch thick
Salt and pepper
Cooked couscous
⅓ cup extra-virgin olive oil, plus more
   for brushing
½ cup dry white wine
1 bay leaf
Juice of 2 lemons and 1 orange

1 tablespoon red wine vinegar
1 tablespoon chopped shallots
¼ cup pitted kalamata olives,
   quartered lengthwise
¼ cup pitted green olives
Red Pepper Garnish
2 tsp chopped fresh rosemary, for
   garnish
2 ounces crumbled feta cheese, for
   garnish

Blanch 8 grape leaves in simmering water for about 3 minutes. Remove and drain. Cut off the stem ends.

Season the fish with salt and pepper. Place two overlapping grape leaves (dull sides facing up), in front of you, and top with a few spoons of couscous mixture. Center the fillet bottom-side up on the couscous, then fold first the sides, then the top and bottom of the grape leaves over the fish to enclose it like a package. Place the "package" seam-side down in a roasting pan with a lid. Repeat with remaining fillets, brush each wrapped fish with olive oil, and pour wine and ½ cup water over the fish. Add the bay leaf, cover, and bake 15–17 minutes, basting from time to time. While the fish is baking, place the reserved lemon and orange juice in a small saucepan with the vinegar. Bring to a boil and cook until reduced to 3 tablespoons of liquid. Pour into a small bowl and whisk in the ⅓ cup olive oil, shallots, and olives, and season to taste. Place the fish on a platter or individual plates. Sauce with the vinaigrette, and garnish with the red pepper triangles, rosemary, and feta cheese.

Seared Scallops with Corn Cream and Maque Choux

MAKES 4 SERVINGS   PREP TIME: 45 MINUTES

I always envied folks who grew up in corn country and got to taste those gold and silver ears cooked fresh from the field, just exploding with sweetness. I had a friend whose mother used to say, "Go run and get the corn, and if you drop any on the way back, don't stop to pick it up!" I love the *urgency* of it.

So, when we get a case of really sweet corn at the restaurant, I like to use it two ways: I make this sweet Corn Cream, which goes beautifully with big, juicy sea scallops, and I serve it with the *maque choux*, so you also get the crisp crunch from the corn kernels in addition to the creamy sauce.

If corn isn't in season and you're just dying to make this, use frozen sweet corn.

CORN CREAM

3 ears sweet white or yellow corn, all
　　silk removed
1 tablespoon butter

Pinch of salt
½ cup heavy cream

Cut the kernels off the cobs with a serrated knife, being careful not to cut too close. Place the corn with the butter, 1 cup of water, and salt in a small saucepan over medium-high heat and bring to a boil. Reduce the heat and simmer for about 5 minutes, or until tender. Remove from the heat and let cool completely. Pour into a blender jar and pour the cream into the empty pot. Bring the cream to a boil, then reduce the heat and simmer while you blend the corn mixture to a smooth puree. Strain the corn puree through a fine sieve into the saucepan with the cream, and whisk. Warm the sauce gently and taste for seasoning. Adjust to desired thickness by reducing it a little or thinning with a little more cream or water. Keep warm until ready to serve.

When pureeing a mixture that contains more solids than liquid, add the solids first, then pulse the blade to break them down, then add liquid. Use caution when blending a hot sauce, and never fill the blender more than a third full. Otherwise, the heat will force the top off the machine.

MAQUE CHOUX

3 ears sweet white or yellow corn, all
   silk removed

1 tablespoon butter

½ medium yellow onion, finely
   chopped

1 medium ripe tomato, peeled,
   seeded, and diced

2 tablespoons thinly sliced scallions

Salt and pepper

Cut the kernels from the cob, being careful not to cut too close. Melt the butter in a medium skillet over medium-high heat and cook the onion, stirring, until softened, about 6 minutes. Add the corn and stir, cooking 4–5 more minutes, then add the tomato. Cook, stirring, until tomatoes are warm, then stir in the scallions. Taste and adjust seasoning with salt and pepper.

TO ASSEMBLE

20 to 24 large sea scallops
   (10–20 count, about 1¼ pounds
   total), untreated or "dry pack"

Salt and pepper

1 tablespoon olive oil

Corn Cream

Maque Choux

Place a large skillet over high heat.

   Pat scallops dry with a paper towel, then season with salt and pepper.

   Pour the olive oil into the skillet and when very hot (but not quite smoking), add the scallops, being careful not to crowd them. Cook at high heat until the first side is a deep golden brown, 2–3 minutes, then turn the scallops and cook on the other side for about 2 more minutes. Scallops should be firm but not hard. Drain on paper towels. Deglaze the pan with 2 tablespoons water, scraping up the brown bits. To serve, pool some of the Corn Cream onto each plate, then pile a little *Maque Choux* in the center of each plate. Place 3–4 scallops around the *Maque Choux* and drizzle with pan juices. Serve immediately.

Maque Choux

Choux *is French for "cabbage," but the translation is not literal—there is no cabbage in this dish. Since corn was not a staple of the Acadians' diet, it's believed that the Indians taught the French settlers of Louisiana to make* maque choux. *This dish is essentially smothered corn or a Cajun version of Yankee succotash made with tomatoes, onions, and green pepper.*

Mediterranean Roasted Shrimp
with Crispy Risotto Cakes

MAKES 12 SERVINGS   PREP TIME: 1 HOUR

It's not hard to imagine eating this dish at a table on the coast in Portofino, Italy. Warm spices, garlic, fresh thyme, and sunny citrus flavors create an irresistible marinade for sweet shrimp. I prefer to pour the marinated crustaceans right onto a baking sheet and roast them (a great no-fuss technique for dinner parties) until they're just cooked. However, you could certainly sear the shrimp in a hot skillet as well. Crispy Risotto Cakes are the perfect starch to serve alongside the shrimp. Drag a forkful of the flavorful rice through the marinade and you'll understand why this dish has been one of my entertaining staples for years. For an extra swath of color (and flavor), serve this dish with Butternut Squash Puree (p. 189).

Risotto Cakes

3 cups Vegetable Stock (p. 204) or Chicken Stock (p. 206) or a combination of the two

2 teaspoons plus 2 tablespoons olive oil

⅓ cup each finely diced onion, celery, and fennel bulb

1 cup arborio rice

⅓ cup sherry or white wine

Salt and pepper

⅓ cup grated Parmesan or Grana Padano cheese

2 tablespoons each chopped fresh basil and snipped chives

¼ cup diced fontina or mozzarella cheese

Roasted Shrimp

Bring the stock to a boil in a small saucepan, then reduce the heat and keep warm. Melt the 2 teaspoons oil in a heavy-bottomed skillet over medium heat and sweat the onion, celery, and fennel for about 5 minutes. Add the rice and stir for 2–3 minutes, then add the sherry and stir until it is absorbed. Using a ladle, start adding the stock a cup or so at a time, and stir until the liquid is absorbed. About halfway through add a little salt and pepper. When all the stock is added, taste the rice. It should be tender but not mushy. (It's okay if the rice is still a little firm, as it will continue to cook after it is removed from the heat.) Add the Parmesan and the herbs, then remove it from the heat and let cool a couple of minutes before stirring in the fontina. Check the seasoning one more time, then pour the rice into a pan and refrigerate for at least 30 minutes (until the rice is cool enough to handle). Use your hands to form 3- to 4-inch cakes (they should be a little smaller than hockey pucks) and set aside. Meanwhile, prepare shrimp.

Heat the remaining 2 tablespoons olive oil in a large nonstick skillet over medium-high heat. Sauté the cakes (two or three at a time so as not to overcrowd the pan) until golden and crispy, 3–4 minutes on each side. Serve the warm cakes alongside the roasted shrimp.

Mediterranean Roasted Shrimp

½ cup extra-virgin olive oil

¼ cup butter, melted

1 teaspoon each toasted and crushed fennel seeds and coriander seeds

½ teaspoon each crushed black pepper and red pepper flakes

2 garlic cloves, minced

2 teaspoons chopped fresh thyme

1 teaspoon each grated lemon zest and orange zest

1 bay leaf, preferably fresh

1 teaspoon salt

3 dozen shrimp (16–20 count, about 2¼ pounds total), peeled and deveined

Preheat the oven to 425°F (on the convection setting, if possible). Combine the marinade ingredients in a large bowl. Add the shrimp and use a rubber spatula (or your hands) to toss and coat the shrimp thoroughly. Allow the shrimp to marinate at least 30 minutes at room temperature, or up to 4 hours in the refrigerator. To cook the shrimp, divide them evenly between two baking sheets and roast for about 10 minutes, until just cooked through (they will firm up and turn light pink). Remove them from the pan, and strain and reserve any juices left in the pan. If not much juice is left, deglaze the sheets with a little white wine; reserve the juice. Pour thickened juices back over the roasted shrimp and toss to combine.

If you run your hands under cold water before forming the Risotto Cakes, the rice mixture will be less likely to stick to them.

The Risotto Cakes can be sautéed in advance and held in a low oven. To give this dish a bit more color (and a nice touch of acidity), garnish with a fine dice of tomatoes dressed with a little vinegar and olive oil. Micro greens or celery leaves would also make a nice crown for the crispy cakes.

Arborio Rice

This short-grain Italian rice is the star of risotto because of its high starch content. As the kernels cook and begin to break down, the starch creates the desired creamier texture for warm risotto, and it also helps hold these cakes together.

Big City Salmon with Martini Sauce

MAKES 4 SERVINGS   PREP TIME: 25 MINUTES

A few years ago I created a menu of regional American dishes (both traditional and invented) for a special Fourth of July wine dinner. I wanted something particularly clever to represent Manhattan. I kept thinking of sophisticated New Yorkers drinking martinis and decided to try my hand at making a sauce with similar ingredients. I like the double dose of juniper with the deep, rich taste of wild salmon, and the olives add a distinctive briny note.

---

4 (6-ounce) salmon fillets

Salt and pepper

Chopped fresh parsley, as desired

2 tablespoons olive oil (if sautéing)

Martini Sauce

Season each piece of salmon with salt and pepper and sprinkle with a little chopped parsley. If sautéing, heat the olive oil in a wide skillet and cook the fish, about 3 minutes on the first side, then about 2 minutes on the second side to achieve a medium-rare temperature. (Increase the cooking time by about 90 seconds on each side if you want the salmon to be cooked through.) You may also grill or broil the salmon, as desired.

Spoon the Martini Sauce over (or alongside) the cooked salmon and serve immediately. This salmon is delicious with boiled new potatoes or rice.

MARTINI SAUCE

1 tablespoon minced shallot

¼ cup gin

¼ cup dry vermouth

1 teaspoon chopped whole juniper
   berries

1 teaspoon dried or brined green
   peppercorns, optional

¼ cup heavy cream

2 teaspoons butter

6 pimiento-stuffed queen olives,
   sliced into rings

Fresh lemon juice

Salt and pepper

Place the shallots, gin, vermouth, juniper berries, and green peppercorns in a small saucepan and bring to a boil. Lower the heat and simmer until reduced to about 3 tablespoons liquid. Add the cream and reduce to ¼ cup.

Strain and return the liquid to the saucepan (discard the solids). Whisk in the butter. Add the olives and season to taste with lemon juice, salt, and a little pepper. Cover and keep warm while you prepare the salmon.

Gulf Coast Bouillabaisse

MAKES 8 SERVINGS   PREP TIME: 1 HOUR 30 MINUTES

Although I had never tasted it myself, I decided to try my hand at bouillabaisse after listening to my dad reminiscing for years about the one he'd had in Marseilles, in a café overlooking the bustling port. Eventually, after much research, I felt I knew what it *should* taste like, but I was still overwhelmed when I had my first bowl in Nice many years later—it was even more complex and deeply flavored than Dad's memories had suggested.

This is one dish where a paticularly flavorful version of Fish Fumet (p. 205) is essential. Because we don't have the same fish as they do in France (such as *rascasse,* the bony fish that makes a true bouillabaisse), I use Gulf fish and shellfish in the stock. I put in a mix of flounder, snapper, and trout bones along with shrimp shells (and heads, if available), and a couple of gumbo crabs for good measure. Make enough so that you can freeze a batch for the next time you make this stew. My one concession: mussels. We don't get them in the Gulf, but it's just not bouillabaisse without 'em. Roasted Red Pepper Rouille (p. 184) and thin slices of toasted baguette are the essential condiments for this soup.

3 tablespoons olive oil

2 onions, chopped

1 fennel bulb, chopped

3 leeks, split lengthwise, rinsed, and
    thinly sliced

3 garlic cloves, minced

1 scant teaspoon saffron threads

4 cups Fish Fumet (p. 205)

2 cups diced tomatoes

½ cup fresh orange juice

1 tablespoon grated orange zest

1 tablespoon chopped fresh thyme

2 tablespoons Pernod, Herbsaint, or
    other anise liqueur

Bouquet Garni (p. 145)

Salt and freshly ground pepper

1 pound white fish

1 pound shrimp (25–30 count)

16 oysters, shucked

1½ pounds mussels

½ pound scallops, optional

Toasted baguette croûtes (p. 88)

Roasted Red Pepper Rouille (p. 184)

In a 1-gallon pot, heat half the olive oil over medium-high heat and sauté the onions, fennel, and leeks for 5–7 minutes, then add the garlic and saffron and cook for 2 additional minutes, until vegetables are softened but not browned (lower the heat to medium, if necessary, to prevent this). Add the Fish Fumet, tomatoes, orange juice, orange zest, thyme, liqueur, and Bouquet Garni, and

bring to a boil. Reduce the heat and simmer for about 20 minutes, stirring occasionally, until thickened. Taste for seasoning and add salt and pepper; keep warm.

Heat the remaining olive oil in a large pot over medium heat and add the fish, cut into ½-inch dice, and the shrimp, and sauté for 2–3 minutes. Add the oysters, mussels, and scallops, and ladle in some of the broth and vegetable mixture (approximately 1 cup per person). Stir, bring it to a boil, reduce the heat, and cover. Cook until the mussel shells open, then taste for seasoning and divide among 8 bowls. Serve with the baguette rounds and Roasted Red Pepper Rouille (p. 184).

When it comes to cleaning mussels, there's not much to it. Just throw them in a sink with enough cold water to cover. Rinse them off (I use my fingers), then press the mussel closed with one hand and use the other to pull off the beard (that little stringy cord that hangs out). After that, you'll want to cook them immediately, so don't clean them until you're ready to cook. If any mussels are open, give them a sharp rap on the counter and set aside. If they don't close within a minute or two, discard them.

Speedy Shrimp with Tomatoes, Feta Cheese, and Basil

MAKES 4 SERVINGS   PREP TIME: 30 MINUTES

This is a dish I make often, especially for informal parties. It is delicious, easy, and pretty, and makes a great buffet item, especially when paired with all those other Mediterranean dishes I love to cook and eat, such as Eggplant Caviar and Black Olive Tapenade (p. 191), Artichoke Dolmades with Lemon Sauce (p. 20), and Simple Orzo Salad with Black Olives and Feta (p. 115). The tomato sauce is also a good base for moussaka or baked stuffed eggplant, or just tossed with noodles and some sharp Greek cheese, such as kasseri. The dish can be completed up to the final baking point and kept refrigerated for several hours or even overnight. Bring it to room temperature before baking, or it will overcook.

1 tablespoon olive oil

24 shrimp (16–20 count, about 1½ pounds total), peeled and deveined

1 tablespoon slivered garlic

1 teaspoon Herbsaint, Pernod, or ouzo, optional

½ cup thinly sliced scallions

Salt

Tomato Sauce

2 tablespoons fresh basil leaves, torn in pieces

½ cup crumbled feta cheese

Preheat the oven to 450°F. Heat the olive oil in a large skillet over medium-high heat. Add the shrimp and sauté until pink and just cooked through. Add the garlic and toss. Remove from the heat and sprinkle lightly with liqueur. Return the skillet to the heat, stir in the scallions, and cook for 30 more seconds. Season lightly with salt, then mix the shrimp with the tomato sauce, fold in the basil, and pour into a wide, shallow casserole dish or 4 individual (10-ounce) ovenproof dishes. Sprinkle with the feta cheese and bake for 10–15 minutes, or until cheese is slightly brown and casserole is nice and hot.

TOMATO SAUCE

2 tablespoons olive oil

1 onion, finely diced

1 fennel bulb, finely diced

½ teaspoon each dried oregano and
dill, or 1 teaspoon each fresh

3 cups diced fresh tomatoes, or
1 (28-ounce) can diced tomatoes
with their juice (for fresh, peel and
seed before dicing)

Bouquet Garni (p. 145) made with
1 bay leaf, 1 bunch parsley stems,
and a 1-inch piece of cinnamon
stick

Salt

Crushed red pepper flakes

Heat the olive oil in a 2-quart saucepan over medium-high heat, then add the onion and fennel and cook for about 5 minutes, until translucent. Stir in the herbs and cook for 1 minute, then add the tomatoes, Bouquet Garni, and 1 cup of water. Bring to a boil and let simmer for about 15 minutes. Season to taste with salt and pepper flakes, but go easy on the salt, as the feta will be salty too. Remove the sauce from the heat and set aside until ready to use. Remove the Bouquet Garni.

Serve with orzo pasta tossed with kalamata olives and/or artichoke hearts, plus crusty bread to sop up all the sauce. A cucumber-onion salad makes a good starter.

Sautéed Snapper
with Grapefruit-Basil Butter

MAKES 4 SERVINGS   PREP TIME: 30 MINUTES

One of the great things about living in Louisiana is the plethora of sunny citrus fruits available during winter. When my grapefruit tree started producing more than I could use at home, I developed this recipe to serve at Bayona. Fresh basil is commonly partnered with lemon or orange, but I love how the faint anise flavor of the herb plays off the bright, tart-sweet punch of grapefruit (and since it rarely freezes in New Orleans, we can typically grow basil all year round as well). Citrus and fish is such a great match—this sauce is delicious with pompano, amberjack, or just about any fish.

4 red snapper fillets (6–7 ounces each), skin on or off
Salt and pepper
3 tablespoons olive oil
Grapefruit-Basil Butter
Grapefruit segments

Season the fish with salt and pepper. Heat half the oil in a large skillet over high heat and place 2 of the fillets skin side down (if serving skin-on). If the skin is off, place the fish in the pan presentation side down first. Reduce the heat to medium and cook for 4–5 minutes, pressing with a spatula so that the skin makes contact with the pan and becomes crispy. Turn and cook on the other side for about 2 more minutes, until the fish is just cooked through. Repeat with the other 2 fillets and the remaining oil. Pour half the Grapefruit-Basil Butter on plates or a platter, and place fish and grapefruit segments (see Grapefruit-Basil Butter) on top. Drizzle with the remaining Grapefruit-Basil Butter. This dish is excellent with plain basmati rice.

GRAPEFRUIT–BASIL BUTTER

1 large ruby red grapefruit, cut into
    segments (see p. 179), juice
    reserved (about ⅔ cup)
Juice of 1 medium orange (about
    ⅓ cup)
¼ cup white or rosé wine

1 medium shallot, chopped
2 tablespoons butter
4–6 large fresh basil leaves, blanched,
    shocked, and finely chopped
Salt

Place the grapefruit juice, orange juice, wine, and shallot in a small saucepan and bring to a boil. Lower the heat and simmer until you have about 2 tablespoons of liquid (about 10 minutes). Whisk the butter slowly into the juice, until you have a creamy sauce. (Remove it from the heat and cover if not serving immediately.) When ready to use, stir in the basil, season with salt, and reheat if necessary.

I often cook fish with the skin on, because I love the taste and texture of the crispy skin, and it actually helps keep the fish moist.

Shrimp or Crayfish Clemenceau

MAKES 4 SERVINGS   PREP TIME: 45 MINUTES

I'm not sure what the connection is between this old New Orleans favorite and the French politician—perhaps it was created when he visited the city—but whatever the reason, it is an enduring part of the Creole repertoire.

The potatoes are most often deep-fried to a light golden brown (a preparation known as "brabant potatoes") before joining the other ingredients in the pan, but it works just as well to blanch them in water, then crisp them. This makes a tasty complete meal when paired with a ripe tomato salad or a platter of crudités.

1 cup diced potatoes (about ½-inch dice)

Salt

3 tablespoons olive oil

5 tablespoons butter

½ pound button mushrooms, quartered

1 pound shrimp (16–20 count), peeled and deveined, or 1 pound crayfish tails

2 cups peas (frozen or fresh) or cut-up sugar snaps or snow peas (blanched)

Pepper

Hot sauce

1 medium shallot, finely diced

¾ cup white wine

3 tablespoons fresh lemon juice

2 garlic cloves, minced

3 scallions, finely chopped

Preheat the oven to 325°F.

Place the potatoes in a small saucepan and cover with cold water; add a pinch of salt. Bring to a boil, then reduce the heat and simmer until the potatoes are just cooked through (they will become opaque and should be tender, but not overly soft, when pierced with a paring knife). Drain them, rinse with cold water, and cool. Pat the dice dry with paper towels.

Heat 1 tablespoon olive oil in a medium skillet until hot but not smoking, and add the potatoes and 2 tablespoons butter. Cook until evenly browned and crispy, and transfer to a large bowl. Keep them warm in the oven.

Return the skillet to the heat (no need to clean), pour in the remaining 2 tablespoons olive oil. When the oil is hot, add the mushrooms and cook, stirring, until they are lightly browned and crispy. Add the mushrooms to the potatoes. Add the shrimp or crayfish tails to the skillet and cook a few more minutes. Add the peas, season lightly with salt, pepper, and hot sauce, and transfer the mixture to the bowl of potatoes. Toss mixture to combine and return to oven to keep warm. Deglaze the pan with the shallots, wine, and lemon juice and scrape up the bits. Bring to a boil and reduce to about 4 tablespoons of liquid. Stir in the garlic, then whisk in the remaining 3 tablespoons butter, a little at a time, to make a creamy sauce. Season with salt, pepper, and hot sauce.

Pour the sauce over the shrimp, sprinkle with scallions, and serve immediately. Or divide among four plates, top with potatoes and scallions, and drizzle with sauce.

The potatoes can be blanched in advance and held in water. This dish is best served as soon as it's made (it gets a little soggy, and the peas will shrivel, if it sits too long).

Southern Shrimp Stew

MAKES 4 SERVINGS   PREP TIME: 45 MINUTES

Shrimp and okra go together like oysters and artichokes (which is to say, they're made for each other). And to my mind it's no coincidence that corn and tomatoes are at their peak around the same time as the okra. In this recipe, they all find themselves swimming happily in a broth scented with allspice and thyme, and zippy with fresh jalapeños. If you are leery of that much spice in the broth, leave out the jalapeños and just serve some chopped up alongside, for the daring ones among you.

2 tablespoons canola or olive oil

1 tablespoon butter

1 medium yellow onion, chopped

1 red bell pepper, chopped

1 poblano pepper, chopped

1 quart Shrimp Stock (p. 229)

1½ cups fresh or canned diced
    tomato

1 garlic clove, minced

½ teaspoon chopped fresh thyme
    leaves

½ pound okra, stemmed and sliced
    (about 2 cups)

2 teaspoons cider vinegar

1 cup fresh corn kernels, cut from the
    cob, or 1 cup frozen kernels

24–28 shrimp (16–20 count; about
    1½ pounds), peeled and deveined

Salt and pepper

Hot sauce

¼ cup thinly sliced scallions

2 thinly sliced jalapeños, optional

Heat 1 tablespoon oil and the butter in a large heavy-bottomed pot over medium-high heat. Add the onion and peppers and cook, stirring, for about 5 minutes. Add stock, tomatoes, garlic, and thyme and bring to a boil. In another skillet, heat the remaining tablespoon oil over high heat until very hot but not smoking. Add the okra and sauté for 4–5 minutes, tossing. When the okra is starting to brown a little, drizzle in the vinegar, toss, and add them to the tomato mixture. Reduce the heat and simmer the stew for about 15 minutes, then add the corn and shrimp and cook 5 minutes. Taste, and adjust the seasoning with salt, pepper, and hot sauce. Serve hot, sprinkled with sliced scallions and jalapeños.

If you want to make this a complete meal, add diced cooked potatoes or sweet potatoes to the stew, or serve it over rice.

Shrimp Stock

2 tablespoons canola or olive oil

Heads and shells from at least
   1 pound shrimp

1 medium onion, chopped

2 celery ribs, chopped

1 carrot, chopped

2 cups white wine

2 quarts water

3 tablespoons tomato paste

2 jalapeños, stemmed, seeded, and
   chopped

3–4 smashed garlic cloves

Bouquet Garni (p. 145), made from
   parsley stems, thyme, and bay
   leaves

1 teaspoon whole allspice

1 teaspoon whole black peppercorns

Heat the oil over medium-high heat in a 1-gallon pot. When the oil is almost smoking, add the shrimp heads and shells and stir. Cook over medium-high heat for about 5 minutes, then add the onion, celery, and carrot, and cook for 5–7 more minutes, stirring frequently. Add all the other ingredients, whisking to mix in the tomato paste. Bring to a boil, then reduce the heat and simmer for about ½ hour. Let it cool; strain. You should have at least 1 quart. If you have more, you may reduce it to the desired amount (for a more concentrated flavor) or simply freeze the extra. If you have less, just add a little water.

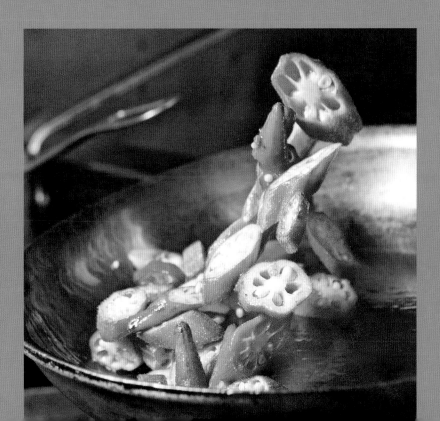

Seared Yellowfin Tuna
with Walnut Red Pepper Sauce

MAKES 4 SERVINGS   PREP TIME: 30 MINUTES

This dish's vibrant, savory sauce is my version of *muhamarra*, a mildly spicy and slightly fruity Turkish red pepper condiment. It is easy to prepare and goes great with just about any grilled meat or fish (or with thick slices of grilled eggplant). Pole-caught yellowfin tuna is a good sustainable choice; its meaty texture and flavor stand up well to the thick pesto-like puree. Swordfish would be a good alternative, cooked the same way as the tuna. A green vegetable, baked or grilled eggplant, or rice pilaf would make a great side dish.

4 pieces yellowfin tuna (6–8 ounces each)

Salt and pepper

¼ teaspoon plus ½ teaspoon ground cumin

¼ teaspoon each coarsely ground fennel and coriander seed

2 roasted red bell peppers (see roasting technique, p. 122), seeded and chopped

¼ cup walnuts, toasted

Juice of 1 medium lemon (about 3 tablespoons)

1 garlic clove, minced

1 teaspoon pomegranate molasses (see below)

Pinch of crushed red pepper flakes

½ cup plus 2 tablespoons olive oil

Season the tuna with salt, pepper, ¼ teaspoon of the cumin, and the fennel and coriander.

Tuna is delicious served medium-rare. If you are used to eating your fish cooked through, do yourself a favor and try cooking it for a little less time.

   Many versions of this style of sauce call for lightly toasted bread crumbs. Feel free to add about ¼ cup to this recipe, if desired.

   Pomegranate molasses (or syrup) is tart, tangy, and fruity and is usually available in Middle Eastern or specialty food markets.

Combine the red peppers, walnuts, lemon juice, garlic, molasses, remaining ½ teaspoon cumin, and crushed red pepper in a food processor and pulse on and off for 1 minute. Slowly drizzle in ½ cup of olive oil and season with salt and pepper.

Heat the remaining 2 tablespoons olive oil in a large skillet until hot but not smoking. Add the tuna and cook about 2 minutes on each side. (My recommended doneness for tuna is rare to medium-rare.) Serve the tuna with a dollop of the sauce. (It's thick and concentrated, so you won't need much.)

Salmon with Choucroute and Gewürztraminer Sauce

MAKES 4 SERVINGS   PREP TIME: 45 MINUTES

This unexpected salmon preparation borrows flavors from Alsace. The usual partner for choucroute is a medley of pork meat sausages, but the oceany flavor of the best wild salmon works surprisingly well. The tart sauerkraut and spicy Gewürztraminer balance the richness of the fish. Juniper berries lend a distinct perfume. Needless to say, the perfect wine for this dish is the one that you used to make the sauce.

CHOUCROUTE

1 tablespoon olive oil

1 red onion, thinly sliced

1 carrot, peeled and julienned

1 (16-ounce) jar sauerkraut, rinsed

1 cup Chicken Stock (p. 206)

¼ cup white wine

½ teaspoon coarsely chopped whole juniper berries

½ teaspoon fresh thyme

1 bay leaf

¼ teaspoon black pepper

Snipped fresh chives, for garnish

Heat the olive oil in a large skillet over medium-high heat. Add the onion and carrot and cook, stirring, until just wilted. Stir in the sauerkraut, stock, wine, and seasonings. Bring to a simmer and cook, covered, about 15 minutes, then set aside, still covered, to keep warm.

GEWÜRZTRAMINER SAUCE

1 cup Gewürztraminer (you can substitute Riesling or another Alsatian white wine)

2 tablespoons apple cider vinegar

2 tablespoons finely chopped shallots

4 tablespoons (½ stick) butter

Pinch of salt

Combine the wine, vinegar, and shallots in a small saucepan and bring to a boil. Lower the heat and simmer gently until the liquid is reduced to

2–3 tablespoons. Gradually add butter, in small pieces, whisking constantly, until all the butter is incorporated. The sauce should be a shiny, creamy yellow. Add salt. Taste, and adjust seasonings.

SALMON

4 salmon fillets (about 6 ounces each)	2 tablespoons olive oil
Salt and pepper	1 tablespoon butter
1 cup dry bread crumbs, mixed with	
2 tablespoons chopped fresh	
parsley	

Season the salmon with salt and pepper and coat with the bread crumb mixture. Heat the olive oil in a wide skillet over medium-high heat. When it is very hot but not smoking, add the salmon, presentation side down. Lower the heat to medium, add the butter, and use a spatula to lift the salmon, to allow butter to run under each fillet. Cook until it is golden brown, about 3 minutes. Turn and cook about 3 more minutes, until salmon is just medium-rare. Cook a little longer if you like it more done, but not long enough to dry it out.

TO SERVE

Divide the choucroute among four plates, top with a piece of salmon, and drizzle the sauce around the fish. Garnish with chives.

At Bayona, we use plain bread crumbs for this dish. But for a little more texture, try panko, *Japanese bread crumbs (available at specialty markets and many grocery stores).*

Beurre blancs, or butter sauces, are known for breaking. Luckily it's a cinch to repair them. To fix a broken beurre blanc, skim the butter off the top and reserve the separated part of the sauce. In a small clean saucepan, heat 1 tablespoon of water to a simmer and whisk in the reserved sauce. Over a very gentle heat, whisk in the butter, a bit at a time, and the reserved sauce base should pull together.

A Mess of Main Courses

Pan-roasted Quail with Dried Cherries and Pinot Noir Sauce

Roasted Duckling with Orange–Cane Syrup Sauce

Seared Duck Breasts with Pepper Jelly Glaze

Seared Pork Chops with Satsuma-Horseradish Marmalade

Jalapeño-roast Pork

Soy-glazed Pork with Quick-fried Rice

Pork "Saltimbocca" with Marsala Sauce

Grilled Steak with Arugula, Tomato, Blue Cheese, and Shoestring Salad

Seared Steak with Rosemary and Broccoli Rabe

Filet of Beef with Herbed Cream Cheese Filling and Bordelaise Sauce

Turkish Stuffed Eggplant with Spicy Lamb and Rice

Herb-roasted Lamb Loin with Goat Cheese and Zinfandel Sauce

Sautéed Sweetbreads with Sherry-Mustard Butter

I loved fairy tales as a child, and a line from one of my favorite stories has stayed with me all these years. A princess is asked to declare her love and loyalty for her father, the king, and she says, "I love him as meat loves salt." Those words could just as easily describe my approach to cooking. The main thing I've learned in my twenty-seven years in the professional kitchen, where I've handled just about every cut of every animal imaginable, is that when it comes to preparing meat and poultry successfully, two things are paramount: technique and *seasoning.* If you've ever enjoyed a juicy piece of smoked brisket or a perfectly grilled rib eye with a sprinkling of coarse sea salt, then you know what I mean. Whether you roast, sauté, braise, grill, or broil, it's all in the handling, timing, and seasoning—done before, during, and after cooking. Incidentally, this approach translates to cooking vegetables to their full potential too, so I've included a few of my favorite meatless entrées in this chapter.

Just remember that a tough, cheap cut of beef, lamb, or pork can be turned into the most succulent, tasty dish imaginable with a long, slow simmer. Then again, the finest, dearest center-cut filet can turn out dry and tasteless if overcooked. From simple sautés to savory stews and braises, these recipes offer choices for every real-life occasion, from a late-working weeknight dinner to a leisurely, knock-'em-dead Saturday night dinner party.

Vegetable and Cheese Enchiladas with Ancho-Tomato Sauce

MAKES 4 SERVINGS   PREP TIME: 2 HOURS

While these are definitely a contemporary take on a Mexican classic, vegetable enchiladas are as satisfying and flavorful as any meat version. The preparation takes some time, but they're a cinch to assemble. My advice is to make the sauce a day in advance or to start this early in the day before you get too hungry.

The only difficult part about this recipe is deciding what vegetables to leave out. There are countless choices, but I've narrowed it down to a tasty combination that works well with the mildly spicy sauce. Substitute or add your seasonal favorites, including—but not limited to—chayote squash (known as mirliton in New Orleans), corn, yellow squash, pumpkin, eggplant, and so forth. If you want to fire up the grill, that's another great way to prepare the vegetables. Just keep the veggies in large pieces, brush them with a little olive oil and seasoning, and grill a few minutes on both sides; then cool them and cut into smaller pieces. You also have a number of cheeses to choose from, such as white cheddar, Monterey Jack, and pepper Jack.

ANCHO-TOMATO SAUCE

1 large dried ancho chile
1 medium white or yellow onion, cut into ¼-inch slices
4 garlic cloves, unpeeled
1 teaspoon red wine vinegar
8 roma tomatoes

Salt
1 tablespoon olive oil
Water, Chicken Stock (p. 206), or Vegetable Stock (p. 204), for thinning the sauce

Lay a piece of aluminum foil on the bottom of a cast-iron skillet (for easier cleanup, as juices have a tendency to weep and scorch the pan) and set it over medium heat. Place the ancho chile on the foil and cook about 2 minutes, turning once, until the chile smells toasty. Remove the chile and set aside, then add the onion and garlic and cook 10–15 minutes, turning the vegetables once or twice as they brown. Or place the vegetables on a baking sheet under a broiler and cook 6–7 minutes, turning them once halfway through the cooking process.

Discard the stem and seeds from the cooled chile and tear it into pieces. Place the chile in a small bowl, cover with hot water, and add the vinegar. Let it soak for about 10 minutes. Peel the garlic cloves and place them in a food processor or blender along with the onions.

Char the tomatoes in the same pan on the foil or under the broiler, turning several times so they are evenly blistered, about 10 minutes. Chop the tomatoes (skin and all) and add to the food processor. Save the chile soaking liquid and add the pieces of chile. Pulse to blend the sauce thoroughly. If necessary, add a little of the chile liquid to thin the sauce (it should have the consistency of thick tomato juice). Season to taste with salt. Heat the olive oil in a medium saucepan and carefully pour in the sauce. Cook, stirring, over medium-high heat for about 10 minutes. The sauce will darken and thicken a little.

Add some water or, preferably, Chicken or Vegetable Stock to adjust the consistency. Simmer gently for about 5 more minutes and adjust the seasoning to taste. Hold the sauce at room temperature while you make the vegetable filling. (Alternatively, the sauce can be made a day in advance.)

VEGETABLE FILLING

3 tablespoons vegetable or olive oil

1 medium white or yellow onion, thinly sliced

1 poblano pepper, thinly sliced

2 portobello mushroom caps, wiped clean with a damp cloth, gills scraped (see technique, p. 55), and cut in ¼-inch strips

½ teaspoon each dried Mexican oregano and ground coriander

Salt

2 medium zucchini (about 8 ounces), cut lengthwise in ¼-inch pieces, then crosswise into ¼-inch dice

4 scallions (green and white), chopped

Black pepper

½ bunch cilantro, cleaned and chopped (about ¼ cup)

Heat 1 tablespoon oil in a large skillet over medium-high heat. When the pan is very hot but not smoking, add the onion and poblano and toss to coat evenly with oil.

Cook for 4–5 minutes, then scrape the vegetables into a large bowl and return the skillet to the heat. Heat another tablespoon of the oil; add the mushrooms and cook, tossing or stirring, until they are wilted and starting to get brown and crispy, 3–4 minutes. Stir in the oregano and coriander. Season with a little salt and add to the bowl of vegetables. Heat the remaining tablespoon of oil, toss in the zucchini pieces, and cook for 4–5 minutes, or until tender. Season with salt, stir in the scallions, and scrape the zucchini into the bowl with the other vegetables. Grind a little black pepper over the vegetables and stir in the cilantro.

TO ASSEMBLE

Vegetable oil, for greasing dish

Ancho-Tomato Sauce

8–12 corn tortillas

Vegetable Filling

2½ cups shredded white melting
    cheese (such as *queso fresco,* mild
    white cheddar, Monterey Jack,
    whole milk mozzarella, or
    asadero)

½ cup chopped onion, for garnish

Chopped cilantro, as desired, for
    garnish

Sliced jalapeños, fresh or pickled, as
    you prefer, for garnish

Preheat the oven to 350°F.

Use a pastry brush to grease a 13 × 9-inch baking pan or shallow oblong baking dish with vegetable oil. Ladle about ½ cup of the sauce into the bottom of the greased pan and spread evenly. Place about half the remaining sauce in a 10-inch skillet and warm gently. Submerge one tortilla in the sauce and let it warm until it is soft and pliable (about 5–10 seconds), then lift it out, draining the excess sauce back into the skillet. Place the tortilla on a work surface, spoon on about 3 tablespoons of the vegetable mixture, sprinkle with a little cheese, and roll it up into a snug cylinder. Place the enchilada seam side down in the baking pan. Fill more tortillas in the same manner. They should fit snugly in the pan, in one layer. Pour the rest of the sauce over the enchiladas and sprinkle with the remaining cheese. Bake for about 15 minutes, until they are hot all the way through and the cheese is bubbly. Garnish with onion, cilantro, and jalapeños and serve.

Polenta Gratin with Savory Vegetables

MAKES 6 TO 8 SERVINGS   PREP TIME: 2 HOURS

This is what I call a "close your eyes and sigh" dish—one of those fragrant and comforting meals that remind us what makes eating such a soul-satisfying experience. It can be served as a vegetarian entrée or as a side dish with chicken, veal, or lamb. Polenta provides the creamy base that melds alternating layers of cheese and vegetables. During baking, the flavors intermingle, and the fontina and roasted garlic provide a pleasing gooey texture. A simple tomato basil sauce brightens up the mellow flavor of the polenta. The result: a perfect confluence of luscious Italian flavors.

If you have never had real Val d'Aosta fontina cheese, this is an excellent time to try it. The difference is noticeable: Val d'Aosta is firm and has a savory, slightly grassy flavor.

If you are short on time, forgo the sauce; this polenta is delicious without it.

POLENTA

Olive oil or butter, for greasing

1 cup whole or low-fat milk

1 cup polenta or good-quality stone-
    ground cornmeal

½ teaspoon salt

2 tablespoons butter

½ cup grated Grana Padano or
    Parmesan cheese

Savory Vegetable Topping

3 cups grated fontina cheese

Brush an 8-inch square baking dish with a thin coating of olive oil or butter.

Bring the milk and 3 cups of water to a boil in a heavy-bottomed 2-quart saucepan over medium-high heat. Slowly pour in the polenta, whisking constantly. Continue whisking or stirring until the mixture boils. Reduce the heat and simmer, stirring occasionally, for about 15 minutes. Add a little more water if the polenta gets too thick (it should be loose enough to pour, but not runny). Stir in the salt, butter, and the Grana Padano cheese, and pour the mixture into the baking dish. Using a spatula, smooth the polenta into an even layer, ⅜ to ½ inch thick. Gently press a sheet of plastic wrap directly

---

If you can't find fontina, you can use any other flavorful melting cheese, such as aged provolone or mozzarella. You might also consider a combination of fontina and grana cheeses.

---

onto the surface of the polenta and let it cool for 10 minutes at room temperature, then refrigerate it until needed. Meanwhile, prepare the vegetables.

When all the vegetables are ready, top the polenta with the eggplant, then sprinkle with a little fontina cheese and spread the spinach on top. Arrange the mushrooms and garlic confit over the spinach, then a little more cheese. Finish with the red peppers and the remaining cheese.

Bake for about 15 minutes, until the polenta is heated through. Serve with a tomato basil sauce if desired.

If you are not serving the polenta immediately, let it cool for 15 minutes, then cover it with plastic wrap, place another pan of the same size on top, and weight it down, using 3 or 4 pounds. Refrigerate for at least ½ hour. Pressing the vegetables in this manner helps them meld with the polenta; however, you shouldn't use so much weight that you make a flat "pizza." This also makes the gratin easier to cut into neat squares. Then you can serve this dish as I do at the restaurant—simply reheat individual squares in the oven. Portions can also be tightly wrapped in plastic and frozen for up to 2 months.

SAVORY VEGETABLE TOPPING

1 ½ cups Garlic Confit (p. 193)

2 large or 3 medium red bell peppers, roasted and peeled (see roasting technique, p. 122)

1 large eggplant, peeled and cut into ½-inch dice (about 3 cups)

6 tablespoons olive oil

Salt

½ pound mushrooms (button, cremini, or wild), stemmed and sliced

Pepper

2 (10-ounce) bags or 1 bunch fresh spinach, washed, or 1 (10-ounce) package frozen spinach, defrosted and squeezed to remove excess moisture

Prepare 2 recipes of Garlic Confit. Preheat the oven to 375°F.

Remove the seeds from the peppers and cut them into strips or dice. Set aside. Place the eggplant in a large bowl with 1 cup of water, 3 tablespoons olive oil, and a generous pinch of salt. Toss the eggplant well to coat, then transfer it to a baking sheet and roast for 15 minutes (flipping once), or until golden brown and soft. Use a metal spatula to flip the eggplant once during cooking.

Heat 2 tablespoons olive oil in a medium skillet over medium-high heat. Add the mushrooms and sauté them (in batches, if necessary, to avoid overcrowding the pan) until golden brown and crispy, about 5 minutes. Season them with salt and pepper, then transfer to a plate and cool. Wipe the skillet with a paper towel, if necessary, and heat the remaining tablespoon of olive oil over medium-high heat. Add the spinach and a pinch of salt and cook, turning frequently with tongs, for 2–3 minutes, until just wilted. Use a strainer to drain it.

"Cajun-style" Chicken Breast with Chili Bean Maque Choux

MAKES 4 SERVINGS   PREP TIME: ABOUT 30 MINUTES

A simple smear of Creole mustard (which gets added heat from horseradish) and a little extra seasoning gives a chicken breast new sass. Here, the chicken is paired with a speedy version of *maque choux*, a Louisiana sauté of beans and corn. You'd be hard-pressed to find a simpler, more satisfying weekday supper. For this dish the chicken breasts can be broiled, grilled, or pan-seared.

4 boneless, skinless chicken breasts (about 6 ounces each)
1 tablespoon olive or other vegetable oil, plus 1–2 tablespoons vegetable oil, for sautéing
2 tablespoons Creole or whole-grain mustard

1 teaspoon salt
½ teaspoon each black and cayenne pepper

Maque Choux
2 tablespoons chopped scallion

If you plan on grilling the chicken, light the coals about ½ hour before you're ready to cook.

Rinse the chicken breasts and pat dry. Combine the olive oil, mustard, salt, and spices and smear it on the chicken.

Refrigerate for at least 15 minutes, or up to several hours, until you're ready to cook. Meanwhile, make the *maque choux*.

To cook the chicken, heat the vegetable oil in a large nonstick skillet over medium-high heat. Pat excess marinade from the breasts and then sear for 3–4 minutes on each side, or until nicely browned. Alternatively, you can grill the chicken over hot coals or broil it.

To serve, place a scoop of *maque choux* on each plate, garnish with chopped scallions, and top with a chicken breast. The corn and beans together provide a good amount of starch, so this dish needs nothing more than a tossed salad or a simple green vegetable. Of course, a big slice of warm corn bread would be delish too.

Maque Choux

2 ears sweet white or yellow corn,
  shucked and silk removed, or 1½
  cups frozen corn kernels, thawed
1 tablespoon olive or vegetable oil
2 tablespoons butter
½ medium yellow onion, diced
1 jalapeño, seeded and minced
1 garlic clove, minced
½ cup peeled, seeded, and diced fresh
  tomato, or canned tomato (with
  juices)

1 (14-ounce) can red beans, kidney
  beans, or chili beans (for a bit
  more heat), drained and liquid
  reserved
Salt
Hot sauce

Cut the corn kernels from the cob, being careful not to cut too close to the cob (where the kernels become dry and starchy). Heat the oil and 1 tablespoon butter in a skillet to foaming. Add the onion and cook for 2–3 minutes. Then add the corn, jalapeño, and garlic and stir to mix. Cook for about 3 more minutes, then add the tomato, beans, and ¼ cup water or reserved bean liquid and season to taste with salt and a little hot sauce. Stir and cook until heated through, then swirl in the remaining tablespoon of butter. Keep the vegetables warm while cooking the chicken.

Pan-roasted Chicken Breast with Vinegar, Mustard, and Tarragon

MAKES 4 SERVINGS   PREP TIME: ABOUT 30 MINUTES

This, to me, is the essence of French home cooking: a simple sauté and flavorful pan sauce made with vinegar, mustard, and tarragon (the quintessential French herb). If you can't find fresh tarragon, you can use tarragon vinegar instead and finish the dish with chives, but it's just better with fresh tarragon. For the best results be sure to use a flavorful Chicken Stock (p. 206). If yours tastes a little weak, start with two cups instead of one (as called for below) and let it reduce longer to concentrate the flavor.

4 chicken breasts (about 6 ounces each), with or without skin, as preferred

Salt and pepper

2 tablespoons canola or olive oil

1 cup Chicken Stock (p. 206)

6 tablespoons apple cider or wine vinegar

2 tablespoons butter, softened

2 teaspoons Dijon mustard

2 teaspoons coarsely chopped fresh tarragon leaves

2 teaspoons snipped fresh chives, optional

Preheat oven to 325°F.

Season the chicken breasts with salt and pepper. Heat the oil in a large skillet over medium-high heat, and when it is almost smoking, add the chicken breasts, skin side down. Lower the heat to medium and cook the breasts 6–7 minutes, then turn them (they should have an even, golden brown color) and continue cooking for about 5 more minutes. Rotate the skillet if the heat on your burner is uneven, so that you don't get any dark or burned spots, and reduce the heat if the chicken seems to be browning too quickly. When the chicken is cooked, remove it to a platter and keep warm in the oven (don't cover). Pour the excess grease from the pan and deglaze with the stock and vinegar, whisking to scrape up the browned bits on the bottom of the pan. Let the liquid bubble briskly in the pan, whisking, until it's reduced to about ½ cup, then whisk in the butter, mustard, and tarragon.

The sauce should have a slightly creamy consistency. If it's too acidic, whisk in a little more butter or stock. Remove it from the heat and spoon over the warm chicken breasts. Sprinkle with chives, if desired.

This simple dish makes a meal with virtually any green vegetable and/or roasted potatoes or rice.

Roasted Chicken with Olives, Lemon, and Garlic

MAKES 4 SERVINGS   PREP TIME: 1 HOUR 15 MINUTES

Think there's no way to improve upon perfectly roasted chicken? Think again. At Herbsaint we would have to appoint someone to guard the pans while these birds cooled, or they would all end up wingless! In this recipe, the addition of rosemary, garlic, lemon, and olives perfumes the meat and suggests a world of accompaniments: steamed artichokes, just-cooked angel hair pasta, fluffy couscous, a salad of pungent greens with crusty bread for sopping up the juices. When it comes to wine, consider serving a rosé or a white from the Rhone valley.

---

1 chicken (2½ to 3 pounds)

2 lemons, zested and quartered

12–15 garlic cloves, crushed and peeled

3 tablespoons olive oil

Salt and pepper

Crushed red pepper flakes

6–8 sprigs rosemary (strip half the sprigs of their leaves and chop coarsely)

1 medium onion, peeled and cut into 8 wedges

1 cup pitted kalamata or picholine olives, or a combination of both

Preheat the oven to 450°F. Place a 13 × 9-inch roasting pan in the oven.

Rinse the chicken and use paper towels to pat it dry, inside and out. Squeeze 1 of the lemon quarters over the skin and rub the juice around with your fingers. Using your fingers to gently separate the skin from the breast, place a couple of the garlic cloves and some of the lemon zest under the skin of the breast on each side. Let it sit about 10 minutes, then pat the bird dry again, rub the skin with 2 tablespoons olive oil, and season with the salt, pepper, red pepper, and some of the chopped rosemary. Make an incision on the inside of each thigh and insert a garlic clove. Place 3 of the garlic cloves in the cavity, along with the rosemary sprigs and 2 of the lemon quarters.

You may tie the legs together over the cavity, if you like. Place the chicken breast side up in the preheated roasting pan. Bake for about 30 minutes, watching to make sure the chicken starts to brown. Carefully loosen the chicken from the pan with a spatula and turn it over to brown the underside.

At this point, lower the oven heat to 400°F. Add the remaining table-spoon olive oil to the pan, then scatter the onion, olives, remaining garlic, lemon quarters and zest, and chopped rosemary around the chicken and cook for about 15 minutes. Turn the chicken over again and stir the onion, olives, and garlic around a little. Cook another 10–15 minutes to re-crisp the skin.

When the chicken is a deep golden brown, remove it from the oven and let it sit for about 5 minutes. Transfer the chicken to a plate and collect any juices that drain. Tilt the roasting pan and spoon off the fat, if desired. Stir the olives, onion, and lemon around, pressing on the lemon a little to extract the juice. Add the chicken juices to the pan and scrape the brown bits off the bottom of the pan to incorporate them into the mixture. Spoon the juicy olive-onion mixture around the chicken and serve.

This is a good time to splurge on a "natural" or free-range bird, which will be juicier and more flavorful than the more common mass-produced bird. Trust me on this—try it once and you'll taste the difference.

Crispy Turkey Piccata

MAKES 4 SERVINGS   PREP TIME: 45 MINUTES

Here's another dish that works for the kids as well as my husband and me. I dish theirs up plain (with ketchup on the side) and then make a quick little pan sauce for us. At your grocery store, you can find the turkey tenderloin already cut into slices, but for a little less you can get them whole and slice them yourself—it's easy! Pasta is the perfect companion for the crispy turkey, which makes us all happy.

1¼ pounds turkey tenderloin

1 cup milk

1 egg

Salt and pepper

1½ cups dry bread crumbs

¼ cup Grana Padano or Parmesan cheese, optional

2 tablespoons fresh chopped parsley (if cooking for adults only!)

4 tablespoons olive oil, more if needed

½ cup white wine (or just use a few extra tablespoons lemon juice)

Juice of 2 medium lemons (about ⅓ cup)

2 tablespoons capers

4 tablespoons butter, at room temperature

If you're slicing the tenderloin yourself, you'll want to use a sharp, thin-bladed knife. First, lay the tenderloin on a flat, even surface. If you wish, remove the piece of white sinew that runs through it by turning it over and cutting into the underside of the meat with the tip of a paring knife, trimming the meat away on either side, then pulling the sinew free. Reshape the tenderloin, turn it over, and lay it flat. Picture it as a teardrop shape and, starting at the thinner, rounder end, start slicing at a 45-degree angle from the top of the meat to the cutting board. Move the knife about ⅜ inch back toward the pointy end and make a parallel slice down. Continue in this way, making slices close to the same size and thickness, until you come to the larger end. If your slices are a little thick or uneven, you can pound them out evenly between two sheets of plastic wrap.

Pour the milk into a wide, shallow bowl and add the egg, beating with a fork; season with salt and pepper. Soak the turkey slices in the mixture (in batches if necessary, to avoid overcrowding), turning to coat.

Place the bread crumbs in another bowl or on a plate, and mix with the cheese and parsley. Lift a turkey slice out of the milk and let it drip for a moment before placing it into the crumbs. If you can remember to use one hand for wet and one hand for dry, it will be easier, but you will probably still end up with all fingers breaded in the end. Press the slices into the crumbs, then lift and shake them to remove the excess. You can either put the slices directly into the hot pan or set them on a clean plate and finish breading before you start cooking. The latter is probably easier.

Heat half the oil in a large skillet over medium-high heat, and when the oil is shimmering, add enough slices to cover the pan in one layer without overlapping. Try to have the oil hot enough to keep the meat sizzling, but not so hot that the crumbs start burning. Cook about 2 minutes on each side and remove the slices to a platter while you cook the rest, using the remaining oil. You will need to add more oil in between batches. When the turkey is finished cooking, wipe the skillet out with a paper towel and add the wine, lemon juice, and capers. Bring the liquid to a boil and let it bubble for 2–3 minutes, then whisk in the butter, a spoonful at a time, until you have a light, creamy sauce. Divide the turkey among four plates or serve it on the platter, with the sauce spooned evenly over the top.

Indian-spiced Turkey Breast with Creamy Red Lentils

MAKES 4 SERVINGS   PREP TIME: ABOUT 1 HOUR

This dish just scratches the surface of the marvelous world of Indian cuisine. In European and American cooking we have embraced the virtues of fresh herbs, but it is in the Indian kitchen that we begin to understand how spices can work together in fragrant and intense combinations, creating lingering flavors. In this dish the warmth of cinnamon romances cumin and other savory spices. The yogurt tenderizes and adds moisture to the lean turkey meat, and the creamy lentils eliminate the need for sauce. This dish needs nothing more than a scoop of warm basmati rice, but it's also delicious with Brown Butter Cauliflower (p. 296).

2 (8-ounce) pieces boneless turkey
    breast
Juice of 1 medium lemon (about
    3 tablespoons)
Salt
Zest of 1 medium lemon, grated
    (about 2 teaspoons)
1 cup plain yogurt (low-fat is fine),
    preferably a Middle Eastern or
    organic brand
1 serrano chile, seeded and minced,
    or ½ teaspoon cayenne pepper

1 tablespoon olive oil
¼ teaspoon ground cinnamon
¼ teaspoon ground cumin
¼ teaspoon ground coriander
½ teaspoon grated fresh ginger
¼ teaspoon minced garlic
Vegetable oil, for greasing the baking
    sheet
Creamy Red Lentils
Chopped fresh cilantro and lemon
    wedges, as garnish

Rinse the turkey breasts and pat dry. Pour the lemon juice over the turkey and sprinkle it lightly with salt. Let it sit for about 10 minutes. Combine the lemon zest, yogurt, chile, olive oil, spices, ginger, and garlic in a shallow bowl. Turn the turkey over in the marinade and let it sit at room temperature for at least ½ hour, or chill overnight.

Preheat the oven to 475°F or turn on the broiler.

Place an oiled baking sheet in the preheated oven for about 5 minutes.

Remove the turkey from the marinade and strip off the excess marinade with your fingers. Place the turkey on the hot baking sheet and cook for about 5 minutes, then use a spatula to flip it and cook another 5 minutes, or until just cooked through. Remove it from the oven and allow to rest before slicing. If you're using the broiler, broil the turkey 8–10 minutes, turning once.

To serve, place a generous spoonful of the lentils on the plate, then place a few slices of the turkey alongside. Garnish with a sprinkling of chopped cilantro and a wedge of lemon.

Creamy Red Lentils

1 tablespoon vegetable oil
1 small yellow onion, finely chopped
1 garlic clove, minced
½ teaspoon grated fresh ginger
1 cup red lentils, rinsed with cold
    water

Cilantro stems and a bay leaf, tied
    together with string
½ teaspoon ground cumin
Salt

Heat the oil in a 2-quart saucepan over medium-low heat. Add the onion, garlic, and ginger and cook for about 5 minutes. Add the lentils and pour in 3½ cups water, then add the cilantro bundle and cumin and bring to a simmer. Lower the heat and cook gently for about 45 minutes, adding a little more water if necessary.

When the lentils are tender and ready to serve, remove the cilantro stems and season with salt.

Hoss's Rabbit 'n' Dumplin's

This may be the all-time favorite Bayona family meal, created by Greg Collier, aka "Hoss," one of my all-time favorite sous chefs (he's now executive chef of Redfish Grill, which is also in the French Quarter). Hoss adapted his family's chicken and dumplin' recipe, and the staff still clamors for it whenever there's a chill in the air.

This recipe takes a little time, but it's worth it. For this preparation, the "dumplin's" are baked atop a thickened stew (rather than boiled or steamed in broth). Because we use mainly the hind legs and backstrap, or tenders, of the rabbit for the menu, we end up with lots of forelegs and breast meat to use for other things, such as sausage, confit, and crew food. (Naturally, we use the bones to make stock.) You can prepare the meat and stew up to a day ahead, then reheat gently and bake it with the dumplin's. If you just can't eat bunnies, chicken may be substituted.

RABBIT

2 tablespoons olive or canola oil

6 hind legs of rabbit, or 6 whole
   chicken legs

Salt and pepper

3 cups Chicken Stock (p. 206)

Bouquet Garni (p. 145)

1 onion, quartered and pierced with
   2 whole cloves

Heat the oil in a large skillet or Dutch oven over medium-high heat until hot but not smoking. Season the rabbit well with salt and pepper and sear it in the hot pan, turning to brown on all sides. For the best results, don't overcrowd the pan, and try not to fuss with the pieces until they have a chance to brown. Pour off the excess oil and add the Chicken Stock, Bouquet Garni, and onion. Add enough water to just cover the rabbit and bring it to a boil. Cover the pan. Reduce the heat and let it simmer, either on top of the stove or in a 350°F oven, turning the meat once or twice, until rabbit is tender and coming away from the bone, about 40 minutes. Remove the pan from the heat, cool, and strain the stock, reserving it. You should have 4 cups; add additional Chicken Stock if necessary. When the meat is cool enough to handle, pick it off the bones and set aside. Discard the bones.

STEW

2 tablespoons olive oil or butter

2 medium turnips, peeled and diced

2 medium carrots, peeled, split lengthwise, and cut into ½-inch pieces

1 onion, diced

2 celery stalks, diced

1 garlic clove, minced

1 teaspoon chopped fresh thyme

½ teaspoon chopped fresh sage

4 tablespoons flour

1 cup milk

4 cups stock from cooking the rabbit

Bouquet Garni (p. 145)

Cooked rabbit meat

Salt and pepper

Dumplin' dough

Preheat the oven to 400°F.

Heat the olive oil in a large, heavy-bottomed ovenproof pot or Dutch oven over medium heat. Add the turnips, carrots, onion, and celery and cook for about 7 minutes. Add the garlic, thyme, and sage, then sprinkle in the flour and cook, stirring, for 2–3 minutes. Whisk in the milk, add 1 cup of the stock, and bring to a boil. Whisk in the remaining stock and add the Bouquet Garni. Return the mixture to a boil, then reduce the heat. Add the rabbit meat and a little salt and simmer gently, stirring from time to time, about 12 minutes, until the vegetables are tender when pierced with a paring knife. Meanwhile, make the dumplin' dough. Remove the stew from the heat, taste and season as needed with salt and pepper.

Drop spoonfuls of dumplin' dough onto the surface of the stew. Place the pot in the oven and bake, uncovered, for 12–15 minutes, until dumplin's are golden brown.

DUMPLIN'S

1½ cups flour

½ cup cornmeal

1 tablespoon baking powder

¾ teaspoon salt

1 egg, beaten with a fork

2 tablespoons butter, melted

¼ cup finely chopped onion

½ cup milk

Black pepper

Mix the flour, cornmeal, baking powder, and salt in a medium bowl. Beat the egg, butter, onion, and milk together in a large bowl. Stir the dry ingredients into the wet ingredients until a sticky batter forms. Grind in a little black pepper.

Pan-roasted Quail with Dried Cherries and Pinot Noir Sauce

MAKES 4 SERVINGS   PREP TIME: ABOUT 35 MINUTES

I love the rich and "wild" taste of quail. I'm not alone: because the flavor is appealingly gamey (but not as liver-y as squab), it's one of the most popular and accessible game birds on the menu. At Bayona, I use Mississippi bobwhite quail, which is particularly plump and tender, but any variety will work in this recipe. When marinated and grilled, quail makes for the ultimate finger food. But the birds become sexy and sophisticated when paired with a lovely red wine sauce, plumped tart cherries, and sautéed spinach. Add a wedge of crispy polenta or some herb-roasted potatoes and you have a sweet and savory main course.

---

1 cup pinot noir

¼ cup dried sour cherries

2 tablespoons finely chopped shallots

1 teaspoon red wine vinegar or
    raspberry vinegar

2 cups Chicken Stock (p. 206), or
    stock made from quail bones

1 tablespoon red currant jelly

3 tablespoons butter, softened

Salt

8 quail, partially boned

Pepper

2 tablespoons olive or canola oil

1 (10-ounce) bag spinach, or
    2 bunches, washed and dried

Heat the pinot noir, cherries, shallots, and vinegar in a small saucepan over medium heat. Bring to a boil, then reduce the heat and simmer until reduced by half, about 10 minutes. Add the stock and simmer until the liquid is reduced to about ⅓ cup. Whisk in the currant jelly, then whisk in 1 tablespoon butter. Season to taste with salt. The sauce should be pleasantly fruity, not too sweet, and slightly viscous, with a nice sheen. Keep it warm while cooking the quail.

    Season the quail with salt and pepper. Heat 1 tablespoon olive oil in a large skillet over medium-high heat, then add half the quail, breast side down.

Cook about 4 minutes, then turn and cook about 4 minutes on the underside. Maintain a lively heat and keep a little space between the quail so they do not start to steam: you want the skin golden brown and a little crispy. Heat the remaining olive oil and repeat with remaining quail.

Heat the remaining 2 tablespoons butter in a large skillet over medium-high heat. Add the spinach and a pinch of salt and cook until just wilted, 2–3 minutes. Squeeze the spinach with tongs to remove excess moisture and divide it among four plates. Place 2 quail on each bed of spinach and spoon the warm sauce over the quail.

Roasted Duckling
with Orange-Cane Syrup Sauce

MAKES 2 TO 4 SERVINGS   PREP TIME: 2½ HOURS

Every once in a while I crave an old-school, crispy-skin roasted duck with a fruity but not-too-sweet sauce to drizzle over the top. Most of the fat will render out during the roasting process if you are patient and let it cook long enough. Cane syrup, which is made from sugar cane and has a deep, bittersweet flavor, is a Louisiana twist, but maple syrup or honey will work just as well. This duck is delicious with simple sides like wild or pecan rice, haricots verts, or sugar snap peas, or, on the fancier side, warm Butternut Squash Spoon Bread Soufflé (p. 316).

---

1 duck (about 5 pounds)

1 onion, quartered

1 medium orange (or satsuma, a Louisiana mandarin), zested and quartered

1 teaspoon each chopped fresh sage and thyme

1 teaspoon salt

½ teaspoon freshly ground black pepper

Orange–Cane Syrup reserve liquid

Orange–Cane Syrup Sauce

Rinse and pat the duckling dry and trim away some of the excess fat around the cavity. Stuff the bird with the onion and orange quarters. Tie the duck legs closed with string. Combine the orange zest, sage, thyme, salt, and black pepper. Prick the duckling skin lightly all over and rub it generously with the herb mixture. Set aside at room temperature for 1 hour, or refrigerate up to 12 hours.

About 2 hours before serving time, preheat the oven to 425°F and place a 13 × 9-inch roasting pan in the oven.

Place the duck breast side up in the preheated pan. Roast for 30 minutes, then reduce the heat to 400°F. Turn the duck, baste it, and roast for 30 more minutes. Finally, turn the duck breast side up again, baste it, and roast for 40 more minutes, until the skin is crisp and the juices run clear when you prick the thigh. Remove the duck from the heat and let it rest for 10 minutes.

You may serve the duck whole, or remove the breasts and legs from the carcass, then serve the breasts sliced and the legs whole. Spoon the warm sauce over the duck or serve it on the side.

ORANGE–CANE SYRUP SAUCE

2 cups fresh-squeezed orange or
    satsuma juice

1 cup cane vinegar or apple cider
    vinegar

2 medium shallots, minced

¼ cup cane syrup

2 cups Chicken Stock (p. 206)

2 tablespoons butter, softened

Salt

Place the orange juice, vinegar, and shallots in a small saucepan and bring to a boil. Lower the heat and simmer until it has reduced to about 1 cup. Whisk in the cane syrup and divide the mixture in half. Reserve one half for basting the duck later. In another saucepan, bring the Chicken Stock to a boil. Lower the heat and simmer until the stock is reduced to ½ cup, then whisk in the orange juice mixture and simmer for about 7 minutes, until slightly syrupy. Whisk in the butter a tablespoon at a time, until you have a light, creamy sauce. Taste for seasoning and add a little more salt if necessary. The sauce should be balanced between sweet and tart. If it's too tart, add a little more syrup. Keep it warm while the duck is roasting.

Carving a Duck

Place the bird on a cutting board. Disjoint and remove a leg from the side nearest you. Use a knife to remove the wings (they will come off easily). Slicing along the breastbone, gently remove the whole breast in one piece. Slice the breast on the slant to make nice medallions. Repeat with the other side.

Seared Duck Breasts with Pepper Jelly Glaze

MAKES 4 SERVINGS   PREP TIME: ABOUT I HOUR

A sweet, hot pepper glaze is just the thing to complement the rich flavor of duck. In this recipe, the duck breast is scored, rubbed with herbs, and pan-seared. Be sure to get the pan nice and hot before adding the duck, to ensure a crispy, well-browned skin. A fine dice of jalapeño adds a bit more fire to the sauce, while red bell pepper offers sweetness. This dish can be served with any number of sides, from Honey-glazed Carrots and Turnips (p. 294) to Wild and Dirty Rice (p. 311).

---

4 boneless duck breasts (about 6 ounces each), skin on and fat trimmed

2 tablespoons kosher salt

1 teaspoon ground black pepper

1 teaspoon chopped fresh thyme

1 teaspoon chopped fresh rosemary

1 bay leaf, crumbled

Pepper Jelly Glaze

Lightly score the skin side of the duck, being careful not to go all the way through to the meat. Mix the seasonings and herbs together in a small bowl. Gently rub the salt and herb mixture on the skin of the breasts. Before cooking, refrigerate for several hours or let stand at room temperature about ½ hour. Meanwhile, make the Pepper Jelly Glaze. Sear the duck breasts skin side down in a large, dry skillet over medium-high heat for 8–10 minutes, to render the fat and crisp the skin. Turn over and cook for about 3 more minutes. Remove the duck from the heat, let stand for about 2 minutes, then slice into 5–6 pieces and arrange in a fan on a plate, skin side up. Drizzle with warm Pepper Jelly Glaze.

PEPPER JELLY GLAZE

2 cups veal stock, or broth made from
    roasted duck bones
½ cup sherry wine vinegar
2 tablespoons finely chopped shallots
2 tablespoons hot pepper jelly

2 tablespoons butter
Salt
1 fresh jalapeño and/or ½ red bell
    pepper, seeded and finely minced,
    optional

In a small saucepan combine the stock, vinegar, and shallots and bring to a boil. Lower the heat and simmer until the liquid is reduced to about ⅓ cup. Whisk in the pepper jelly and butter. Season to taste with salt and, if the sauce is too sweet, add more vinegar (or jelly if the sauce is too acidic). Add the jalapeño and/or the red bell pepper.

If you're searing in a skillet and too much fat accumulates when you're cooking on the skin side, take the pan off the heat, tilt it slightly, and spoon out some of the excess fat (you can discard it or use it to roast your potatoes). Either way, you'll want to turn on an exhaust fan when frying the duck.

Seared Pork Chops with Satsuma-Horseradish Marmalade

MAKES 4 SERVINGS   PREP TIME: ABOUT 5 HOURS (INCLUDING 4 HOURS OF BRINING)

This is a recipe I created to celebrate satsuma season. Satsumas are sweet, juicy tangerines that flourish in Louisiana during the winter. (If you can't find them in your area, any tangerine will do.) You can certainly make the marmalade in larger quantities—it keeps well and is terrific with any grilled or roasted meat, served hot or cold. Try it with grilled quail, duck breast, or even smoked pork sausage or ham.

Brining is a technique that serves many purposes. It tenderizes, flavors, and keeps meat juicy. This brine can be used with chicken, turkey breast (I'd leave the soy out), and pork loin or tenderloin. You can throw in herbs or spices appropriate to the dish, but you'll want to keep the salt/sugar ratio the same. Green beans with shallots make the perfect accompaniment to this dish.

2 tablespoons brown sugar

1 tablespoon salt plus additional for
   seasoning pork before cooking

1 tablespoon soy sauce

5 allspice berries

1 star anise

½ teaspoon whole black peppercorns

1 bay leaf

4 (10-ounce) center-cut pork loin
   chops or T-bone chops

Pepper

Satsuma-Horseradish Marmalade

Place all the ingredients except pork chops, pepper, and marmalade in a medium saucepan and add 3 cups water. Bring the brine to a boil, whisking to dissolve the sugar and salt, then simmer for about 5 minutes. Remove from the heat and cool completely, stirring occasionally. When cool, pat the pork chops dry and place in a Ziploc bag. Pour in the brine, seal the bag, and place in a bowl. Refrigerate at least 4 hours or overnight, flipping the bag at least once to be sure the chops are evenly marinated. Meanwhile, make the Satsuma-Horseradish Marmalade.

When ready to serve, remove the chops from the brine, pat dry with paper towels, and let sit at room temperature for about 10 minutes. Season with salt and pepper. Sear (over medium-high heat), grill, or broil for 5–6 minutes on each side. Serve hot with the marmalade on the side.

SATSUMA-HORSERADISH MARMALADE

6 satsumas (or large tangerines)

1½ cups sugar

1 small onion, diced

3 roma tomatoes, peeled, seeded, and
diced

3–4 tablespoons apple cider vinegar

2 teaspoon grated fresh ginger

Prepared horseradish

1 tablespoon ketchup

Salt

Juice 2 of the satsumas, removing the seeds. Grate the zest of the remaining 4 satsumas, then peel and cut the flesh into smallish pieces, removing the seeds and reserving the juice.

Place the juice, zest, and satsuma pieces in a 2-quart saucepan with the sugar, onion, tomatoes, vinegar, ginger, and 1 cup water, and bring the mixture to a boil, stirring to dissolve the sugar. Simmer gently over low heat, stirring occasionally, for 30–45 minutes. When the mixture is thickened and almost syrupy, stir in horseradish to taste, then add the ketchup. Season with salt and let cool.

Jalapeño-roast Pork

MAKES 8 TO 10 SERVINGS   PREP TIME: 4 HOURS

This slow-roasted pork dish came to me from my Bayona partner, Regina Keever. The succulent meat lends itself to two fantastic preparations. For a Latin-inspired meal, serve it with Green Rice (p. 309). Or make ciabatta sandwiches with Pickled Cabbage and Creole Mustard (p. 154), from the leftovers.

---

1 boneless pork shoulder (about
    6 pounds)

Juice and zest of 2 oranges (about
    ⅔ cup)

2 jalapeños, stemmed, seeded, and
    diced

2 tablespoons chopped fresh thyme

2 tablespoons minced garlic

2 tablespoons kosher salt

2 tablespoons cracked black pepper

2 tablespoons olive or vegetable oil

Preheat the oven to 325°F.

Rinse the pork shoulder and pat dry. Using a paring knife, make several ½-inch-deep incisions on both sides of the meat. Mix the juice, jalapeños, thyme, garlic, salt, pepper, and oil, either by hand or by pulsing in a food processor until just mixed. Rub the meat with the mixture, being sure to massage some down into the incisions.

Place the meat in a roasting pan fat side up, cover with foil, and roast for 3–4 hours, or until the meat is fork-tender. Cool, remove it from the pan, then shred or slice the pork as desired. After the meat has been removed, add a little water or broth to the roasting pan and stir to dissolve any brown bits, then strain the juices and pour them back over the sliced or shredded meat.

Soy-glazed Pork with Quick-fried Rice

MAKES 4 SERVINGS   PREP TIME: ABOUT 45 MINUTES

Pork loves the salty, "meaty" flavor of soy sauce just as tomatoes love basil. This quick little sweet-and-hot marinade, fragrant from garlic and ginger, permeates and perfumes the meat, and helps it to caramelize over the heat. Flavored with crunchy vegetables, Quick-fried Rice makes a fresh one-pan accompaniment that is nutritious and provides great leftovers. Feel free to add a few stalks of celery or a cup of broccoli florets to the rice. If you're pressed for time, plain white or brown rice is perfectly fine.

---

2 pork tenderloins (10 to 12 ounces each), or 4 (6-ounce) center-cut pork chops

2 tablespoons honey

2 tablespoons soy sauce

2 garlic cloves, minced

1 teaspoon minced or grated ginger

1 teaspoon *sambal oelek* (or other red chile paste)

½ teaspoon 5-spice powder

2 teaspoons canola, peanut, or olive oil, plus 1 tablespoon for cooking pork

Quick-fried Rice

Use paper towels to pat the pork dry. Mix the other ingredients in a small bowl, then brush the pork generously with the marinade. Marinate pork at least ½ hour (or up to 12 hours) in the refrigerator. Meanwhile, make Quick-fried Rice.

To cook the pork, preheat the oven to 375°F.

Use paper towels to pat the pork dry of excess marinade. Heat the oil in a large ovenproof skillet over high heat until shimmering (almost smoking), then add the pork and reduce the heat to medium-high. Sear the pork on all sides (or both sides for chops), then baste with marinade and place the pan in the oven. Cook about 10 minutes, turning once and basting generously with marinade (which will probably bubble and blacken a little because of the honey). The chops will probably cook faster than the tenderloin, depending on how thick they are. Remove from the oven and tent the pork in aluminum foil until ready to serve, then slice and serve alongside Quick-fried Rice.

Quick-fried Rice

2 teaspoons canola, peanut, or olive
  oil
2 eggs, lightly beaten with a fork
Salt
1 medium carrot, split in half
  lengthwise and cut thinly on a
  diagonal
1 cup cabbage, spinach, bok choy, or
  other greens, thinly sliced

2 garlic cloves, minced
3 cups cooked white rice
1 bunch scallions (white and green
  parts), thinly sliced
2 tablespoons soy sauce
Sesame oil, as desired
Pepper

Heat 1 teaspoon oil over medium-high heat in a medium nonstick skillet until almost smoking. Pour in the eggs and a pinch of salt and scramble with a plastic spatula for a minute, then let the eggs set. Stir and lift to make sure the eggs are cooked and no liquid remains, then transfer to a plate and cool. Coarsely chop the eggs and set aside.

Wipe out the skillet (or rinse, if necessary), put in the carrot and ¼ cup water, and lower the heat to medium. Simmer the carrot for about 3 minutes, until tender-crisp. Raise the heat to medium-high, pour off any remaining water, add the remaining teaspoon oil, the cabbage, and garlic, and toss. When the greens are wilted, add the rice and eggs and stir over medium-high heat. Stir in the scallions and soy sauce and a drop or two of sesame oil. Taste and adjust seasoning with salt and pepper.

It's always a good idea to pat dry a piece of meat before and after marinating. Before marinating, removing excess moisture from the meat ensures that the flavors of the marinade won't get diluted. When it comes to cooking after marination, drying the meat ensures a crispier crust (overly moist meat has a tendency to steam) and also helps keep a sugary-sweet marinade from burning.

Pork "Saltimbocca" with Marsala Sauce

MAKES 4 SERVINGS　　　PREP TIME: ABOUT 30 MINUTES

This dish requires a little effort ahead of time but finishes quick and easy, making it perfect for a casual weeknight dinner. It's an adaptation of *saltimbocca* (Italian for "jump in your mouth"), traditionally made with thin slices of veal sautéed with prosciutto and sage. Since veal can be a little harder to find, and pricier, I use a less expensive cut of meat and splurge on an embellishment: a genuine Fontina Val d'Aosta, from the Piedmont region in Italy. This combination will literally jump in your mouth! I recommend serving it with tender asparagus.

---

8 pork medallions (2½ to 3 ounces each, about 1½ pounds total), pounded thin

Salt and pepper

4 thin slices Fontina Val d'Aosta cheese (about 4 ounces total) or other fontina

8 sage leaves

4 thin slices prosciutto (about 4 ounces total)

3 tablespoons olive oil

1 cup marsala

Juice and zest of 2 lemons

1 garlic clove, minced

1 cup Chicken Stock (p. 206)

2 tablespoons butter

Preheat the oven to 325°F.

Season the pork medallions lightly with salt and pepper. Place one slice of cheese on top of each of 4 medallions and top each slice with 2 sage leaves. Cover the sage leaves with the prosciutto, then top with another pork medallion, making 4 "sandwiches." Place each sandwich between two sheets of plastic wrap and smack with a mallet or the side of a cleaver to flatten slightly.

Heat the olive oil in a large ovenproof skillet and, when almost smoking, add the pork sandwiches. Cook over medium-high heat until a nice brown crust forms, 2–3 minutes, then flip and repeat on the other side. Place the pan in the oven and cook for an additional 3–4 minutes, until you can see the cheese start to ooze out of the middle. Place the pork on a platter and keep warm in the oven while you make the sauce.

Pour off any grease from the pan, then pour in the marsala, lemon juice, zest, and garlic. Bring to a boil, then simmer until the liquid is reduced by half. Add the stock and return to a boil. Simmer over medium-high heat until reduced to 3–4 tablespoons. Whisk in the butter and season to taste with salt. Spoon over the pork and serve.

As an alternative to marsala pan sauce, try the Sun-dried Tomato–Pistachio Pesto (p. 186), moistened with enough olive oil and vinegar (to taste) to make a vinaigrette consistency.

Grilled Steak with Arugula, Tomato, Blue Cheese, and Shoestring Salad

MAKES 2 SERVINGS   PREP TIME: ABOUT 45 MINUTES

Like of lot of folks these days, I have gotten away from eating beef very often, but when I do, give me the real deal—a thick, juicy, medium-rare steak sprinkled with good salt. Given a choice between a well-marbled rib eye and a lean center-cut filet, I'll take the rib eye every time, for the chewy texture and the deep flavor it delivers. Hanger steak, or the "butcher's tender," is another cut that lots of restaurants are serving these days as a less expensive but delicious alternative to tenderloin. You probably won't find it at your average supermarket, but you might find it at an upscale market or a good butcher. It may not look like much, but it cooks up tender and tasty (as long as you don't cook it past medium). These steaks don't need any sauce, just something savory to serve alongside—my choices being a pungent salad (with the indulgence of some rich blue cheese) or some broccoli rabe with garlic and olive oil. Hold the baked potato.

STEAK

2 steaks of your choice	Olive oil
(6 to 10 ounces each)	Salt and pepper

Preheat your grill or broiler. At least 10 minutes before cooking, pat the steak dry with paper towels, rub it with a little olive oil, and season with salt and pepper. Grill or broil on high heat to brown and sear the meat, then lower the heat slightly to finish cooking to desired doneness. If you like it rare, you probably don't have to lower the heat, just get a good sear on both sides and pull it off. If you like it medium-rare to medium, you will want to cook it about 3 minutes per side for a 1-inch-thick piece of meat.

If you're serving rib eye, strip, or filet, serve it whole. For hanger steak, it's best to let it rest about 3 minutes, then slice it across the grain into thin slices.

Shoestring Salad

1 russet potato

Oil for frying

Salt

2 handfuls of arugula

1 ripe tomato, sliced or diced

Classic French Vinaigrette (p. 90)

2 tablespoons blue cheese

Peel the potato, cut it crosswise into ⅛-inch-thick slices, then cut into thin matchsticks. Rinse the matchsticks thoroughly in cold water, then drain and shake or pat thoroughly dry in a kitchen towel. Heat 2 inches of oil in a deep saucepan over medium heat until it registers about 350°F. Fry the matchsticks to golden brown and crisp, 4–6 minutes, stirring a little to cook them evenly. Drain on paper towels and salt lightly. When they've cooled completely, you can store them in a Ziploc bag or an airtight container, and they will stay crisp for several days.

Place the arugula and tomato in a bowl and dress with the vinaigrette. Toss, crumble in the blue cheese, and add a big handful of shoestrings. Toss again and serve.

I go a little bit light on the salt when preseasoning the steaks, as I like to sprinkle on some coarse sea salt after the steak is cooked. I love the crunch and the way coarse salt brings out the flavor.

Seared Steak with Rosemary and Broccoli Rabe

MAKES 2 SERVINGS   PREP TIME: 30 MINUTES

2 steaks of your choice (6 to 10
    ounces each)
Salt and pepper
Olive oil or other cooking oil, plus 3
    tablespoons extra-virgin olive oil
2 tablespoons chopped fresh
    rosemary leaves

1 bunch (about 12 ounces) broccoli
    rabe leaves and stems, washed and
    coarsely chopped
1 garlic clove, minced
Crushed red pepper flakes

Generously season the steaks with salt and pepper. Heat a large skillet to very hot. Pour in a very small amount of olive oil (about 1 teaspoon) and immediately add the steaks to the pan. (If you have an exhaust fan, this is a good time to use it!) Sear the steaks on both sides to a nice crusty brown. Sprinkle steaks with half the rosemary leaves, then turn them over. Lower the heat and cook about 3 minutes on each side for medium-rare (for a 1-inch-thick piece of meat). Sprinkle with the remaining rosemary after cooking the first side. Remove the steaks from the skillet. Pour 2 tablespoons water and 1 tablespoon extra-virgin olive oil into the skillet and swirl over the heat. Pour the juices over the steaks, then pour the remaining 2 tablespoons olive oil into the pan and return it to the heat. When the skillet is hot, add the broccoli rabe and toss or stir with tongs. Cook over medium-high heat for about 2 minutes, then stir in the garlic, and season with salt and red pepper. Cook about 2 more minutes, until the stems are tender-crisp. Serve with the steak.

Filet of Beef with Herbed Cream Cheese Filling and Bordelaise Sauce

MAKES 4 SERVINGS   PREP TIME: ABOUT 50 MINUTES

This sumptuous steak dish makes for a spectacular celebration meal. Beef tenderloin steaks are stuffed with a garlicky cream cheese mixture, seared in a hot skillet, and served with a warm, fragrant red wine sauce. The trick is chilling the stuffed steaks to firm up the cream cheese so it stays put while the steaks are cooking. All this meal needs is your favorite potato dish (simple roasted new potatoes with herbs would be my choice), a simple salad, and a lusty bottle of red wine. I suggest drinking the same style of wine that you use to make the sauce. If you are short on time, these steaks are great without the sauce too.

---

4 (1½-inch-thick) center-cut beef tenderloin steaks (6 to 8 ounces each)

Salt and freshly ground pepper

4 ounces cream cheese, at room temperature

1 garlic clove, minced

2 teaspoons chopped assorted fresh herbs, such as thyme, tarragon, chives, and parsley

2 tablespoons olive or canola oil (reserved for searing steaks)

Bordelaise Sauce

Season the steaks with salt and pepper. Set aside.

In a small bowl, combine the cream cheese with the garlic, herbs, and salt and pepper, to taste. Chill until the mixture firms up, at least 15 minutes.

Cut an "X" into the top of each filet, almost but not quite all the way through the steak. Open the "X" with your fingers and stuff with 1 or 2 tablespoons of the cream cheese mixture, packing the cheese well and level with the top of the steak. Chill the steaks in the refrigerator for at least 15 minutes, to firm up the cheese. Meanwhile, make the Bordelaise Sauce.

To cook the steaks, preheat the oven to 400°F.

Heat the oil in a large ovenproof skillet until very hot but not smoking. Sear the steaks, cut side down, until nicely browned, about 5 minutes. Flip the steaks carefully, using a spatula to get under the crispy cheese crust so it doesn't stick to the pan. Sear the other side for 1–2 minutes, then finish them in the oven to the desired doneness (6–8 minutes for medium-rare). To serve, spoon warm Bordelaise Sauce over the steaks.

BORDELAISE SAUCE

1 cup cabernet sauvignon or
  Bordeaux wine
2 tablespoons diced shallots
1 teaspoon chopped fresh thyme
  leaves, or ½ teaspoon dried thyme

1 cup rich veal stock or demi-glace
  (may be purchased in specialty
  stores)
2 tablespoons butter
Salt and pepper

Place the wine, shallots, and thyme in a small saucepan, bring to a boil, then simmer until reduced to ¼ cup. Add the stock and reduce again to about ¼ cup. Whisk in the butter, bit by bit, until the sauce is thick and glossy. Season to taste with salt and pepper, and keep warm.

Turkish Stuffed Eggplant with Spicy Lamb and Rice

MAKES 4 SERVINGS   PREP TIME: ABOUT 1 HOUR 15 MINUTES

Aaaaahhh, Mediterranean comfort food! Think of this as a heady, warmly spiced alternative to your mom's stuffed bell pepper. The baked eggplant flesh becomes a tender bed for the luscious meat and rice filling, and the whole is so succulent and moist that no sauce is needed. Some chilled sliced cucumber and onion with olive oil and vinegar would be a good starter or side dish.

LAMB AND RICE FILLING

- 1 tablespoon olive oil
- 1 small onion, diced
- 1 small poblano pepper, seeded and diced
- 2 large garlic cloves, minced
- 6–8 ounces ground lamb, or a combination of lamb and beef
- 1 teaspoon salt
- ½ teaspoon Aleppo pepper, or ¼ teaspoon cayenne
- ¼ teaspoon each ground cinnamon, allspice, and cumin
- 1 cup diced tomatoes, canned or fresh (peeled and seeded)
- 1 tablespoon tomato puree
- ¼ cup Chicken Stock (p. 206), lamb stock, beef stock, or water
- 2 cups cooked rice
- 1 tablespoon chopped fresh parsley
- 1 teaspoon chopped fresh dill, optional

Heat the olive oil in a medium skillet over medium heat, then add the onion and pepper, stir, and cook for 3–5 minutes. Stir in the garlic and crumble in the ground meat. Raise the heat to medium-high and cook, stirring, for 5–6 minutes, until the meat has lost its pink color and the mixture is starting to dry out and brown a little in the pan. Tilt the pan and spoon out any excess fat from the lamb. Sprinkle in the seasonings, stir, then add the tomatoes and puree, then the stock. Stir and scrape the bottom of the pan to dissolve the brown bits that have accumulated. Add the rice and herbs, and stir and cook a couple of minutes, until warmed through. Taste and adjust seasoning to your liking. When the filling is well mixed, moist, and flavorful—but not wet—remove it from the heat and let it cool.

EGGPLANT

¼ cup olive oil

2 teaspoons fresh lemon juice

½ teaspoon paprika or Aleppo pepper

½ teaspoon ground cumin

½ teaspoon salt, plus additional for
    salting the eggplant if necessary

2 medium to large eggplants (about
    2 pounds total)

Preheat the oven to 400°F.

Combine all the ingredients except the eggplants in a small bowl.

Cut the stem end from each eggplant, then cut it in half lengthwise. Take a look at the flesh, and if it is creamy white and not too seedy, don't worry about salting it. However, if it is a little darker, with numerous seeds, there's a good chance the juices will be slightly bitter, so you'll want to extract them. To do this, sprinkle the cut sides with about a teaspoon of salt each and place them cut side down on a plate or tray lined with a double thickness of paper towels. Place another plate or tray on top and weight that with a couple of pounds (cans of beans work well). Set aside for 10–15 minutes, then remove the weight and brush the salt off the surface, or rinse with running water and pat dry. Cut a shallow crosshatch pattern in the cut surface of the eggplant and brush generously with the flavored oil. Place the eggplant halves cut sides up on a lightly oiled baking sheet and bake for about 20 minutes, rotating the pan once, until the eggplants are very soft when you squeeze the sides and the surface is golden brown. Cool completely.

TO ASSEMBLE

Cooked eggplant

Lamb and rice filling

¼ cup Cheesy Bread Crumb Topping
    (p. 42), or plain dry bread crumbs
    moistened with a little olive oil

With your fingers or a spoon, press the tender eggplant flesh to the sides, making a bed for the filling. Divide the filling among the halves. Sprinkle the bread crumb topping evenly over the filling and pat it lightly. Bake the filled eggplants for about 15 minutes, or until they're heated through and the crumbs are browned.

After you've made this recipe once, you may want to embellish the filling a bit with some additional ingredients, such as toasted pine nuts, artichoke hearts, or a handful of lightly soaked currants. Or you may want to vary the herbs with oregano, cilantro, or mint. I've also added some small cubes of feta cheese.

Herb-roasted Lamb Loin with Goat Cheese and Zinfandel Sauce

MAKES 4 SERVINGS   PREP TIME: ABOUT 45 MINUTES

I loved the idea of pairing lamb and goat—since that's how I think of them, frolicking in a field together (what do I know, I'm a city girl). The idea for a pairing led me to this dish. The tasty goat cheese, herbes de Provence (a mixture of herbs that includes basil, fennel, rosemary, thyme, summer savory, and lavender), and pancetta mixture was initially a stuffing for the lamb, but it was quite tricky to assemble. I made it simpler for the staff and now for you (you don't always have to take the most difficult route!) by simply crumbling the topping over the roasted lamb. The rich, glossy zinfandel sauce really pulls the flavors together.

GOAT CHEESE FILLING

3 ounces fresh goat cheese, at room temperature

¼ pound pancetta, diced and cooked until crisp

2 tablespoons diced marinated sun-dried tomatoes

1 teaspoon herb es de Provence or fresh herbs of your choice (such as rosemary, thyme, and/or basil)

1 garlic clove, minced

This cheese filling can be made one day in advance. Using a fork, combine the goat cheese, pancetta, tomatoes, herbs, and garlic in a small bowl. Chill the mixture for a few minutes to allow the flavors to meld. When ready to use it, let the cheese mixture soften slightly at room temperature.

ZINFANDEL SAUCE

1 cup zinfandel or full-flavored red
    wine
1 medium shallot, finely minced
2 sprigs fresh thyme or rosemary, or a
    combination

2 cups lamb stock (or substitute rich
    Chicken Stock [p. 206])
2 tablespoons butter, cut in 4 pieces
Salt and pepper

Place the wine, shallot, and herb in a small saucepan and bring to a boil. Lower the heat and simmer until the liquid is reduced by half. Add the stock, bring to a boil, then lower the heat and let it simmer until reduced to ½ cup of liquid. Remove the herb sprigs.

    Whisk in the butter, 1 piece at a time. The sauce should be glossy and slightly syrupy (but not so thick that it sticks your lips together; add a tablespoon or two of hot water if it gets too thick). Taste and season with salt and pepper.

LAMB

1½ pounds boneless lamb loin, cut
    into 4 (6-ounce) portions
Salt and pepper

1 tablespoon olive oil
Goat Cheese Filling
Zinfandel Sauce

Season the lamb with salt and pepper. Heat the olive oil in a medium skillet over medium-high heat until almost smoking. Sear the lamb on both sides for a minute or so, to brown, then reduce the heat and cook each side 3–4 minutes longer. Transfer to a plate and let rest. You may serve the loins whole or sliced, with equal portions of the goat cheese mixture crumbled along the top and Zinfandel Sauce spooned over it.

Sautéed Sweetbreads with Sherry-Mustard Butter

MAKES 6 APPETIZER OR 4 DINNER SERVINGS   PREP TIME: 2 HOURS 30 MINUTES (INCLUDES 1 HOUR CHILLING)

This recipe will not be for everyone—gland lovers only!

Chef Daniel taught me how to prepare sweetbreads many years ago (his technique follows), and I have been serving them ever since. Of all the offals, it is the most appealing to me, because of its mild flavor and creamy texture.

This particular preparation is my mom's favorite dish, so it will never go off the menu. One of the most challenging parts of preparing sweetbreads is finding a place to buy them. You will probably have to special order them from your market's meat department, but once you have them, then the real fun begins! For those intrepid cooks who dare to tackle this rather involved recipe at home, read on. . . .

SAUTÉED SWEETBREADS

2 pounds veal sweetbreads	A few black peppercorns
1 tablespoon olive or canola oil	Pepper
1 onion, chopped	Flour, for dusting
1 carrot, chopped	3 tablespoons olive oil or butter
1 celery stalk, chopped	Sherry-Mustard Butter
1 cup white wine, or ¼ cup vinegar	Sliced mushrooms, optional
1 bay leaf	Chopped fresh parsley and snipped
Salt	fresh chives, for garnish

Place the sweetbreads in a container, cover them with cold water, and soak them in the refrigerator overnight. The next day, take them out and rinse them under cold running water to remove any remaining blood. Heat the olive oil in a large pot over medium-high heat. Add the onion, carrot, and celery and cook, stirring, for about 5 minutes. Lay the sweetbreads on top of the vegetables, pour in the wine, and cover with cold water by 2–3 inches. Add the bay leaf, a little salt, and the peppercorns and bring to a boil. Reduce the heat and simmer gently for 10–12 minutes. Test the sweetbreads for doneness by removing one piece (with tongs or a slotted spoon) and placing it in an ice-water bath; it should be firm but neither hard (overcooked) nor too flabby (undercooked) when cool. (Chef Daniel used to say that they should have the feel of a firm, young breast, and of course he would say that looking directly at me, to see me blush!) If it is done, chill all the sweetbreads in the ice bath.

Place the sweetbreads in a pan or on a large plate with another pan or plate on top of them, and 2–3 pounds of weight (cans of beans work well) evenly distributed on top. Refrigerate and press for at least 1 hour. This process will firm the sweetbreads and create a uniform thickness that helps them cook more evenly.

With a paring knife, clean the sweetbreads of outer membranes, fat, and any tendons or rubbery bits. If they are plump enough (at least 1 inch thick), the best method is to slice them in half. This shows you any little pinkish parts that you want to remove, which you can do by grasping the end between the tip of your paring knife and your thumb and gently tugging to extract them without breaking the sweetbread apart.

Do not overdo the cleaning, but do try to get these chewy bits out. You can do this while the Sherry-Mustard Butter is cooking.

Season the sweetbreads with salt and pepper. Dust with flour, shaking off the excess. Heat the olive oil in a large skillet over medium-high heat. When the pan is hot, cook the sweetbreads until golden brown and crispy on both sides. Drain them briefly on paper towels and serve on a plate or platter with sauce ladled over the top. If you like, throw some sliced mushrooms into the pan and sauté to a crispy brown. Season lightly, then spoon on top of the sweetbreads. Finish with chopped parsley or chives.

SHERRY-MUSTARD BUTTER

½ cup white wine

¼ cup medium dry sherry

2 tablespoons sherry vinegar

1 medium shallot, diced

4–6 tablespoons butter, cut in small
   pieces, at room temperature

1 teaspoon Creole mustard

1 teaspoon Dijon mustard

Salt and pepper

Combine the wine, sherry, vinegar, and shallot in a small saucepan. Bring to a boil, lower the heat, and simmer until the liquid is reduced to about 3 tablespoons, about 5 minutes. Whisk in the butter, 1 tablespoon at a time, until the mixture is smooth and has a creamy consistency. Whisk in the mustards and season to taste with salt and pepper.

Sweetbreads normally come in sets: the noix ("nut," in French), which is the rounder, meatier part (although a little fatter), about the size and shape of the palm of your hand, and the "gorge" (throat), which is the longer, gnarlier part, requiring more work for less yield. Ask your butcher or meat department for "heart-breads," which will be just the noix. Heartbreads cost a little more but are a lot easier to deal with.

Show-stealing Sides

Smoked Vegetables

Honey-glazed Carrots and Turnips

Braised Red Cabbage

Brown Butter Cauliflower

Smothered Greens with Smoked Onions

Five-bean Picnic Salad

Shiitake Mushroom Sauté with Asian Flavors

The Best Stuffed Artichokes, Italian-style

Eggplant Roulades with Garlic Goat Cheese and Roasted Tomatoes

Spinach and Artichoke Phyllo Crisps

Fragrant Basmati Pilaf

Red Rice, Green Rice

Caribbean Crab Pilaf with Coconut Milk

Wild and Dirty Rice

Rice Calas

Alice's Spoon Bread

Bayona Extra-cheesy Spoon Bread

Butternut Squash Spoon Bread Soufflé

Alice's Bread and Herb Stuffing

Shrimp, Corn Bread, and Andouille Stuffing

Creole Cream Cheese Spaetzle

Onion and Carrot *Bhajis*

Sweet Potato Brioche

When I read the menu at a restaurant, it's often the side dishes that seduce me into ordering a particular entrée. And when I shop for dinner fixin's for my family, it's often an alluring vegetable (artichokes, hmmm . . .) or a craving for a specific carb (creamy black beans, fragrant basmati rice, a comforting spoon bread soufflé) that steers the decision-making ship. This chapter, made up of my very favorite side dishes, is devoted to such temptations. The sources of inspiration stretch back to my childhood and extend forward to the present, to the treats that have recently captured my imagination. Most of these recipes are ones I've turned to again and again (for holiday meals, dinner parties, and simple weeknight suppers), and they have yet to lose their luster.

Whether you are looking for guidelines for preparing an essential staple, such as how to cook perfect rice, or for a dish loaded with personality to elevate a grilled chicken breast or tuna steak, you'll find delicious options in the pages that follow. But don't be surprised if you find yourself planning a meal around, say, Eggplant Roulades with Garlic Goat Cheese and Roasted Tomatoes (p. 303), Brown Butter Cauliflower (p. 296), or sweet-as-candy Honey-glazed Carrots and Turnips (p. 294). Sides tend to steal the show that way.

Smoked Vegetables

PREP TIME: ABOUT 35 MINUTES

Though we have a cabinet-style smoker at the restaurant, you can do the same thing at home with a domed barbecue grill or smoker. Get your chips going, then fill the drip pan with ice. Lay the veggies out on the grill, close the cover, and let it smoke. The smaller vegetables like mushrooms need less time. Check them periodically and take them off when they look and smell ready.

HERE'S WHAT WE DO

Button mushrooms, whole, about 10 minutes (Experiment with other kinds—we tried chanterelles and didn't like them, but creminis and portobellos would be great)

Onions, cut in half (or whole, if they're small), 20–30 minutes

Tomatoes, whole, about 15 minutes

OTHER SUGGESTIONS

Ears of corn (shucked or unshucked)
Red or yellow bell peppers

Use these vegetables to enhance vinaigrettes, sauces, salsas, and stuffings. Add the smoked onions anywhere you might use bacon or smoked ham.

Honey-glazed Carrots and Turnips

MAKES 4 SERVINGS   PREP TIME: ABOUT 30 MINUTES

Sweet, sticky, and full of flavor, glazed carrots and turnips are the perfect complement to roast meat of any kind, although lamb comes to my mind first. This dish is also a good way to show off a favorite fancy honey, but even the plainest squeezie-bear type works well.

1 large or 2 small carrots, peeled, cut lengthwise and then on the bias into ½-inch pieces	Salt
	2 tablespoons butter
	2 tablespoons honey
1 large or 2 small turnips, peeled and cut into wedges	3–4 sprigs of fresh thyme

Place the carrots and turnips in a medium saucepan and just barely cover with cold water. Add a little salt and bring to a boil. Lower the heat and simmer for about 2 minutes, until the vegetables are tender but still firm. Drain and shock the vegetables in ice water.

Melt the butter in a large skillet over low heat and stir in the honey. Add the vegetables, thyme sprigs, and about 3 tablespoons water. Raise the heat to medium and cook, stirring now and then, until the liquid becomes a light, syrupy glaze and the vegetables begin to brown. Sprinkle in a little more water if they are browning too fast or start to look greasy. Season to taste with salt, and serve.

If you're a fan of parsnips, feel free to throw in a couple of those as well. Simply increase the amounts of water, butter, and honey to accommodate the additional vegetable.

Braised Red Cabbage

My mother always served this dish with roast pork, or sometimes goose, and tiny boiled potatoes. I have served it with our Seared Duck Breasts with Pepper Jelly Glaze (p. 264) for a long time, and I never get tired of it. It's easy to prepare, and yet, to please Alice, my mother, it must be "just so."

2 tablespoons butter
1 small red onion, thinly sliced
1 small head red cabbage, quartered,
   cored, and sliced as thin as
   possible

Salt
2 tablespoons brown sugar
2–3 tablespoons red wine vinegar

Melt the butter in a Dutch oven or heavy-bottomed skillet over medium heat. Add the onion and cabbage and stir to mix. Sprinkle with salt and cook over medium-low heat for about 10 minutes, until the cabbage is starting to wilt. Stir in the brown sugar and vinegar and cover. Cook for about 15 minutes, stirring from time to time to prevent the vegetables from getting too brown.

Remove the cover and raise the heat a little to evaporate the liquid in the pot. Cook for about 5 more minutes, stirring often. The cabbage will be very tender and a dark reddish purple when ready. If the color is still light and opaque, you need to keep cooking and stirring, until the cabbage is moist and tender but not wet or mushy. Taste for seasonings (it should be a balance of sweet and sour) and add vinegar or salt as necessary.

Brown Butter Cauliflower

MAKES 4 SERVINGS   PREP TIME: 30 MINUTES

Years ago I drove through France with English friends on our way down to Provence. We were trying to decide where to stop for the night and couldn't agree, so we kept passing by pretty country inns until finally it was dark, options were limited, and we were all tired and cranky. We agreed to stay at the *very next* place we came to that offered rooms, which turned out to be a rather dismal box of a building with very little charm. Just our luck! We went in and asked the woman who greeted us if we could possibly have a meal as well as a room. She told us to take a fifteen-minute walk, and then she would be ready. We stumbled around in the dark, hungry, weary, and not expecting much. When we returned to the house, we were greeted by a lovely platter of crudités, a country terrine with mustard and cornichons, sautéed river trout with lemon, and cauliflower that had been browned in butter. Needless to say, we were lucky after all! I'm sure there was dessert too, but the thing I dreamed about long after was the cauliflower. This preparation is still one of my favorite things to eat.

---

1 small head or ½ large head
    cauliflower, cut or broken into
    smallish pieces, roughly 1 inch or
    so (about 2 cups)

Salt
2 tablespoons butter

Blanch the cauliflower in a large pot of boiling salted water for about 2 minutes, then shock in ice water. Drain and pat dry with paper towels.

Heat ¼ cup of water with 1 tablespoon butter in a medium skillet over medium-high heat. When the water is simmering, add the cauliflower and lower the heat to medium-low. Toss or stir the cauliflower and cook gently for about 10 minutes, stirring now and then and adding a little water if the pan dries up. Add the rest of the butter and a sprinkle of water and keep cooking and stirring until the florets are evenly browned on all sides. Season with salt, as desired, and serve hot.

Smothered Greens with Smoked Onions

We first developed this recipe as a side for a vegetarian dish we were serving at Bayona. We wanted to create the traditional smoky pork flavor of southern greens without using pork. That's when we thought about smoking the onions. The smokiness imparts a tremendously satisfying and "meaty" flavor, but if you want to prepare this dish in the real southern way, don't hesitate to throw some bacon, ham, or salt pork in the pot. Also, we tend to cook ours a little drier (mainly for presentation, so it plates up neater), so if you want more pot liquor, add more water early on.

1 tablespoon olive oil or rendered
    bacon fat
1 medium raw onion and 1 medium
    smoked onion (see Smoked
    Vegetables, p. 293), diced
1 garlic clove, minced

4–6 cups greens, such as mustard,
    turnip, or collard greens,
    stemmed, washed, and chopped
2 teaspoons apple cider vinegar
Salt and pepper
Hot sauce

Heat the olive oil in a wide, heavy-bottomed skillet over medium heat. Add the onions and sauté for about 5 minutes, stirring often, until softened but not brown. Add the garlic and cook 1 more minute. Stir in the greens and cook over medium-high heat until wilted, about 5 minutes. Add about 1 cup of water, cover the pan, and cook 20 minutes more. Remove the cover and turn up the heat to evaporate some of the liquid. Taste the greens: if they're slightly bitter, reduce the heat and cook a little longer. When the greens taste nice and sweet, sprinkle with vinegar and season to taste with salt, pepper, and hot sauce. Keep warm until ready to serve.

When it comes to selecting greens, a mixture of two or three varieties is the most delicious. Feel free to include red chard, beet tops, kale, or other hearty greens in the mix. Whichever you choose, be sure to wash them thoroughly (we do it twice), as they tend to be sandy and even a little grit can spoil the finished product. My husband, Chip, swears by adding a bottle of beer and a pinch of sugar to the pot—your call.

Five-bean Picnic Salad

MAKES 10 TO 12 SERVINGS   PREP TIME: 1 HOUR

If you're going to buy and chop up all the vegetables for this salad, you might as well make a big batch that will last you a few days. This colorful, incredibly satisfying combination keeps well and makes for a terrific side dish to just about anything you care to sauté, fry, or grill. And because this salad feeds a crowd, it's perfect for picnics and backyard barbecues.

½ pound green beans, cut into 1-inch pieces

½ pound yellow wax or romano beans, cut into 1-inch pieces

1 pound fresh shelled field peas, such as limas, black-eyed peas, or purple hull beans (or 2 cups canned or frozen beans, prepared accordingly)

1 (15-ounce) can red beans, drained

1 (15-ounce) can chickpeas, drained

¾ cup sugar

¾ cup apple cider vinegar

¼ cup Crystal or Louisiana brand hot sauce, or other hot sauce

1 teaspoon salt

1 garlic clove, minced

¾ cup olive oil

1 large onion, finely chopped (about 1½ cups)

3 celery stalks, finely chopped (¾ cup)

1 red bell pepper, finely chopped (1 cup)

1 bunch scallions, finely chopped (1 cup)

Bring a large pot of salted water to a boil. When the water is near to boiling, fill a large bowl with ice water. Blanch the green beans, yellow wax beans, and field peas, one bean variety at a time, in the boiling water for 3–4 minutes and transfer them to the ice water to shock. Be sure to let the water return to a rolling boil before dropping in each batch. (Putting a lid on the pot will speed up this process, but leave it off when cooking the beans.) Drain and dry the beans, and place them in a large bowl with the drained red beans and chickpeas.

Place the sugar and vinegar in a medium saucepan and bring to a boil. Reduce the heat and simmer for about 7 minutes, then add the hot sauce and cook 2 more minutes. Remove from the heat, whisk in the salt and garlic, and pour over the beans. Add the olive oil and toss thoroughly. Add the remaining vegetables and toss again. Adjust the seasoning to taste.

Shiitake Mushroom Sauté with Asian Flavors

MAKES 4 SERVINGS   PREP TIME: 30 MINUTES

This is a tasty little combination that can be used on top of or alongside any Asian-inspired meat or fish entrée or mixed with shrimp or crabmeat to make a light and tangy starter. I love it with tuna, brushed with a little hoisin sauce, or with medallions of pork tenderloin.

2 tablespoons canola oil

½ pound shiitake mushrooms, stemmed and sliced

1 teaspoon grated fresh ginger

1 garlic clove, minced

2 tablespoons *ketjap manis* (see p. 14), or 5 teaspoons soy sauce mixed with 1 teaspoon molasses

Juice of 1 medium lime (about 2 tablespoons)

½ teaspoon *sambal oelek* (red chile paste)

1 teaspoon sesame oil

1 small carrot, peeled and cut into matchsticks

½ medium red onion, thinly sliced

4 scallions, thinly sliced on the diagonal

½ bunch cilantro, cleaned and chopped, optional

Salt, optional

Heat 1 tablespoon canola oil in a medium skillet over high heat until hot but not smoking. Add the mushrooms and stir, then lower the heat to medium-high and cook for 4–5 minutes. When the mushrooms are lightly browned and crisp, stir in the ginger and garlic and cook 1 more minute. Scrape the mushrooms into a bowl and stir in the *ketjap manis,* lime juice, *sambal oelek,* sesame oil, and remaining canola. Stir to combine, then add carrot, onion, scallions, and cilantro.

The sauté should be moist and well seasoned. Add a little salt, if desired, and adjust the flavor to taste with more sesame oil, *ketjap manis,* or *sambal oelek.* Serve warm or at room temperature.

The Best Stuffed Artichokes, Italian-style

MAKES 4 SERVINGS   PREP TIME: 45 MINUTES

Preparing fresh artichokes takes some effort, but it's worth it because they are so delicious. In *The French Laundry Cookbook* Thomas Keller says that cleaning artichokes is one of his favorite things to do. I'm just the opposite. When I started out at Louis XVI, I had to clean two cases a day. My fingers were perpetually dried out and stained a nasty tobacco brown, and they didn't want to come clean, no matter how much lemon I rubbed on them. I still clean the occasional case myself, and cuss under my breath the whole time.

So, if you're not put off by this introduction, read on to learn how to clean, cook, and stuff your way to happiness.

ARTICHOKES

1 lemon	1 bay leaf
1 orange	Salt
4 large artichokes	

Grab a pot just large enough to hold the artichokes and fill with cold water. Cut the lemon and the orange in half, squeeze them both into the water, and drop the rinds in as well.

For the next part of the process, I use two knives: a small serrated knife (also called a tomato knife) and a sharp paring knife. Lay the artichoke horizontally on a cutting board and with the serrated knife, cut off the top third, which should remove most of the sharp, pointy tips. Holding the artichoke upright in your left hand, snap off two or three of the outer leaves. Take the paring knife in your right hand and, using a sawing, up-and-down motion, but keeping the knife in one place, turn the artichoke against the knife with your left hand so that you are cutting away the outer layer (about 2 leaves deep) of the artichoke. Be careful not to cut too deep, as that will take away some of the bottom, which is the prize. The object is to remove anything that is darker green and get down to the light yellow-green flesh. After you have done that, you will still have a sort of skirt around the bottom and the stem. Turn the artichoke upside down and, with your paring knife pointed at the stem, trim away the tough darker green down to the yellow-green, all around. Then peel the stem with downward strokes of the knife. When you finish, it should all be light yellowish green and should retain its round shape. Place the turned artichoke into the pot and continue with the others. When you are finished, add the bay leaf and some salt to the pot, place it over high heat, and bring to a boil. You may lay a small plate or a piece of parchment or wax paper on the artichokes to keep them submerged. Lower the heat and simmer for about 12 minutes. To check for doneness, remove one artichoke with tongs and plunge it into ice water. Carefully open the center leaves to reveal the choke. Dip it in cold water again, as it is usually still hot in the center. Try to pull or push the choke out with your thumb. If you can do this easily, it is ready. If it is still too hard, return the artichoke to the pot and cook 4–5 minutes more. Remove from the heat and cool in the ice water. When ready to use, remove the choke from the artichokes, while still keeping them intact. They are now ready to stuff.

At this point you could also slice and sauté the artichokes, fry them, or eat them cold with aïoli or vinaigrette.

STUFFING

½ cup olive oil

1 small onion, finely chopped

1 medium zucchini, grated and
squeezed dry of excess moisture

1 garlic clove, minced

Grated zest and juice of 1 medium
lemon (about 2 teaspoons zest and
3 tablespoons juice)

½ cup dry bread crumbs

¼ cup grated Parmesan, Grana
Padano, or pecorino

2 tablespoons chopped Italian parsley

1 teaspoon chopped fresh rosemary

¼ teaspoon crushed red pepper flakes

Salt, to taste

Preheat the oven to 350°F.

Heat 2 tablespoons olive oil in a medium skillet over medium heat and cook the onion for 4–5 minutes, until wilted. Add the zucchini and garlic and cook, stirring, until most of the moisture from the zucchini is gone, about 5 minutes. Scrape into a bowl and cool a few minutes, then add the remaining ingredients (including the remaining olive oil). Taste and adjust the seasoning.

TO ASSEMBLE

Stuffing

Cooked artichokes

Olive oil for drizzling

Lemon wedges, for garnish

Use a spoon to pack the mixture into the artichokes (mostly in the center, but some inside the leaves, too), dividing evenly.

Place the stuffed artichokes in a baking pan, add about half an inch of water to the pan, drizzle the artichokes with a little more olive oil, and cover with foil. Bake for about 15 minutes, then remove the foil and cook another 10 minutes, until stuffing is hot and slightly crusty. Serve hot or at room temperature with lemon wedges.

This recipe gives a more arduous but elegant presentation for stuffed artichokes, allowing you to eat the entire thing without creating a pile of tooth-scraped leaves. However, most folks simply trim the top third off the artichoke, cook it, scrape the choke out with a spoon, and stuff it, and that's fine too. For a delicious appetizer, you could also cut the (chokeless) artichokes in half, add some crabmeat to the stuffing, then bake and serve with a drizzle of lemon butter.

Eggplant Roulades with Garlic Goat Cheese and Roasted Tomatoes

MAKES 4 SERVINGS AS A SIDE DISH OR 2 AS A MAIN COURSE   PREP TIME: 45 MINUTES
(NOT INCLUDING GARLIC CONFIT OR ROASTED TOMATOES)

This is one of my favorite dishes for entertaining. The tender roasted eggplant sheets are used like cannelloni pasta and rolled around the savory cheese filling. The sweet roasted tomatoes add just enough acidity. If you are short on time, fresh tomatoes marinated in oil and vinegar are a great alternative. If you want to get fancy, secure each bundle with a blanched chive for a beautiful presentation.

ROASTED TOMATOES

4–6 roma tomatoes, cored and cut in
  half lengthwise
2 tablespoons olive oil
2 garlic cloves, thinly sliced

Salt and pepper
Crushed red pepper flakes
6 sprigs fresh herbs, such as thyme
  and rosemary

Preheat the oven to 300°F.

In a small bowl, toss the tomatoes with the olive oil, garlic, seasonings, and herbs. Lay the tomatoes cut side up on a baking sheet and roast for about 45 minutes to an hour, or until the tomatoes look slightly dehydrated and the skins are wrinkled. Let the tomatoes cool to room temperature, then transfer them to a bowl or storage container (be sure to include any of the richly flavored tomato oil that's left on the baking sheet). These can be prepared up to 2 days in advance and kept covered in the refrigerator (bring to room temperature before using). You may keep the tomato halves whole or chop them up.

GARLIC GOAT CHEESE

¼ cup Garlic Confit (p. 193)
½ cup fresh goat cheese, softened

Salt and pepper, to taste

Place the Garlic Confit and the softened goat cheese in a small bowl and mash with a fork. Taste and adjust seasonings. Set aside until the eggplant is ready. The garlic goat cheese can be prepared the day before, but remove it from the refrigerator to soften before assembling the dish.

EGGPLANT

2 tablespoons olive oil

1 teaspoon lemon juice

½ teaspoon ground cumin

Salt and pepper

1 large eggplant (about 1–1¼ ounces), peeled and sliced lengthwise into ¼-inch slices (should make 8 usable slices)

Preheat the oven to 400°F.

Combine the olive oil with the lemon juice, cumin, and a little salt and pepper.

Brush the eggplant slices on both sides with the seasoned oil and lay them out on a baking sheet. Bake about 5 minutes, then use a metal spatula to turn the slices and continue baking until eggplant is cooked through and is a light golden brown. Leave the oven turned on.

TO ASSEMBLE

Baked eggplant

Garlic Goat Cheese

8 blanched chives (see blanching technique, p. 118), to secure roulades, optional

Roasted Tomatoes

Remove the eggplant from the oven. Lower the oven to 350°F. Loosen the slices with a spatula and let them cool. Spread each slice with about 2 tablespoons of the goat cheese mixture and roll up from the smaller end to the larger. If you like, tie each roulade with a blanched chive. Place the roulades on a baking sheet and, when you're about ready to serve, return them to the oven for 10 minutes or until heated through. Serve the roasted tomatoes alongside the roulades.

Spinach and Artichoke Phyllo Crisps

This is my twist on classic Greek spanakopita, a spinach and phyllo pie. I add fennel and artichoke hearts. I've never met anyone who doesn't go mad for these crisp and savory little pastries.

FILLING

3 tablespoons olive oil

¾ pound fresh spinach, washed and
   dried

Salt

1 small onion, finely chopped

½ small fennel bulb, finely chopped,
   optional

1 garlic clove, minced

1 (15-ounce) can artichoke hearts,
   drained, cleaned, and coarsely
   chopped, or 1 (9-ounce) package
   frozen, thawed and chopped

3 tablespoons flour

1 cup milk

Pepper

Hot sauce

1 (8-ounce) package cream cheese

2 tablespoons chopped fresh dill

½ cup finely chopped scallions

1 teaspoon fresh lemon juice, plus
   more if desired

1 to 1½ cups crumbled feta cheese

Heat 1 tablespoon olive oil in a large skillet over medium-high heat, then add the spinach and stir with a pair of tongs or a spatula. Season the spinach with a little salt and cook until it is just barely wilted. Remove it from the pan and drain in a colander.

When the spinach is cool enough to handle, squeeze out the excess water and chop. Add the remaining olive oil to the skillet and sauté the onion, fennel, and garlic for 3 minutes. Add the artichokes and cook for 2 more minutes, then add the flour and stir to evenly coat vegetables. Whisk in the milk and bring to a boil. Season with salt, pepper, and hot sauce. Cook for about 5 minutes, then add the chopped spinach and mix thoroughly. Remove from heat and cool about 5 minutes. Place in a food processor and add the cream cheese, cut into pieces. Pulse to combine mixture. Add the dill, scallions, lemon juice, and feta and pulse once or twice more. Taste and adjust the seasoning. Scrape the filling into a container and cool completely or refrigerate until needed.

PHYLLO CRISPS

½ pound phyllo dough

¼ pound (1 stick) butter, melted

½ cup dry bread crumbs

Spinach and artichoke filling

Lay 1 sheet of phyllo on a clean work surface with the long side facing you. Brush evenly with melted butter and sprinkle with bread crumbs. Repeat brushing and sprinkling with 2 more sheets, stacking them on top of the first. Slice the sheets vertically into 5 equal strips. Place 1 heaping tablespoon of filling on the bottom corner of each strip. Fold the corner up over the filling to form a triangle, then continue folding, flag style, until you reach the top. Brush the top with butter and sprinkle with bread crumbs. Continue with remaining strips, until all filling is used up. Refrigerate (or freeze) until ready to bake.

Preheat the oven to 425°F.

Place the crisps on a greased baking sheet, leaving a little space between them, and bake until golden brown, about 6–8 minutes. (If frozen, preheat the oven to 350°F and bake about 15 minutes.) Serve warm.

Fragrant Basmati Pilaf

MAKES 4 SERVINGS　　　PREP TIME: 45 MINUTES

Basmati wins my vote for the best all-around rice because it is easy to cook, incredibly fragrant, and complements so many different dishes. Best of all; it's so rich in flavor that it needs little enhancement. Before I discovered basmati I used to love to eat butter with my rice. This pilaf is definitely delicious enough to eat on its own, but I especially like it with a sprinkling of chopped scallions. (What can I say—I'm a Crescent City girl.)

1 tablespoon butter or oil

3 tablespoons diced celery

3 tablespoons diced onion

1 cup basmati rice

1½ cups water

¼ teaspoon salt

Melt the butter or heat the oil in a 1-quart saucepan over medium heat. Add the celery and onion and sweat until soft, then add the basmati rice and stir until the kernels are coated with butter. Cook over low heat, stirring, for about 2 minutes, until the rice turns opaque. Add the water and salt and bring to a boil. Lower the heat to a simmer, cover, and cook for 15 minutes. Remove the pan from the heat and let it sit, covered, for 5 minutes. When ready to serve, fluff the rice with a fork.

Depending on what you're serving it with, you can flavor this basic pilaf with any number of ingredients, such as a few slices of ginger, cilantro stems, a teaspoon of garam masala, or a few cardamom pods. Add them with the water and cook as directed. Or mix in a tablespoon of chopped fresh herbs before serving.

Red Rice, Green Rice

MAKES 4 SERVINGS   PREP TIME: 35 MINUTES EACH

Can you tell I love rice? I can't say which one of these recipes I prefer—the spicy, tomatoey red rice or the poblano and herb flavors in the green rice variation. They are both full of flavor and complement countless dishes. Serve either one with Jalapeño-roast Pork (p. 269), and your favorite spicy black beans or grilled fish, chicken, or shrimp.

RED RICE

3 tablespoons olive oil

1 small onion, chopped

4 garlic cloves

4 roma or 2 large tomatoes, halved

2 ancho chiles, toasted

1 teaspoon dried Mexican oregano

¼ teaspoon ground cloves

¼ teaspoon ground cumin

2 cups Chicken Stock (p. 206) or
    Vegetable Stock (p. 204)

2 cups medium- or long-grain rice

1 teaspoon salt

Preheat the oven to 450°F.

Toss 2 tablespoons olive oil with the onion, garlic, and tomatoes and spread on a baking sheet. Roast for 15 minutes, turning once, until the vegetables are charred and breaking down. Place the chiles in a small bowl and cover them with hot water. Soak for 15 minutes, then drain, stem, and seed. Scrape the charred vegetables into a food processor or blender with the chiles and spices and process with 1 cup of stock, until you have a liquidy paste. Heat the remaining tablespoon of oil in a 2-quart saucepan or deep skillet with a tight-fitting lid over medium-high heat, and add the rice. Cook, stirring briskly, for about 5 minutes, until the rice becomes opaque and is just starting to turn lightly golden. Add the chile paste and cook for about 2 minutes, then add the remaining stock and salt and bring to a boil. Lower the heat, cover, and cook for 15 minutes, then remove the pan from the heat and let it stand, covered, for another 5–10 minutes. Fluff the rice with a fork and serve.

GREEN RICE

1 medium onion, chopped

2 poblano peppers, roasted, peeled, seeded, and chopped (see roasting technique, p. 122)

1 cup coarsely chopped cilantro

½ cup chopped scallions

2 garlic cloves, coarsely chopped

½ teaspoon ground cumin

2 cups Chicken Stock (p. 206) or Vegetable Stock (p. 204) (unsalted)

2 tablespoons olive oil

2 cups medium- or long-grain rice

1 teaspoon salt

Place the onion, peppers, cilantro, scallions, garlic, and cumin in a blender and puree with 1 or 2 cups of the stock. Heat the olive oil in a 2-quart saucepan or deep skillet with a tight-fitting lid over medium-high heat and add the rice. Cook, stirring briskly, for about 5 minutes, until the rice becomes opaque and is just starting to turn light golden. Stir in the puree and cook for 2–3 minutes, then add the salt and remaining stock. Bring the rice to a boil, cover, lower the heat, and cook for 15 minutes. Remove the pan from the heat, still covered, and let it sit for another 5 or 10 minutes. Fluff the rice with a fork and serve.

Caribbean Crab Pilaf with Coconut Milk

MAKES 4 SERVINGS   PREP TIME: 45 MINUTES

This is a fantastic dish that I came across when I was researching Caribbean food on the Internet. The recipe was cryptic—just a list of ingredients with no measurements or instructions. But I was so intrigued by the use of curry, black pepper, and Angostura bitters that I developed my own method (and added fresh herbs). This pilaf is substantial enough to eat on its own, but heavenly when served alongside grilled fish or shrimp.

---

1 tablespoon vegetable oil

1 tablespoon butter

1 medium onion, finely chopped

1 medium carrot, finely chopped

2 garlic cloves, minced

1 tablespoon curry powder

½ teaspoon black pepper

2 cups medium- or long-grain rice

1 large tomato, peeled, seeded, and diced

1 pound lump crabmeat, picked free of shells

1½ cups canned unsweetened coconut milk

1 teaspoon Angostura bitters

1 tablespoon lime juice

1 teaspoon salt

Hot sauce

¼ cup finely sliced scallions

¼ cup each chopped fresh basil and/or cilantro, optional

Heat the oil and butter in a 2-quart saucepan over medium-high heat and add the onion, carrot, and garlic. Cook, stirring, for 2 minutes, then add the curry powder and pepper and cook 2–3 minutes longer. Add the rice and sauté for another 2 minutes. Add the tomato, crabmeat, coconut milk, 1½ cups water, bitters, lime juice, and salt and bring to a boil. Reduce the heat, cover, and cook for 15–20 minutes, until the liquid is absorbed. Remove the pan from the heat and let it stand, covered, for an additional 10 minutes. Stir the rice and season it with the salt and hot sauce. Serve garnished with scallions and herbs.

If your pilaf begins to dry out, you may want to moisten it with a little more coconut milk before serving.

Wild and Dirty Rice

MAKES 6 TO 8 SERVINGS   PREP TIME: 35 MINUTES

Plain ole dirty rice is a good thing. Add the earthy, nutty taste and tooth-some texture of wild rice, and you have something even better.

1 cup wild rice

½ pound ground pork

2 tablespoons butter, oil, or bacon fat

1 small onion, diced

2 celery stalks, finely chopped

1 small green bell pepper, finely chopped

½ red bell pepper, finely chopped

2 garlic cloves, minced

½ pound chicken or duck livers, trimmed and coarsely chopped

1 cup long-grain white rice

1½ cups Chicken Stock (p. 206)

1 teaspoon Worcerstershire sauce

1 teaspoon chopped fresh thyme

1 tablespoon chopped fresh parsley

1 small bay leaf

Salt and pepper

Hot sauce

½ bunch scallions, finely chopped (about ¼ cup)

Bring a 2-quart saucepan of water to a boil over medium-high heat. Add the wild rice, reduce the heat, and simmer covered for 30–40 minutes, until the grains are tender and the ends have just slightly popped. Drain the rice in a colander and set aside.

While the rice is cooking, cook the ground pork in a medium skillet over medium heat, stirring to break up any clumps, until it is no longer pink, about 5 minutes. Drain the excess fat and set aside.

Melt the butter in a wide, shallow skillet or Dutch oven over medium-

When cooking rice, I find that covering the surface of the water with a piece of waxed paper or parchment paper cut to fit the shape of the pot helps keep the rice moist and makes it cook more evenly. For more moisture and a richer flavor, stir in a cup of diced sautéed or roasted eggplant when you add the stock.

high heat. Add the onion, celery, green and red peppers, and garlic, and cook, stirring, until softened, 5–7 minutes. Add the livers and cooked pork and cook, stirring, until the livers are browned. Stir in the white rice, Chicken Stock, Worcestershire, thyme, parsley, bay leaf, and ½ teaspoon salt and bring to a boil. Cover and cook over low heat about 15 minutes, until the rice is tender. Stir in the wild rice and cook for 5 more minutes. Remove from the heat and let sit, covered, for an additional 5 minutes. To serve, remove the bay leaf, season with salt, pepper, and hot sauce, and stir in the chopped scallions.

Rice Calas

MAKES 6 SERVINGS   PREP TIME: 40 MINUTES

A cala is a rice beignet or fritter that used to be sold by New Orleans street vendors back in the 1800s. It was a tasty way of using up leftover rice, since rice was a staple on the table pretty much every day. I first researched cala recipes when I started cooking Sunday brunch at Savoir Faire many years ago. I wanted to find an authentic yeast-raised batter, which causes fritters to develop a more interesting (slightly fermented) flavor than when a baking powder version is used. I love to eat these warm, with strawberry preserves and plenty of café au lait.

2 cups cooked rice, a little warmer
   than room temperature
1 package dry yeast, softened in
   ½ cup warm water
2 teaspoons, plus ¼ cup, sugar
3 eggs, beaten

1 cup flour
¼ teaspoon grated nutmeg
½ teaspoon salt
Vegetable oil, for frying
Confectioners' sugar, for serving
Strawberry preserves, optional

Place the rice in a deep mixing bowl and add the dissolved yeast and 2 teaspoons sugar. Stir together with a wooden spoon, mashing the rice slightly, then cover and set in a warm place to rise overnight, or for at least 2–3 hours.

When ready to cook, stir the eggs, ¼ cup sugar, flour, nutmeg, and salt into the rice mixture. Beat 1 minute, then set aside and let rise another 20–30 minutes.

Heat 2 inches of oil in a wide, deep skillet until hot (about 350°F) but not smoking.

Working in batches so you don't overcrowd the skillet, carefully drop the batter by tablespoonfuls into the hot oil and fry for 2–3 minutes, then flip the fritters and cook them until golden brown all over, another minute or so. Drain on paper towels and repeat with the remaining batter.

Sprinkle the calas with confectioners' sugar and serve with preserves on the side for dipping.

Alice's Spoon Bread

MAKES 6 TO 8 SERVINGS   PREP TIME: 45 MINUTES

As almost any southerner will confirm, you can't underestimate the allure of a warm, moist spoon bread. Sometimes the desire for it is downright urgent. Take my first recollection of the dish: when I was five years old, I invited one of my girlfriends to spend the night, and she woke up in the middle of the night wailing for spoon bread. My parents ended up having to take her home, as she would not be consoled.

I can relate to the craving. When Hurricane Katrina forced us to evacuate to Jackson, I had the good sense to throw a pork roast in a cooler. Our first night in exile, we had dinner with our in-laws, and my mom made her spoon bread—served with the pork roast, it was a nice taste of home. My mom's recipe, the one I grew up on (but never demanded at the home of my friends), is simple and delicious. At Bayona we couldn't resist jazzing up her version to go alongside our grilled double-cut pork chops—a match made in heaven!

¼ pound (1 stick) butter, cut in small pieces, plus more for greasing the casserole

Dry, unseasoned bread crumbs

4 cups milk

1 cup cornmeal

Salt and pepper

4 eggs, separated

½ cup grated cheddar cheese

Preheat the oven to 400°F. Butter a 2-quart casserole and coat it evenly with bread crumbs. Shake out the excess crumbs and set aside.

Heat the milk and butter in a medium saucepan over medium-high heat until the butter is melted. Whisk in the cornmeal and bring to a boil. Reduce the heat and cook, whisking constantly, until the mixture has thickened, about 5 minutes. Season generously with salt and pepper. Remove from the heat and cool.

In a clean bowl, beat the egg whites until stiff but still creamy. Beat the egg yolks into the cornmeal mixture, then fold in the egg whites, a third at a time. Fold in the cheese and pour into the casserole. Bake for 25 minutes, until lightly golden and a cake tester inserted in the center comes out clean.

Bayona Extra-cheesy Spoon Bread

MAKES 6 TO 8 SERVINGS   PREP TIME: 45 MINUTES

¼ pound (1 stick) butter, cut in small pieces, plus more for greasing

Dry, unseasoned bread crumbs

1 small onion, finely chopped

2 garlic cloves, minced

4 cups milk

1 cup cornmeal

Salt and pepper

4 eggs, separated

1 cup grated white cheddar cheese, plus extra for topping

Preheat oven to 400°F. Butter a 2-quart casserole or 8 individual ramekins and coat with bread crumbs. Shake out excess crumbs.

Melt the butter in a 2-quart saucepan over medium-high heat. Add the onion and garlic and cook, stirring, for about 5 minutes. Add milk and bring almost to the boil. Whisk in cornmeal and bring to a boil. Reduce heat and cook, whisking constantly, until the mixture has thickened, about 5 minutes. Season generously with salt and pepper.

Remove from heat and let cool.

In a clean bowl, beat the egg whites until they're stiff but still creamy. Beat the egg yolks into the cornmeal mixture, then fold in the egg whites, a third at a time. Fold in the cheese and pour into casserole or spoon into ramekins.

Top the spoon bread with a little extra cheese. Bake until the surface is lightly golden and a cake tester inserted in the center comes out clean—about 25 minutes if you're using a casserole, 20 minutes if you're using the individual ramekins.

Butternut Squash Spoon Bread Soufflé

MAKES 4 TO 6 SERVINGS   PREP TIME: 1½ HOURS (INCLUDES SQUASH-BAKING TIME)

I created this soufflé for a magazine article about Thanksgiving in New Orleans. I wanted a side dish that was seasonal and distinctly southern—and this filled the bill. Imagine how nice it would look on your table in your prettiest casserole or soufflé dish. This soufflé dresses up a simple roast chicken or pork loin. But I'd encourage you to try it with Roasted Duckling with Orange–Cane Syrup Sauce (p. 262).

¼ pound (1 stick) butter, plus more for buttering soufflé mold and dish

Flour, for the soufflé mold

2 cups pureed roasted butternut squash (from a 2-pound squash; see below)

1 cup finely chopped onions

1 teaspoon chopped fresh sage, optional

2 cups milk

1 tablespoon chestnut (or other strongly flavored) honey or molasses

½ cup cornmeal

Salt and pepper

4 eggs, separated, plus 2 additional egg whites

Preheat the oven to 400°F. Butter and flour a 1½-quart soufflé mold or 6 individual soufflé molds.

Slice the squash in half lengthwise and scoop out the seeds. Place the squash cut side down on a buttered or oiled baking dish and pour 1 inch of water in the dish. Roast for 30–40 minutes, until the squash is very soft and tender.

Remove the squash from the oven, turn it over, and, when cool enough to handle, scrape the meat away from the skins. Mash with a fork or puree in a food processor. Place in a strainer to drain off any excess liquid.

Melt the butter in a 2-quart pot over medium heat. Add the onions and cook, stirring, for 3–4 minutes, until softened. Add the sage and continue to stir. Pour in the milk and honey and bring almost to a boil. Whisk in the cornmeal and bring to a boil. Reduce the heat and whisk or stir the mixture for 5 more minutes, until it is quite thick. Remove the mixture from the heat and scrape it into a large bowl. Add the squash puree and mix thoroughly. Season with salt and pepper. Mix in the 4 egg yolks and set aside.

In a separate bowl (or an electric mixer), beat the egg whites until stiff but not dry. Fold the whites into the squash mixture, a third at a time. Scoop the batter into the prepared mold (or divide evenly among individual molds) and bake at 400°F for about 30 minutes (25 for individual soufflés). Insert a wooden skewer into the soufflé to test for doneness. If it is dry, it's done; if it's wet, bake a few more minutes.

Alice's Bread and Herb Stuffing

MAKES 12 SERVINGS   PREP TIME: 30 MINUTES

My strongest memories of Thanksgiving are the mingling smells of chopped parsley, melted butter, and chicken broth going into the stuffing, and the sounds of cheering and yelling as we all watched the Army-Navy football game.

At Bayona we always serve two different stuffings with our roast turkey. One is my mom's simple bread stuffing, and the other is loaded with local flavors like shrimp (or crayfish) and andouille. I still like my mom's the best. I call for both stuffings to be baked in casseroles, but you can also follow your favorite method for baking them inside a bird.

½ pound (2 sticks) butter

1 bunch celery, finely chopped (about 2 cups)

2 medium onions, finely chopped (about 2 cups)

2 bunches scallions (white and green), finely chopped (about 2 cups)

1 tablespoon each finely chopped fresh thyme and sage

6 cups dried bread, torn in ½-inch pieces

4–5 cups Chicken Stock (p. 206)

1 bunch fresh Italian parsley, chopped (about ¾ cup)

Salt and pepper

Preheat the oven to 350°F.

Melt one of the sticks of butter in a large skillet over medium heat. Add the celery, onions, and half the scallions and cook for 5–7 minutes. Add the thyme and sage and cook another 2–3 minutes. Scrape the vegetables into a large bowl and add the bread. In a separate saucepan, bring the stock to a boil and add the other half of the butter to it. Pour this over the bread mixture, then add the remaining scallions and parsley, season with salt and pepper, and stir well to soak all the bread. Place in a medium casserole dish, cover with foil, and bake for 15–20 minutes. Uncover and cook for about 10 more minutes, until the top is crusty and golden brown.

Shrimp, Corn Bread, and Andouille Stuffing

MAKES 12–15 SERVINGS   PREP TIME: 45 MINUTES

6–8 cups diced corn bread (about one 8-inch square pan)

1 pound andouille sausage, cut in quarters lengthwise, then in ½-inch slices

4 tablespoons (½ stick) butter

2 medium onions, chopped (about 2 cups)

4 stalks celery, chopped (about 1½ cups)

2 cups chopped red and green bell peppers

2 bunches scallions (green and white), chopped (about 2 cups)

1 pound small or medium shrimp, peeled, deveined, and coarsely chopped

3 garlic cloves, minced

1 tablespoon each chopped fresh thyme and sage, or 1 teaspoon each dried

6 cups Chicken Stock (p. 206) or Shrimp Stock (p. 229)

Salt and pepper

Hot sauce

½ cup chopped fresh Italian parsley

Preheat the oven to 350°F.

Crumble the corn bread into a large bowl and set aside to dry. Cook the andouille in a large skillet over medium heat, just until the fat is rendered. Use a slotted spoon to transfer it to the corn bread bowl. Melt the butter in the same skillet and add the onions, celery, peppers, and half the scallions. Cook until the vegetables are wilted, then add the shrimp, garlic, and herbs. Cook, stirring, for 5 minutes, then add to the corn bread.

In a separate saucepan, bring the stock to a boil, then pour half of it over the corn bread mixture. Stir thoroughly with a rubber spatula and check the consistency. Add more stock, as needed, to moisten the mixture (though it should not be soggy). Season to taste with salt, pepper, and hot sauce, then stir in the remaining scallions and parsley. Transfer the mixture to a large baking dish, cover with foil, and bake for 15 minutes. Remove the foil and bake another 15 minutes, until the stuffing is heated through and the top is crusty and golden brown.

Creole Cream Cheese Spaetzle

MAKES 6 TO 8 SERVINGS   PREP TIME: 40 MINUTES

German for "little sparrow," spaetzle are tiny dumplings that make a delicious side dish to any number of meats. A former sous chef enriched the traditional recipe and came up with this delicious variation that we typically serve alongside medallions of venison.

Creole cream cheese is the secret ingredient here. It has a tart flavor and a texture as rich and thick as mascarpone. It was traditionally eaten as a spoon food, almost like yogurt, topped with sugar or fruit. It was almost lost until the Slow Food movement came along, and people became more interested in artisanal food products. These days it is produced locally and sold at the farmer's market. My favorite variety is made by the Mauthe family (see Sources, p. 384) at their hormone-free dairy north of Lake Pontchartrain.

---

1 pound flour (about 3 cups)

1 pound Creole cream cheese

4 eggs

¼ cup chopped fresh herbs (such as parsley, thyme, or chives)

Salt and pepper

Olive oil or butter, to sauté

Place the flour in a bowl and stir in the Creole cream cheese. Whisk in the eggs, one at a time, until you have a smooth batter. (If you still have too many lumps, you can strain the batter through a fine sieve.) Stir in the herbs and season with salt and pepper.

Bring a large pot of salted water to a boil. Select a colander with fairly large holes (about ¼ inch). Pour in about a third of the batter and, with a plastic spatula, scrape the batter through the holes into the simmering water. The spaetzle will rise to the surface when they are ready, in about 3 minutes. Let them simmer on the surface for another 30 seconds or so, then use a slotted spoon or strainer to transfer them to a bowl of ice water. Repeat the process with the remaining batter.

To reserve the spaetzle until serving, drain them and toss with a little oil, then store them in a covered container (don't pack too tightly) and refrigerate until needed.

To serve, sauté the spaetzle in a hot nonstick skillet, with a little olive oil or butter, until they are lightly browned and crusty.

Onion and Carrot Bhajis

MAKES 4 SERVINGS   PREP TIME: 40 MINUTES

The first time I passed through London—long before I started cooking—I figured out that some of the best food was to be found in the ubiquitous Indian restaurants. Fortunately for my traveler's budget, it was also the cheapest! One of my favorite discoveries was an onion *bhaji,* a cluster of fried onion slices bound with a spicy, aromatic batter. The flavors stayed in my memory for a long time, and after much research, I came up with this recipe. The batter is made from high-protein chickpea flour (also called *besan* or *gram* flour at Indian markets), which gives it a rich flavor.

At Bayona we serve *bhajis* with seared scallops and carrot-cardamom sauce, but they are awfully good by themselves for snacking, with a drizzle of cilantro-spiked yogurt or your favorite chutney.

Vegetable oil, for frying
½ cup flour
½ cup chickpea flour
½ teaspoon baking soda
½ teaspoon grated fresh ginger
1 garlic clove, minced
¼ teaspoon ground cinnamon

½ teaspoon cayenne
½ teaspoon ground cumin
¾ cup yogurt
1 cup thinly sliced onion
1 cup julienned carrots
Salt

Heat 2 inches of oil in a wide skillet to 350°F.

In a medium bowl, combine the flours, baking soda, ginger, garlic, and the spices. Stir in the yogurt. Add just enough water to make a batter the consistency of thickened cream.

In another bowl, mix the onion and carrots, then stir in enough batter to

To achieve crisp, golden results when frying, it's important to heat the oil to 350°F. If you don't have a thermometer, you can test the temperature by dropping in a cube of bread. If the oil is hot enough, it should brown the bread in about 15 seconds.

just barely coat the vegetables. (Test one or two to ensure you have the perfect amount of batter to hold them together.) Drop by spoonfuls into the hot oil, being careful not to overcrowd the skillet, and cook for 2–3 minutes, turning once. Use tongs to give them a gentle squeeze, which helps hold the *bhajis* together. Cook for another 3–4 minutes, until golden. Remove the *bhajis* from the oil and drain on paper towels. Salt lightly.

Sweet Potato Brioche

This recipe was adapted from one I found in the Jackson, Mississippi, Junior League cookbook, *Come on In!* We have served them at Bayona forever, and they go fast. The sweet potato gives these rolls a beautiful color and rich, moist texture.

---

1 envelope active dry yeast

1 teaspoon sugar plus 2 tablespoons
    sugar

1 cup mashed baked sweet potato
    (approximately 1 large or 2 small
    sweet potatoes)

5 eggs plus 1 beaten egg

¼ cup whole milk

3½ cups flour

1 teaspoon salt

½ pound (2 sticks) cold butter, cut
    into small pieces

In a small bowl, dissolve the yeast and 1 teaspoon sugar in 2 tablespoons warm water. Place the mashed sweet potato in the bowl of a mixer. Using the paddle attachment, beat 1 minute at medium speed, then add the 5 eggs, milk, and yeast mixture and beat for 1 minute. Add the flour, the remaining 2 tablespoons sugar, and salt and mix for about 5 minutes at medium speed. Let the mixture rest for 10 minutes, then beat in the cold butter, a third at a time. Remove the bowl, cover it lightly with plastic wrap, and allow the dough to rise at room temperature until doubled in size.

Close your hands into fists and gently punch down the dough to release air pockets and reduce its size. Cover the dough and place it in the refrigerator to rise overnight, or at least 6 hours.

Remove the dough from the refrigerator and scoop it into a buttered 6-cup brioche mold, 9 × 5-inch loaf pan, or individual molds (such as buttered muffin tins). Allow the dough to rise at room temperature until doubled.

Meanwhile, preheat the oven to 400°F. Brush the surface of the dough with the beaten egg and prick it in several places with a toothpick. Bake for 10 minutes, then lower the temperature to 325°F and continue baking until golden brown, about 20 more minutes for a large mold, or about 10 minutes for individual rolls. Cool for 10 minutes in the molds, then invert and cool completely on a wire rack.

Sweet Endings from Crescent City and Beyond

Best-ever Almond Cookies

Spice Inc. Mudslides

Old-fashioned Glazed Pumpkin Cookies

Double Ginger Gingersnaps

Banana–Chocolate Chip Cake with Peanut Butter–Cream Cheese Icing

Pecan Roulade with Praline Mousse

Silky Butterscotch-Banana Pie

Epiphany Lemon Tart

Classic Crêpes

Sumptuous Chocolate Crêpes

Lemon Crêpes with Goat Cheese Filling and Louisiana Kumquat Compote

Crispy Cinnamon-dusted Banana Fritters

Espresso Pôts de Crème

Danish Rice Pudding with Dried Cherry Sauce

Sicilian Cannoli with Bittersweet Chocolate Filling

Galaktaboureko—Greek Semolina Custard Baked in Phyllo

Coconut Cream Pie

Brandy Crème Brûlée

Molasses Gingerbread with Lime Cream

French Semolina Cake with Pistachio Crème Anglaise

Mint Julep Ice Cream

Cashew Meringues with Chocolate Basil Mousse

Chocolate Hazelnut Phyllo Turnovers

Scotch Almond Tart

Some people are ruled by their sweet tooth, but I am not necessarily a dessert person. At the end of a satisfying meal, rather than order my own, I'm much more likely to say, "I'll just have a bite of yours" (much to my husband's dismay). But there are two notable exceptions: homemade ice cream and the recipes in this chapter. I just can't refuse either.

Most of these irresistible desserts have been in my repertoire for years and represent deeply personal memories. Epiphany Lemon Tart (p. 340), for instance, transports me to a carefree summer in France. My mom's Danish Rice Pudding (p. 351) is a sweet taste of childhood. French Semolina Cake with Pistachio Crème Anglaise (p. 363) is a delicious lesson that I learned as a young apprentice.

Let's get one thing straight: I am not a bona fide pastry chef. This should reassure you. All good cooks need to know the basics of baking and eventually have a few solid desserts up their sleeve. For me, the recipes in this book are those mainstays. They are fun to make, immensely satisfying to serve, and a joy to eat. Even if, like me, you claim not to have a sweet tooth, chances are these temptations will have you sneaking "just one more bite" off your neighbor's plate quite a few times.

Best-ever Almond Cookies

MAKES ABOUT 24 COOKIES   PREP TIME: 30 MINUTES

This is the classic almond macaroon. Bet you can't eat just one!

8 ounces almond paste (not marzipan; buy in tube or bar form)

¾ cup granulated sugar

2 egg whites

1 teaspoon pure vanilla extract

1 teaspoon good-quality almond extract

Whole or slivered blanched almonds, as garnish

Confectioners' sugar, for dusting

Preheat the oven to 350°F and line baking sheets with parchment paper.

Cream the almond paste and granulated sugar in an electric mixer fitted with the paddle attachment. Add the egg whites, vanilla, and almond extract and beat at medium speed until just blended. Fit a pastry bag with a small (¼- to ½-inch) plain tip and use a rubber spatula to fill the bag with the dough. Pipe the cookies into 1½-inch circles on the parchment. Decorate each cookie with a whole almond or almond slivers before baking. Bake for 10–12 minutes, until golden brown. Cool the cookies completely on the baking sheets. Dust with confectioners' sugar and serve.

When I am feeling really decadent, I drizzle melted bittersweet chocolate on these cookies after they are cool. Omit the confectioners' sugar.

Spice Inc. Mudslides

MAKES ABOUT 2 DOZEN COOKIES   PREP TIME: 1½ HOURS (INCLUDES DOUGH-CHILLING TIME)

Talk about a chocolate lover's dream! The deep, dark secret to these cookies is the addition of cocoa nibs—ripe, fermented cocoa beans that have been roasted, then separated from their husks and broken into small bits. They have a crunchy-crackly texture and a rich, winey chocolate essence that rivals the flavor of the best chocolate-covered espresso beans. They are available in most specialty food shops. Make these cookies when you feel a need to splurge.

1½ pounds semisweet chocolate (63% cocoa), coarsely chopped

6 tablespoons butter

1 tablespoon pure vanilla extract

1½ cups flour

¾ teaspoon baking powder

¼ teaspoon salt

6 eggs

3 cups sugar

12 ounces semisweet chocolate chips

2 cups finely chopped toasted walnuts

1 cup cocoa nibs

Melt the chopped chocolate and butter together in a metal bowl over a medium saucepan of hot, barely simmering water. Remove from heat, whisk in the vanilla, and set aside to cool.

Sift the flour, baking powder, and salt together into a large bowl or onto a sheet of parchment paper.

In the bowl of an electric mixer, whisk the eggs and sugar at medium-high speed until they form smooth, glossy ribbons that rest on the batter for a moment after the whisk is pulled out of the batter. Using a rubber spatula, fold in the cooled chocolate mixture and then the sifted ingredients, until just mixed. Then fold in the chocolate chips, walnuts, and cocoa nibs.

Divide the dough into four equal portions. Place each portion on a piece of waxed paper and roll into a log (or long rectangular slab) about 1½ inches thick. Freeze in the waxed paper for at least 1 hour or up to several days.

When ready to bake, preheat the oven to 325°F. Cut the frozen logs into ¼-inch-thick slices and place on parchment-lined baking sheets, allowing at least 2 inches between cookies for room to spread. Bake for 13–15 minutes, until they are slightly crusty on the outside but still gooey in the middle. Let cool completely on the baking sheets.

Freezing the dough is an essential step in this recipe. It makes the cookies easier to slice, and it also helps them hold their shape while baking.

Old-fashioned Glazed Pumpkin Cookies

MAKES 2 TO 3 DOZEN COOKIES   PREP TIME: 35 MINUTES

These cakelike cookies are so irresistible that we sold zillions of them at Spice Inc., and I still have to make them about twice a year for my friend Daniel when he gets a craving. Although pumpkin tends to suggest fall, these moist, spicy cookies can—and should—be made all year round.

---

2 cups flour

1 teaspoon ground cinnamon

½ teaspoon ground ginger

½ teaspoon ground cloves

1 teaspoon salt

1 teaspoon baking soda

½ pound (2 sticks) unsalted butter

¾ cup brown sugar

¾ cup granulated sugar

1 egg

1 cup canned pumpkin puree

1 cup chopped walnuts

1 cup raisins

Preheat the oven to 350°F and grease the baking sheets.

Sift the flour, cinnamon, ginger, cloves, salt, and baking soda into a large bowl or onto a sheet of parchment paper.

Cream the butter and both sugars in the bowl of an electric mixer, using the paddle attachment. Add the egg and pumpkin and mix until fluffy. Stir in the sifted ingredients at a slow speed, until just mixed, then stir in the walnuts and raisins. Drop by the tablespoon onto greased cookie sheets and bake for about 12 minutes, until the tops are set and the cookies are golden around the edges. Use a fork to drizzle glaze onto the cookies after they have completely cooled.

OLD-FASHIONED GLAZE

1 cup confectioners' sugar

½ teaspoon ground cinnamon

1 tablespoon water

Whisk the ingredients together in a small bowl.

Double Ginger Gingersnaps

MAKES 2 TO 3 DOZEN COOKIES   PREP TIME: 40 MINUTES

If you're going to make gingersnaps, you might as well make 'em gingery, right? A combination of fresh and ground ginger does just that. These cookies are buttery and full of flavor, with cloves and cayenne pepper adding an undercurrent of heat. If you like your cookies a little chewy, just take them out of the oven a minute or two sooner.

2½ cups flour

1 teaspoon baking soda

¼ teaspoon salt

1 tablespoon plus 1 teaspoon ground ginger

½ teaspoon ground allspice

¼ teaspoon ground cloves

¼ teaspoon cayenne

½ pound (2 sticks) butter

1 cup sugar

¼ cup molasses

1 teaspoon cider vinegar

1 egg

2 tablespoons grated fresh ginger

Coarse sprinkling sugar, for dipping the cookies

Preheat the oven to 325°F.

Sift the flour, baking soda, salt, ground ginger, allspice, cloves, and cayenne together into a large bowl or onto a sheet of parchment paper.

In an electric mixer fitted with the paddle attachment, cream the butter and sugar until fluffy. Add the molasses and vinegar and beat at medium speed for a few minutes. Use a rubber spatula to scrape the dough down, as needed, then add the egg and fresh ginger and mix well. Add sifted ingredients and mix until just blended. Scrape the dough into a bowl and chill for about ½ hour.

Place the coarse sugar in a small bowl. Scoop the dough into walnut-sized balls, press the tops into the sugar, and place sugar side up on a baking sheet. Press with fingers to flatten slightly.

Bake for approximately 15 minutes, until lightly golden. Cool completely before storing.

Cider vinegar helps gingersnaps achieve a crispy texture.

If you don't have coarse sprinkling sugar, available in most specialty food and baking supply stores, you can use regular granulated sugar.

Banana-Chocolate Chip Cake with Peanut Butter-Cream Cheese Icing

MAKES 8 TO 10 SERVINGS   PREP TIME: 50 MINUTES

I developed this recipe—in very small increments—for a newspaper article celebrating the fiftieth anniversary of the Easy-Bake Oven. My first impulse was to create something very sophisticated, but then I thought I'd appeal to the kid in everyone with bananas, chocolate, and peanut butter. I have since used this cake recipe with a strawberry–cream cheese icing, with great success. And yes, I did have an Easy-Bake Oven when I was a kid!

2½ cups cake flour

¾ teaspoon baking powder

1 teaspoon baking soda

1 teaspoon salt

1½ cups mashed ripe banana (about 2 large)

1½ teaspoons pure vanilla extract

¾ cup buttermilk

¼ pound plus 4 tablespoons (1½ sticks) butter

1 cup sugar

3 eggs

¾ cup semisweet chocolate chips, plus ¼ cup for garnish

Preheat the oven to 375°F. Butter and flour two 8-inch round cake pans.

Sift the cake flour, baking powder, baking soda, and salt together in a large bowl. Whisk together the banana, vanilla, and buttermilk in a medium bowl. In the bowl of an electric mixer fitted with the paddle attachment, cream the butter and sugar until light and fluffy; add the eggs, one at a time, and beat until well mixed.

Add the dry ingredients and banana mixture to the butter mixture in three alternating stages (dry, wet, dry), ending with the dry. Fold in the chocolate chips. Divide the batter between the pans and bake for about 25 minutes, or until springy in the center. Allow cakes to cool in pans for about 10 minutes. Run a knife around the rim of the pan to loosen cake, then invert to release cake. Cool completely on wire racks. Spread icing between the layers, and on the top and sides of the cake. Sprinkle with chocolate chips, if desired.

PEANUT BUTTER–CREAM CHEESE ICING

MAKES ABOUT 2½ CUPS, ENOUGH FOR 1 TWO-LAYER CAKE.

½ cup creamy peanut butter

1 (8-ounce) package cream cheese,
    softened

1¼ cups confectioners' sugar

½ teaspoon vanilla extract

Cream the peanut butter and the cream cheese in a mixer with the paddle attachment, scraping the sides once or twice, until light and fluffy. Beat in the sugar gradually. When completely incorporated, add the vanilla.

Pecan Roulade with Praline Mousse

MAKES 8 TO 10 SERVINGS   PREP TIME: 1 HOUR 15 MINUTES (CAKE AND PRALINE MOUSSE ARE MADE THE DAY BEFORE, IN STAGES; SYRUP IS MADE A DAY OR TWO BEFORE.)

If this recipe looks too daunting at first blush, you might consider making it in stages. The syrup for the praline mousse can be made two days in advance, and the cake can be made the day before the dessert is assembled. Or tackle just the cake the first time, and serve it with some strawberry jam and a little whipped cream on the side. Then imagine how good (and beautiful) the cake will be with the mousse on the inside. I prefer to assemble the roulade in the morning and give it all day to get moist and flavorful in the refrigerator. Some sliced ripe strawberries or peaches send it over the top.

CAKE

7 ounces pecans (about 1 cup), lightly toasted

½ teaspoon baking powder

7 eggs, separated (be careful not to get any yolk in the whites)

½ cup plus 2 tablespoons granulated sugar

Line an 18 × 12-inch baking pan with parchment paper and lightly grease the parchment or spray it with nonstick spray. Preheat the oven to 375°F.

Pulse the pecans in a food processor until you have a coarse meal. Transfer to a medium bowl and toss with the baking powder.

Whip the yolks with ¼ cup of the granulated sugar in an electric mixer at high speed until thick and pale. Stir into the nut mixture. Using a clean beater and a clean mixing bowl, whip the egg whites at medium speed until foamy. Whip at high until soft peaks begin to form. Gradually add the remaining ¼ cup plus 2 tablespoons granulated sugar. Stop the mixer and pull the beater out slowly: if the whites leave stiff peaks in the bowl, the mixture is ready (it should be stiff but not dry).

Fold the whites into the yolk mixture one half at a time. Avoid the urge to overmix. Spread the batter evenly into the prepared pan.

Bake until light golden brown, 10–12 minutes. Remove the cake from the oven and immediately cover with a damp towel; cool completely.

PRALINE SYRUP

1 cup sugar

½ cup water

1 cup heavy cream

1 teaspoon pure vanilla extract

Bourbon or rum to taste

Put the sugar and water in a small, heavy-bottomed saucepan and place over high heat. Stir to combine. Put the cream in another small saucepan and bring it just short of a boil. Remove from heat and set aside.

Bring the sugar mixture to a boil and then down to a steady simmer. When the liquid turns amber, swirl the pan. This will help it caramelize evenly. When it reaches a deep amber color, remove it from the heat and very carefully whisk in the cream. It will bubble up and steam, so watch those fingers! Return the pan to the heat and whisk to dissolve all the caramel. Refrigerate 1 cup of the praline syrup for the mousse filling. Add the vanilla and bourbon to the rest for your sauce.

PRALINE MOUSSE

4 ounces cream cheese (regular or low-fat), softened

1 cup reserved praline syrup

1 teaspoon pure vanilla extract

¾ teaspoon unflavored gelatin

1½ tablespoons dark rum

1 cup heavy cream, whipped to firm peaks

Cream the cream cheese by hand or in an electric mixer fitted with the whisk attachment. Slowly add the praline syrup, scraping the bowl frequently. Add the vanilla. Place the gelatin in a small bowl with about 1 tablespoon warm water. Add the rum to the gelatin and stir to dissolve. Fold a bit of the praline syrup into the gelatin, then fold the gelatin mixture back into the praline syrup. Fold in the whipped cream, one half at a time.

Cake   Praline mousse
Confectioner's sugar   Praline syrup

Run a paring knife around the outside of the cake to release it from the sides of the pan. Lift the edges carefully, feeling under the cake to loosen it. Sift a thin layer of confectioners' sugar onto the top of the cake. Lay a piece of parchment the size of the cake across the top, then turn the pan over to release the cake onto the parchment. With the cake lying on the counter, carefully peel the parchment that is now on top off the cake.

Spread the mousse on the cake, stopping ½ inch from the long edge. Starting with the long edge closest to you, begin rolling the cake up jelly roll style, using the parchment for support. Tuck the rolling edge of the cake in as you go to make it a little tighter and neater. Place the cake back on the baking pan and refrigerate to firm it up.

To serve, sprinkle with confectioners' sugar, cut the slices about 1 inch thick, and serve with a generous drizzle of the reserved praline syrup. Garnish with fresh strawberries or peaches, if desired.

For an easy dessert, try the mousse on its own with shortbread cookies and some fresh strawberries.

Gelatin tends to thicken on standing for even a few minutes. If the mixture seems too thick and granular when you stir in the rum, you might want to place the bowl over hot water to keep the gelatin liquid.

Silky Butterscotch-Banana Pie

MAKES 6 TO 8 SERVINGS   PREP TIME: 45 MINUTES (NOT INCLUDING CHILL TIME)

Next to ice cream (which I consider its own food group), pies are my favorite dessert. This one is an adult version of banana cream pie, with real scotch in the butterscotch (use a blended scotch whiskey, not a single malt). The amount of gelatin is just enough to set the filling, without making it rubbery. For the best texture, be sure to let the pie chill at least 3 hours before serving.

1¼ cups whole milk

1 whole egg plus 2 egg yolks

3 teaspoons cornstarch

3 teaspoons brown sugar

2 teaspoons unsalted butter, softened

2 sheets unflavored gelatin, or
   1½ teaspoons powdered

⅔ cup granulated sugar

1 cup plus ⅓ cup heavy cream

2 teaspoons pure vanilla extract

3 teaspoons scotch whiskey

¼ teaspoon salt

3 bananas, sliced into ¼-inch rounds

Prebaked 9-inch pie (or tart) shell

In a small saucepan, scald the milk over medium-high heat and set aside to cool. Whisk together the whole egg, egg yolks, cornstarch, and brown sugar in a medium bowl, then whisk in the cooled milk. Pour the mixture back into the pan and bring to a boil over medium-high heat, whisking constantly. Remove from heat, strain, and then whisk in the butter. Soften the gelatin in 1 tablespoon cold water and whisk into the egg mixture. Let cool. Caramelize the granulated sugar in a clean, dry pot by adding just enough water to liquefy it (2 or 3 tablespoons) and cooking over medium-high heat until it turns deep, golden brown. Remove from the heat and *carefully* pour in ⅓ cup cream. Whisk together and add the vanilla, scotch, and salt, then whisk into the egg mixture.

Using a wire whisk or an electric mixer fitted with the whisk attachment, whip the remaining 1 cup of cream to stiff peaks. Set aside approximately 1 cup for garnish and fold the remaining cream into the pastry cream in thirds, mixing thoroughly but gently. Fold in two thirds of the sliced bananas and spread the mixture into the baked pie shell. Chill for at least 3 hours, or up to 12 hours. Garnish with the remaining bananas and whipped cream.

When trying to cook caramel to just the right deep amber color, pay attention to the depth of the syrup in the saucepan. If sugar syrup is less than ½ inch deep, it will be ready when it appears deep amber. If it's deeper than ½ inch, the color will actually appear darker in the saucepan than it will when you pour it out—so cook it a little bit longer, to a color slightly darker than deep amber. Once the sugar starts to color, watch it closely and react quickly—it can burn in a flash. For that reason, it's good to have a bowl of ice water handy for setting the pot in to stop the cooking, if necessary.

If you make a 9- or 10-inch tart instead of a pie, chances are you'll have about a cup of leftover filling. No worries—topped with additional sliced banana, it makes a delicious pudding for the cook or cook's helper.

Silky Butterscotch-Banana Pie   339

Epiphany Lemon Tart

MAKES 8 SERVINGS   PREP TIME: 50 MINUTES

I never thought I liked lemon desserts. Then one summer, while visiting friends in the little French village of Hyères, I experienced the most sublime marriage of lemon and butter, in the form of a humble lemon tart. It came from a pastry shop called Le Pâtisserie des Artisans, and I was too shy to ask them for the recipe. So I vowed to myself that I would research every lemon tart recipe I could get my hands on until I found one that came close. Finally, I found this version in an old cookbook called (roughly translated) *Secrets of the Best Restaurants of France*. It is different from any other I've tried, and captures the sunny flavors I can still taste in my memory. I've since returned to Hyères and tried to find that pastry shop (I remember it was near the outdoor market), but I think it closed. Too bad—I would have liked to tell them about my epiphany.

SWEET TART CRUST

1½ cups flour

5 tablespoons sugar

¼ teaspoon salt

7 tablespoons butter, chilled and
   diced

1 egg

1 teaspoon pure vanilla extract

Sift the flour, sugar, and salt into a large bowl. Add the butter and work it in with your fingertips until the mixture is crumbly and well mixed. Mix the egg and vanilla together with a fork and stir into the flour mixture. Gather the dough into a ball and knead just a little. Wrap in plastic and chill until firm, at least 15 minutes.

Preheat the oven to 350°F. Butter and flour a 9-inch tart pan.

Roll out the dough on lightly floured parchment paper to about ⅛ inch thick. Chill again for about 5 minutes. Press the dough into the pan, taking care to tuck the corners in. Fold the excess dough back onto itself to form a lip all the way around, just slightly higher than the rim of the tart pan. (This is important, as the filling is very liquidy, and you want to fill the tart all the way to the rim of the pan. The higher edge will keep the filling from spilling out.) Keep a tiny ball of excess dough to repair any cracks in the baked shell. Line the shell with a piece of foil or parchment and fill with dry beans, making sure to press them up against the sides. Bake for 10–15 minutes, then carefully remove the foil and beans, check for cracks, and use your extra dough as "spackle" to fill them in. Bake an additional 5–10 minutes, until cooked through and light golden brown. Remove the crust from the oven and let it cool for at least 5 minutes.

LEMON FILLING

5 eggs	Juice of 3 lemons and 1 orange (about
1 cup sugar minus 2 tablespoons	¾ cup)
6 tablespoons butter, melted but not	Zest of 2 lemons
hot	Fresh berries, for garnish, optional

Lower the oven temperature to 300°F.

Beat the eggs lightly and whisk in the sugar until well blended. Add the melted butter, then juice and zest. Whisk just until blended. Place the pie shell in the oven and pour in the filling. Bake for 30 minutes, until the filling is just set in the center. Cool and serve, garnished with fresh berries.

This recipe is a little trickier than most lemon tarts that use a precooked curd, but to me the taste is brighter and fresher and the texture smoother than most.

Classic Crêpes

MAKES 16 CRÊPES   PREP TIME: 35 MINUTES

Buttery, golden crêpes, with just a sprinkle of sugar or a warm, luscious filling, are one of the simplest, most appealing, and most versatile of all desserts. They are easy to make ahead and freeze, and a snap to whip up at a moment's notice—what's not to love!

In fact, my earliest cooking memory is making crêpes or "roll-up pancakes," as we used to call them, for my little brother and me while watching Popeye cartoons early on Sunday mornings. My mom taught me how to do it so she could get a little extra sleep! We would roll them up with grape jelly on the inside and confectioners' sugar (probably way too much) on the outside. Hmmm, wonder if our kids, Kelly and Evelyn, want to learn this recipe. . . .

¾ cup milk

2 tablespoons sugar

2 tablespoons butter, melted, plus more for frying

3 eggs

1 cup flour

⅛ teaspoon salt

1 teaspoon lemon zest, optional

Combine the milk and sugar in a small saucepan and cook over medium-high heat until the milk is scalded or just begins to bubble. Add the melted butter and cool until lukewarm. Whisk the eggs in a medium bowl. Gradually add the flour and salt to the eggs to make a paste. Slowly add the milk, whisking to combine. Strain to remove lumps, if necessary. Stir in lemon zest.

Heat 1 teaspoon butter in an 8-inch nonstick skillet over medium heat. Pour ⅛ cup (or 2 tablespoons) of the batter into the pan. Tilt and swirl the pan until batter covers the bottom completely. Keep rolling along the edge so that the edges do not get too thin. When the edges begin to turn golden, flip the crêpe with a plastic spatula. Cook approximately 30 seconds more, then slide the crêpe onto a cooling rack or baking sheet. Repeat until remaining batter is used up.

You can also make the batter by combining all the ingredients in a blender. If you do it this way, it is important to let the batter rest so that you get the air bubbles out.

For savory crêpes, just omit the sugar and add a tablespoon of chopped herbs (such as chives, tarragon, or thyme).

Sumptuous Chocolate Crêpes

MAKES 8 CRÊPES   PREP TIME: I HOUR AND I5 MINUTES (INCLUDES RESTING TIME FOR BATTER)

⅓ cup flour

¼ cup cocoa powder

2 tablespoons sugar

Pinch of salt

1 teaspoon grated orange zest

2 eggs

5 tablespoons butter (2 for batter,
    3 for cooking crêpes)

½ cup milk

¼ cup cream

Sift together the flour, cocoa, sugar, and salt. Add the orange zest. In a medium bowl, whisk the eggs, then whisk in the flour mixture to make a paste. Melt 2 tablespoons butter in a saucepan over medium-high heat and continue cooking until it turns golden brown and has a nutty aroma. Slowly add the butter to the batter. Whisk in the milk and cream. Allow the batter to rest for approximately 1 hour. Batter will separate, so whisk it together again when you are ready to make crêpes.

Heat about ½ teaspoon butter in a 6–8-inch nonstick skillet (or crêpe pan) over medium heat. Swirl the pan, then ladle or pour 2 tablespoons batter into the pan. Immediately tilt and swirl the pan until the batter covers the bottom completely. Keep rolling the batter toward the outer rim of the pan so that the edges do not get too thin. When the edges begin to turn golden, flip the crêpe with a plastic spatula. Cook approximately 30 seconds more, then slide the crêpe onto a cooling rack or baking sheet. Repeat the process with the rest of the batter.

Chocolate batter will become lighter in color as it cooks, so if your crêpe begins to darken, that means it's burning! When it comes to serving them, consider folding the crêpes into triangles (keeping them covered and warm in a low oven, if necessary) and then drizzling with your favorite chocolate sauce, or set alongside vanilla or coffee ice cream.

Lemon Crêpes with Goat Cheese Filling and Louisiana Kumquat Compote

MAKES 16 CRÊPES   PREP TIME: 1 HOUR

My Bayona staff served this dessert at the Taste of the NFL, a huge hunger-relief fund-raiser that we have participated in for over fifteen years. It takes place the night before the Super Bowl in the host city and is attended by more than 2,000 people, dining on food donated and prepared by chefs representing each NFL team. In seventeen years we have raised over $5 million for food banks and relief agencies all over the country. Now *that's* a party with a purpose!

LEMON CRÊPES

¾ cup milk

2 tablespoons granulated sugar

2 tablespoons butter, plus more for frying

3 eggs

¾ cup flour, sifted

¼ cup confectioners' sugar

⅛ teaspoon salt

1 teaspoon each orange and lemon zest

2 drops lemon oil, optional

Heat the milk and granulated sugar in a small saucepan over medium-high heat until the milk is scalded or just begins to bubble. Remove it from the heat and stir in the butter. Place in a blender and add the eggs, flour, confectioners' sugar, and salt. Blend until thoroughly combined, then pulse in the zests. Let the batter rest about 15 minutes to release any air bubbles.

Heat 1 teaspoon butter in an 8-inch nonstick pan over medium heat. Pour ⅛ cup (2 tablespoons) of batter into the pan. Tilt and swirl the pan until the batter covers the bottom completely. Keep rolling the batter toward the outer rim so that the edges do not get too thin. When the edges begin to turn golden, flip the crêpe with a plastic spatula and cook approximately 30 seconds on the other side. Slide the crêpe out of the pan onto a cooling rack or baking sheet. Repeat with the remaining batter.

GOAT CHEESE FILLING

1 cup fresh goat cheese (6–8 ounces)
½ cup mascarpone (4 ounces)
2 tablespoons sugar
1 teaspoon pure vanilla extract
2 tablespoons orange juice

Combine all the ingredients in a food processor, or a mixer with the paddle attachment, and process until smooth and slightly creamy. Taste and adjust sweetness with more sugar or orange juice.

LOUISIANA KUMQUAT COMPOTE

2 cups kumquats (10 ounces),
   quartered lengthwise and seeded
2 cups orange juice
¼ cup fresh lemon juice
1 cup sugar
1 cup water
½ vanilla bean
1 teaspoon grated fresh ginger

Place all the ingredients in a small saucepan and bring to a boil. Reduce the heat and simmer for 30–40 minutes, stirring from time to time, until the mixture is thick and syrupy. Remove from the heat and let cool. Remove the vanilla bean.

TO ASSEMBLE

Lemon Crêpes
Goat Cheese Filling
Louisiana Kumquat Compote

Spread 1½ tablespoons of the cheese mixture on a crêpe and fold in half. Repeat until all the crêpes are filled. (Up to this point, the crêpes can be made ahead, wrapped tightly, and stored overnight.) In a wide nonstick skillet, heat 1 teaspoon butter over medium-high heat. When bubbly, add the crêpes, four at a time (do not overlap), and sauté until lightly browned, turning the crêpes over once. Fold the crêpes a second time, into triangles. Place two crêpes on each plate and top with some of the kumquat compote.

For serious citrus lovers, spread the crêpes with a slather of homemade or good-quality store-bought lemon curd instead of the goat cheese mixture. Then complete the recipe as instructed.

    Lemon oil, which is available in most bakery supply stores, gives these crêpes a particularly concentrated citrus taste.

Crispy Cinnamon-dusted Banana Fritters

MAKES 24 FRITTERS   PREP TIME: 35 MINUTES

These seem to cry, "Brunch! Brunch!" Take the time to make someone special a Sunday morning treat with a big cup of café au lait, and you won't regret it. These fritters, a take on beignets, the French Quarter's most famous doughnut, are a snap to make.

1½ cups flour

¾ teaspoon baking powder

¼ teaspoon plus a pinch of salt

¼ cup sugar

1 teaspoon ground cinnamon

½ teaspoon grated nutmeg

2 eggs, separated

⅔ cup milk

1 tablespoon corn oil

3 bananas, 1 mashed, 2 diced
   (about 2 cups)

Vegetable oil, for deep-frying

Cinnamon sugar (½ cup sugar mixed
   with 1 tablespoon ground
   cinnamon), for rolling

Sift the flour, baking powder, ¼ teaspoon salt, sugar, cinnamon, and nutmeg into a large bowl. Add the egg yolks and ⅓ cup of milk, and stir to form a smooth paste. Stir in the remaining ⅓ cup of milk and the corn oil. Add all the bananas and mix until the batter is smooth. Allow the batter to rest 30 minutes.

Beat the egg whites and the pinch of salt with an electric mixer (or by hand) at high speed until they form stiff peaks. Fold the whites into the batter.

Heat 2 inches of vegetable oil in a deep skillet or pot over high heat until it reaches 350°F (the oil should start bubbling pretty quickly when you drop a small amount of batter into it).

Drop spoonfuls of batter gently into the oil and fry, turning once or twice, until well browned on both sides, 3–4 minutes. Use a slotted spoon or tongs to remove the fritters from the oil and drain on paper towels. While the fritters are still warm, roll them in cinnamon sugar and serve.

Feel free to substitute an equal amount of another fruit (such as mangoes, nectarines, or plums), though it should be diced, not mashed.

Espresso Pôts de Crème

MAKES 8 SERVINGS   PREP TIME: 1 TO 1½ HOURS

We do love our coffee in New Orleans, and we love it strong! Coffee ice cream may be my very favorite dessert, but this runs a close second. It is rich and not too sweet, easy to make, and, because the pôts de crème cook at such a low heat in a water bath, you can make them in pretty, decorative coffee cups and serve them on a saucer.

---

2 cups heavy cream

2 cups half-and-half

½ vanilla bean, split open and
   scraped (see p. 349)

¾ cup sugar

1 tablespoon instant espresso

6 egg yolks

1 teaspoon pure vanilla extract

Whipped cream, for garnish,
   optional

Chocolate-covered espresso beans, for
   garnish, optional

Preheat the oven to 275°F. Heat a kettle of water.

Combine the cream, half-and-half, vanilla bean (and inside scrapings), and sugar in a heavy saucepan. Cook over low heat until the mixture just barely reaches a simmer. Stir in the espresso until dissolved. Whisk the egg yolks in a small bowl, then temper the yolks by whisking in a little hot cream. Add the remaining cream in a slow, steady stream. Whisk the cream mixture back into the pan. Stir in the vanilla, adjusting amount as necessary. Strain the mixture through a fine strainer. Ladle 5 or 6 ounces into eight custard cups, ramekins, or coffee cups. Place the containers in a baking dish and add enough hot water to come halfway up the sides; cover the dish with foil. Bake in the water bath for about 45 minutes or until the cream is set around the edges; the centers will be not quite firm. Let the cups cool in the water bath, then serve at room temperature or chilled, garnished with whipped cream and chocolate-covered espresso beans.

Working with Vanilla Beans

You can't beat the deep flavor and perfume of a fresh vanilla bean. These days they are increasingly available in the produce section of good supermarkets. They are not cheap but are worth the investment for special desserts. The freshest beans will be pliable and leathery (not crackly and dry). If the bean is dry, you can rehydrate it in warm water until it feels soft. To split the bean, lay it on a cutting board and run a paring knife down the center. Use the knife to spread open each half and scrape out the seeds. Be sure to save the leftover pod to flavor sugar (simply tuck it into your sugar jar), sugar syrups, or poaching liquids for fruit.

Danish Rice Pudding with Dried Cherry Sauce

MAKES 6 SERVINGS   PREP TIME: 1 HOUR 40 MINUTES (INCLUDING CHILLING TIME)

This is a fluffy eggless rice pudding scented with sherry and almonds. My mom usually serves it with fresh raspberries, which is the perfect choice when they're in season. But I like it all year round, so I like to make a sauce with dried cherries, which have a similar sweet-tart quality. It is lovely served in elegant stemmed glasses with the sauce spooned over the top. My mom still makes this pudding every year for my birthday. Thanks, Mom!

½ cup rice (white medium-grain or basmati)

3 cups milk

⅓ cup sugar

½ teaspoon almond extract

½ cup sliced almonds, toasted

2 ounces medium-dry sherry

1½ cups heavy cream

Dried Cherry Sauce

Cook the rice, milk, and sugar in a heavy-bottomed 2-quart saucepan over medium heat until the rice is tender and the milk is absorbed, 30–40 minutes. Remove from the heat and stir in the almond extract, almonds, and sherry. Using a rubber spatula, scrape the pudding into a bowl and chill for at least 1 hour. Whip the cream in an electric mixer on high speed (or by hand) until soft peaks form and then get a little firmer, and fold into the chilled pudding. Serve immediately or refrigerate until ready to serve. Top with warm or cold cherry sauce.

DRIED CHERRY SAUCE

4 ounces dried cherries (¾ cup)

1 cup pinot noir or other red wine

2 tablespoons sugar or red currant jelly

Place the cherries in a small saucepan with the wine, ½ cup water, and the sugar or jelly. Bring to a boil, reduce heat, and simmer until the cherries are tender and the juice is syrupy (approximately 10 minutes).

This recipe lends itself to countless variations. You might try a citrus version with a drop or two of orange or lemon oil and a teaspoon of grated zest. It would also be delicious with fresh grated ginger, a splash of rum, and some chopped tropical fruit.

Sicilian Cannoli
with Bittersweet Chocolate Filling

MAKES 12 TO 15 CANNOLI   PREP TIME: 1 HOUR 30 MINUTES

No, I don't have an old Sicilian grandmother, but one of my best friends did, and this is her recipe. You will need 12 to 15 cannoli forms, metal tubes about 5 inches long, available at specialty cooking stores. Or do what I did some thirty years ago: buy ¾-inch wooden dowels and have them cut into 5-inch lengths. If you use the wooden forms, season by frying them in the oil for a few minutes before using them.

CANNOLI SHELLS

2½ cups flour, plus more for rolling

¼ cup sugar

½ teaspoon salt

1 teaspoon ground cinnamon

¼ pound (1 stick) vegetable
   shortening

1 egg, lightly beaten

¼ cup marsala

¼ cup apple cider vinegar

Beaten egg white, as needed,
   optional

Vegetable oil, for frying

Sift the flour, sugar, salt, and cinnamon together and place in the bowl of an electric mixer fitted with the paddle attachment. At a low speed, mix in the shortening, egg, marsala, and vinegar until just blended—do not overmix. The dough should be moist but not too wet (if it is too wet, mix in a bit more flour).

Divide the dough into two equal portions, wrap in plastic, and chill in the refrigerator about 20 minutes. Take the dough portions out one at a time and roll out on a lightly floured surface until very thin. Cut into ovals approximately 3 inches by 4½ inches. (I usually make a template out of cardboard or even parchment paper, but I have also done it freehand.) Place a cannoli form lengthwise on each oval and wrap the dough around the form, overlapping the long edges and pressing to seal. You may want to brush the seam with a little beaten egg white to ensure that it does not come unstuck.

Pour 1½ inches of vegetable oil into a skillet or pan deep and wide enough to hold 4 cannoli at once. Heat the oil to 350°F. Place the shells in the oil and fry, turning once, until deep golden brown, about 4 minutes. The shells should blister a little bit. Remove them from the oil, drain on paper towels, and when just cool enough to handle, remove them from the forms. Cool completely on wire racks before filling.

BITTERSWEET CHOCOLATE FILLING

1 pint ricotta cheese
2 ounces bittersweet chocolate, grated (about ¼ cup)
½ cup brown sugar
1 teaspoon ground cinnamon

1 teaspoon pure vanilla extract
1 tablespoon finely chopped candied orange peel
Cannoli Shells
¼ cup chopped pistachios

Using a rubber spatula, combine the ricotta, chocolate, brown sugar, cinnamon, vanilla, and candied orange peel in a medium bowl. Cover and refrigerate for at least ½ hour. Scrape the mixture into a pastry bag with a ½-inch plain tip and pipe into the cooled cannoli shells. Dip the ends in chopped pistachios. Serve immediately or refrigerate until ready to serve.

It's easier to grate chocolate if you freeze it for 15 minutes beforehand. When it comes to equipment, I like to use a coarse-toothed microplane.

Galaktaboureko—Greek Semolina Custard Baked in Phyllo

MAKES 12 SERVINGS   PREP TIME: 2 HOURS 5 MINUTES (INCLUDING BAKING TIME)

This is a scrumptious home-style Greek dessert that you won't find in many restaurants. *Galaktaboureko*, which might be easier to prepare than pronounce, is made by baking semolina custard in a crispy phyllo package and then drizzling it with sweet syrup. The syrup is traditionally made with sugar and water, but I couldn't resist the urge to infuse it with a little lemon and cinnamon.

SEMOLINA CUSTARD

6 cups milk

1 cup sugar

¾ cup semolina flour (see p. 356)

4 tablespoons (½ stick) butter

2 teaspoons pure vanilla extract

6 eggs, lightly beaten

In a medium saucepan over medium-high heat, whisk 5 cups of milk with the sugar and bring almost to a boil. Whisk in the semolina. Bring to a boil, whisking, then cook over low heat, stirring constantly, until the mixture is thick, about 10 minutes. Remove from heat and add the butter, stirring until incorporated. Cool for 5 minutes, then stir in the vanilla, the remaining 1 cup of milk, and the eggs, mixing thoroughly. Cool, cover with plastic or waxed paper, and refrigerate for at least 1 hour or overnight.

SYRUP

2 cups sugar

1 cinnamon stick

1½ cups water

Zest and juice of 1 medium lemon
(about 2 teaspoons grated zest
and 3 tablespoons juice)

Place the sugar, cinnamon, water, zest, and juice in a small saucepan and bring to a boil. Reduce heat and simmer, stirring, for about 10 minutes, until the syrup thickens and coats a spoon. Remove the cinnamon stick.

½ cup ground almonds

½ cup dry bread crumbs

¼ cup sugar

1 pound phyllo dough (there will be
some sheets left over)

½ pound (2 sticks) butter, melted

Semolina Custard

Sugar syrup

Preheat the oven to 400°F. Butter an 8-inch square baking pan.

In a small bowl, mix together the almonds, bread crumbs, and sugar. Line the baking pan with 8 sheets of phyllo, one sheet at a time (each sheet should overlap its neighbors by an inch or so). Brush each sheet with butter and sprinkle lightly with the almond mixture. The pastry edges should overlap the entire perimeter of the pan. Pour in the cooled custard, spreading evenly, and fold the pastry edges over the custard.

Arrange 8 phyllo sheets over the top of the custard, leaf by leaf, brushing with butter and sprinkling with almond mixture as before. Trim the edges to 1 inch and fold them inward, tucking them down inside the pan. Brush the top with butter and score diagonally with the tip of a sharp knife in two directions, to make diamond-shaped slits in the pastry. Sprinkle the top with water (about 3 tablespoons) and bake for 15 minutes, then lower the heat to 325°F and bake 45 more minutes.

When the top is golden brown and flaky, remove from the oven and immediately pour the cooled syrup over the pastry. Let the custard set until cool, then cut into pieces and serve.

Semolina

Semolina is durum wheat that is more coarsely ground than other flours. It is the primary ingredient in the best pasta and in couscous, and it's also popular as porridge. It gives cakes a heartier, more substantial texture.

Coconut Cream Pie

MAKES 8 SERVINGS   PREP TIME: 1 HOUR 30 MINUTES

This is sinfully rich and creamy, just the way a cream pie should be. It is best made several hours in advance, so that the coconut flavor has a chance to bloom in the filling. The crust is a classic pâte brisée, the rich, flaky French pastry used for both sweet and savory tarts (try it with your favorite quiche recipe). Don't expect leftovers!

PÂTE BRISÉE

1¼ cups flour
1 tablespoon sugar
⅛ teaspoon salt

¼ pound (1 stick) butter, chilled and cut into small pieces, or 4 tablespoons butter and 4 tablespoons vegetable shortening
¼ cup ice water

Sift together the flour, sugar, and salt into a medium bowl. Using a pastry blender, cut in the butter until the mixture resembles oatmeal or coarse crumbs. Use a fork to stir in the water. Turn the dough out onto a lightly floured work surface; it will still be slightly crumbly. Fold it over on itself a few times, just until the dough holds together and becomes more supple and less grainy. Wrap in plastic wrap and refrigerate for at least ½ hour.

Preheat the oven to 350°F and lightly grease a 9-inch pie pan.

Roll out the dough to about ⅛ inch thick and gently drape it on the pan. Cover the dough with a disc of parchment paper and weight down with pie weights or dried beans. Bake for about 12 minutes, until the bottom and sides of the pie shell are starting to turn light golden brown. Remove the pie weights and parchment and bake 2–3 more minutes, until the crust is cooked all the way through but is not too brown. Remove it from the oven and cool completely before filling.

COCONUT CREAM

½ cup milk

½ cup canned unsweetened coconut
   milk

⅓ cup plus 3 tablespoons sugar

½ vanilla bean, split and scraped

2 tablespoons cornstarch

1 cup plus ¼ cup heavy cream

3 egg yolks

1 tablespoon butter, softened

1 cup shredded sweetened coconut,
   lightly toasted

Pâte Brisée

Using a medium saucepan, bring the milk, coconut milk, ⅓ cup sugar, and the vanilla bean (bean and scrapings) to a simmer over medium heat. Whisk the cornstarch into ¼ cup of the heavy cream and then whisk into the milk; remove from heat.

In a bowl, whisk the egg yolks until fluffy. Whisk about ½ cup of the hot milk mixture into the yolks, then pour the egg mixture back into the saucepan, whisking constantly so that the eggs won't curdle. Run the whisk along the bottom of the saucepan to make sure you're getting all the eggs. Return the saucepan to medium heat and start whisking rapidly. The mixture should come to a boil and start to thicken. Lower the heat slightly and cook, whisking, for about 3 minutes. Remove from heat and strain into a bowl. Stir in the butter and cover the surface of the pastry cream with plastic. Cool completely.

Place the cooled pastry cream, 3 tablespoons sugar, and remaining 1 cup of heavy cream in the bowl of an electric mixer and beat at medium-high until stiff. Fold in ¾ cup of the toasted coconut and scoop the filling into the pie shell. Sprinkle the surface with the remaining ¼ cup of coconut and refrigerate until ready to serve.

Brandy Crème Brûlée

Herbsaint, the anise-flavored liqueur that we named the restaurant after, was made in New Orleans for many years. It served as an absinthe substitute, offering a similar licorice taste without the hallucinations. While researching old recipes using absinthe or Pernod, I noticed the liqueurs would frequently be combined with brandy, and this appealed to me, since it tempers the strong anise flavor. Just like a sip of Sazerac, anise is not for everyone. But it's a sophisticated alternative to the classic vanilla version. If you don't like anise, simply substitute another tablespoon of brandy or bourbon.

4 cups heavy cream

¾ cup sugar, plus ½ cup for caramelizing

½ vanilla bean, split and scraped

8 egg yolks

1 tablespoon Herbsaint or Pernod

2 tablespoons brandy

Preheat the oven to 300°F. Place eight 6-ounce ramekin or crème brûlée dishes in a larger baking pan. Heat a kettle of water.

Pour the cream into a heavy-bottomed 2-quart saucepan and whisk in ½ cup of sugar and the vanilla bean, with the scrapings. Bring to a simmer, then remove from heat, cover with plastic wrap, and let sit for about 10 minutes. Whisk ¼ cup of sugar into the egg yolks until well mixed. Gently whisk the cream into the yolks, add the Herbsaint and brandy, then strain through a fine sieve.

I actually prefer to fill the ramekins and water bath when the pan is already in the oven, so I don't spill either when I move them. Place the pan with the ramekins on the middle rack of the oven with the door open, and use a ladle to fill the ramekins with the custard. Carefully pour hot water into the pan about halfway up the sides of the ramekins, cover the pan with foil, then gently slide the oven rack into the oven. Bake the custards for about 40 minutes, rotating once. It is a good idea to take a peek after about 25 minutes and make sure they are not cooking too fast (in which case they would look overly dry and shriveled). This is especially good to do if you are using the shallow, wide variety of crème brûlée dishes. Custard is done when it's just barely set and jiggles when you move the ramekin. Remove them from the oven, uncover, let cool to room temperature, and then refrigerate. The custards should be chilled for about 2 hours before caramelizing with the sugar.

Sprinkle the tops of the custards with a thin layer of sugar and brown under a broiler or with a butane torch held 4–6 inches from the surface. When the sugar starts to bubble and brown, sprinkle lightly with another layer of sugar and brown the second layer. You'll use about ½ cup of sugar in all. For the most crackly top, serve within 10 minutes of caramelizing.

Molasses Gingerbread with Lime Cream

MAKES 12 SERVINGS   PREP TIME: 1 HOUR 30 MINUTES

Moist, spicy gingerbread is one of those simple desserts that people tend to associate fondly with childhood holidays. For me, it harks back to the Christmas seasons that I spent as a kid in Europe where gingerbread is particularly popular. Blending a mixture of baking soda and boiling water into molasses has a magical transforming effect in the oven. The light brown batter becomes very dark, rich, and deeply flavored when baked. Fragrant with warm, fresh ginger, this gingerbread is very moist, simple to make, and irresistible. Lime Cream is an unexpected—but perfect—partner. The recipe makes enough cream for one gingerbread cake. Any leftover cream is delicious slathered over toasted pound cake, buttermilk biscuits, or brioche. Don't reserve this recipe just for holiday baking—it will make your family sublimely happy all year long.

¼ pound (1 stick) butter, plus more
　　for buttering the pan

1 cup sugar

3 eggs

2 cups flour

1 teaspoon ground cinnamon

1 teaspoon ground cloves

2 teaspoons baking soda

1 tablespoon fresh grated ginger
　　(or ½ teaspoon ground ginger)

1 cup unsulfured molasses

2 teaspoons baking soda dissolved in
　　2 tablespoons hot water

Lime Cream

Preheat the oven to 350°F, and butter and flour an 8-inch square pan.

　　Melt the stick of butter, pour into a large bowl, and allow it to cool slightly. Beat the sugar and eggs into the butter. In a separate medium bowl, whisk together the flour, cinnamon, cloves, baking soda, and grated ginger.

　　Bring 1 cup of water to a boil in a small saucepan. Using a wooden spoon, stir the molasses and soda solution into the water. Whisk the dry ingredients into the sugar and eggs, then stir in the molasses mixture.

Pour the batter into the prepared pan and bake for 45 minutes to 1 hour, testing for doneness with a wooden toothpick in the center of the cake (it should pull out clean and free of batter). Another indicator is that the cake will pull away from the sides of the pan when it's done. Cool the cake on a wire rack for 10 minutes. Run a knife around the rim of the pan to loosen the cake, and invert onto a cooling rack and cool completely. Cut into squares and serve with Lime Cream.

LIME CREAM

2 eggs	4 tablespoons (½ stick) butter, cut
½ cup sugar	into small pieces
⅓ cup fresh lime juice	1 cup heavy cream
Zest of 1 lime, grated (about	
1 tablespoon)	

In the bowl of an electric mixer, use the whisk attachment to whip the eggs and sugar at high speed until double in volume and light in color. Lower the speed and blend in the lime juice and zest.

Pour the egg mixture into a medium metal bowl placed over a pot of simmering water (or a double boiler). Cook over high heat, whisking often, until smooth, very thick, and custardlike (about 20 minutes). Remove from the heat and use a wooden spoon to stir in the butter, a few pieces at a time, until it is fully incorporated. If the final mixture is lumpy, strain through a fine sieve. Otherwise, cool to room temperature.

Using an electric mixer or a wire whisk, whip the heavy cream into soft peaks. Gently fold a fourth of the whipped cream into the lime curd. Then fold in the remaining whipped cream.

If you don't have time to make the lime cream, no one is going to complain if you serve this cake with whipped cream sweetened with brown sugar and a couple of tablespoons of bourbon.

French Semolina Cake with Pistachio Crème Anglaise

MAKES 12 SERVINGS   PREP TIME: 1 HOUR 30 MINUTES

I learned this recipe when I spent the summer in the kitchen of the Hotel Sofitel in Paris, some twenty-five years ago. Roland Durand, the chef, graciously accepted me as a *stagiare*, or apprentice, and I was able to work in all sections of the kitchen, including the butcher shop and bake shop. I love this cake for its texture, which is moist and rich-looking but very light, and for its versatility. It goes with so many different things, but it's also delicious all by itself. I like to dress it up with a Pistachio Crème Anglaise and some raspberries or tart cherries.

---

3 cups milk

1 cup sugar

⅔ cup semolina flour

6 tablespoons butter, softened

2 whole eggs, plus 6 separated eggs

2 teaspoons pure vanilla extract

Pistachio Crème Anglaise

Fresh berries or cherries, for garnish,
  optional

Preheat the oven to 350°F. Butter and flour a 9- or 10-inch springform pan, and wrap the outside of the pan with foil (this will ensure that no batter leaks out during the baking process).

In a heavy-bottomed 2-quart saucepan, combine the milk with half the sugar and bring to a boil. Stir in the semolina and cook over low heat, stirring with a wooden spoon, until thickened (about 10 minutes). Stir in half the butter and the remaining sugar. Remove from the heat and cool, stirring now and then. Stir in the remaining butter, the whole eggs plus 6 yolks, and the vanilla. In an electric mixer fitted with a whisk, beat the egg whites until stiff but not dry, and fold by thirds into the semolina mixture. Pour the batter into the prepared pan. Place the pan in a larger baking dish and add warm water to reach about halfway up the cake pan. Bake for 1 hour. Test with a toothpick or skewer to see if the cake is set and the crumb is dry. Remove from the oven and water bath and cool completely before removing from the pan. Serve with the crème anglaise and fresh berries or cherries.

PISTACHIO CRÈME ANGLAISE

1 cup shelled pistachios

2 cups milk

½ cup heavy cream

¼ cup sugar

Pinch of salt

8 egg yolks

¼ teaspoon almond extract

Toast the nuts in a 350°F oven for a few minutes to dry them out and loosen the skins. Wrap the nuts in a dish towel and rub off the skins (as much as possible). When the nuts are cool, grind them very finely. Place the nuts, milk, and cream in a small saucepan and bring just to the boiling point. Remove from heat, cover, and let steep for about 30 minutes. Strain through a fine strainer or cheesecloth and discard the nuts.

Using a 2-quart saucepan set over medium heat, whisk together the sugar, salt, and egg yolks. In a separate small saucepan, heat the pistachio milk just until it begins to boil, then whisk a small amount into the yolk mixture. Gradually add the remaining milk, stirring constantly. Continue to heat the mixture slowly, to just below the boiling point (but do not let it boil), until it thickens and coats the back of a wooden spoon. Remove the pan from the heat, stir in the almond extract, and continue to stir for a few minutes. Strain the custard into a bowl and set aside or refrigerate until ready to use. To serve, spoon a generous pool of the custard onto a small dessert plate and top with a slice of the cake.

Mint Julep Ice Cream

MAKES ABOUT 2 QUARTS   PREP TIME: 1 HOUR

My rule of thumb is "If something tastes good, it will taste even better if you turn it into ice cream." Hence my passion for coffee ice cream—and this divine take on everyone's favorite Kentucky Derby Day libation. The better the bourbon, the better the ice cream. We serve this with short-bread, but it's good with any type of cookies. Shaved or grated bittersweet chocolate would be a delicious addition.

2 cups heavy cream

4 cups half-and-half

½ bunch mint sprigs (about
    2 ounces)

9 egg yolks

2½ cups sugar

½ cup bourbon

Heat the heavy cream, 1 cup of the half-and-half, and the mint in a 2-quart saucepan over medium heat until it is just on the verge of boiling. Turn off the heat, cover, and let it steep for about 30 minutes. Strain the cream into a small bowl. In a large bowl, whisk together the egg yolks and sugar until the mixture is pale yellow. Slowly whisk the cream into the egg mixture and return it to the same saucepan. Cook over medium-low heat, stirring, until the custard has thickened enough to coat a wooden spoon.

Strain the custard into a bowl and cool in an ice bath, then add the remaining 3 cups of half-and-half and the bourbon.

Freeze in an ice cream maker according to the manufacturer's instructions.

Cashew Meringues with Chocolate Basil Mousse

MAKES 6 SANDWICHES (12 ROUNDS OF MERINGUE)   PREP TIME: 2 HOURS 30 MINUTES

When we first conjured up the notion of this dessert, we weren't sure if people would go for the chocolate and basil combination in the mousse. But apparently everyone else dug the combination—the basil's minty quality freshens up the chocolate taste—as much as we did: we couldn't make these fast enough. When the scorching Crescent City summer rolled around, the kitchen got so hot and humid that the meringues wouldn't bake properly (they need dry heat to crisp up), so we had to take them off the menu. We still like to make them from time to time when the temperature finally decides to drop.

CASHEW MERINGUES

½ cup egg whites (about 4 large)

½ cup sugar

Pinch of salt

2 ounces toasted cashews, finely
    chopped (about ¼ tablespoon)

2 ounces (or more, as needed)
    bittersweet chocolate, melted, for
    drizzling

Preheat the oven to 250°F. Line a baking sheet with parchment paper.

Using an electric mixer fitted with a whisk, whip the egg whites at medium-high speed with the sugar and salt, until firm. With a rubber spatula, fold in the chopped cashews. Spoon the batter into a pastry bag with a ½-inch plain tip and pipe it into 4-inch circles on the parchment. You should get 12 meringues.

Bake for about 1 hour, or until the meringues are dry but not too brown. Cool them completely before peeling off the parchment. To finish, drizzle the cooled meringues with the melted chocolate (you can do this with a fork or a squeeze bottle).

CHOCOLATE BASIL MOUSSE

1 tablespoon unsalted butter

8 ounces bittersweet chocolate

2 cups heavy cream

1 ounce (about ½ bunch) fresh basil

3 egg yolks plus 2 whole eggs

3 tablespoons sugar

1½ tablespoons Frangelico, or other hazelnut liqueur

1 tablespoon unflavored gelatin dissolved in 2 tablespoons water

Cashew Meringues

Melt the butter and chocolate together in a small saucepan or microwave-proof bowl; set aside to cool. Using an electric mixer or wire whisk, whip ½ cup of the cream to soft peaks; refrigerate. Combine the remaining 1½ cups of cream and the basil in another small saucepan placed over medium heat, and heat until you can smell the aroma of the basil, about 10 minutes. Cool the cream completely and strain.

Use a mixer fitted with the whisk attachment to whip the egg yolks, whole eggs, sugar, and Frangelico to the ribbon stage, then add the gelatin. Slowly whip in the cooled chocolate, scraping the sides of the bowl often. Use a rubber spatula to fold in the whipped cream and then the basil cream until just mixed. Chill to set.

When you are ready to serve the meringues, pipe or dollop the mousse onto the smooth surface of a meringue round, and top with another, smooth side down. Serve immediately.

The chocolate mousse can be made up to one day ahead.

The "ribbon stage" refers to sugar and eggs that are whipped together until thick and pale. When the whisk is raised, the mixture should fall slowly in thick ribbons that sink back into the batter.

Chocolate Hazelnut Phyllo Turnovers

MAKES 9 TURNOVERS   PREP TIME: 1 HOUR 15 MINUTES

I remember when I came up with the idea for this dessert and surprised myself by how good it was! Of course, it's nice to have a pastry chef on hand who can translate my daydreams into reality. But this one is easy enough for anyone. Try using frozen puff pastry sheets if you don't want to mess with the phyllo dough.

---

6 ounces (1 cup) blanched hazelnuts
    or filberts

1 teaspoon vegetable oil

¼ cup sugar

½ cup dry bread crumbs

¼ pound bittersweet chocolate,
    chopped

¼ pound milk chocolate, chopped

1 cup heavy cream

1 tablespoon Frangelico liqueur,
    optional

½ pound phyllo dough or frozen puff
    pastry

¼ pound (1 stick) butter, melted

Whipped cream or ice cream, for
    serving, optional

Preheat the oven to 350°F.

Place the hazelnuts on a baking sheet and toast in the oven for about 5 minutes, until lightly golden. Watch them carefully so they do not burn! If they are not already skinned, rub the hazelnuts in a kitchen towel to remove as much of the skin as possible. Place ½ cup of the nuts in a food processor and pulse, drizzling in the oil, until you have a paste. Remove the paste from the processor and set aside. When the remaining ½ cup of nuts are cool, pulse them in the processor with the sugar and bread crumbs, until the mixture has the texture of coarse cornmeal. Set aside.

Place the two chocolates in a heat-proof bowl.

Bring the heavy cream to a boil and remove from the heat. Stir in the liqueur and immediately pour over the chocolate. Tap the bowl to settle the chocolate and let it sit for about 2 minutes, then stir with a plastic spatula, using a circular motion. Stir in the hazelnut paste, mixing thoroughly, and let it cool to room temperature.

When the chocolate mixture is cool, unwrap the phyllo dough and lay 1 sheet on the counter with the long edge facing you. Brush the dough lightly with melted butter and sprinkle with about 1 tablespoon of the bread crumb mixture. Layer on 2 more sheets of phyllo, brushing and sprinkling in the same way. Cut the stack into thirds crosswise. Place 3 heaping tablespoons of filling near the bottom right corner of each third. Bring the corner up and over the filling to the opposite edge to form a triangle. Continue in this manner, folding like a flag, until you get to the top end of the dough. If you have any left over, just trim it even with the edge. Brush the tops lightly with butter and sprinkle with a little of the bread crumb mixture. Repeat with the remaining dough and filling. Chill the turnovers for at least 30 minutes.

Preheat the oven to 400°F.

Place the turnovers on a greased baking sheet with a little space between them.

Bake for about 12 minutes, or until golden brown on top and underneath. (Lift with a spatula and check to make sure that the dough is cooked through.)

Serve the turnovers with whipped cream or ice cream on the side, if desired.

When chocolate is melted in heavy cream, the mixture is called a ganache. The result is a rich, satiny glaze that's most often poured over cakes, pastries, and flourless tortes. Butter and/or egg yolks can also be added, along with other flavorings such as extracts and liqueurs. If ganache is not used as a glaze while it's warm, it can be cooled to room temperature and then whipped to twice its volume, to form a mousselike filling for pastries.

Scotch Almond Tart

MAKES 8 SERVINGS   PREP TIME: 1 HOUR 15 MINUTES

This recipe came from Mark Zink, who holds the distinction of being the only male pastry chef we ever had at Bayona. This tart is plenty nutty (no offense, Mark!) and richly flavored, thanks to an abundance of almonds. Just after baking, the tart gets a dousing of scotch while it's still warm—an unusual, aromatic, and delicious twist.

½ cup sugar

½ cup light corn syrup

3 eggs

4 tablespoons (½ stick) butter, melted

½ teaspoon pure vanilla extract

⅛ teaspoon salt

1 Sweet Tart Crust (p. 340)

6 ounces whole blanched almonds, toasted and coarsely chopped (about 1 cup)

2 ounces scotch whiskey

Whipped cream, for garnish

Combine the sugar and corn syrup in a small saucepan and stir over medium heat until the sugar is dissolved. Pour into a bowl, let cool a few minutes, then whisk in the eggs, one at a time, thoroughly incorporating each one. Whisk in the melted butter, vanilla, and salt and refrigerate at least 1 hour (this can be made up to several hours in advance).

Prepare the crust, using a 9-inch tart pan, and bake (see instructions pp. 340–41). After removing it from the oven, lower the temperature to 325°F.

Place the almonds in the warm crust. Pour the cooled filling over the nuts and use a rubber spatula to spread it until the almonds are evenly coated.

Bake for 25–30 minutes, or until firm. Remove the tart from the oven and drizzle the scotch evenly over it. Allow the tart to cool, then serve at room temperature with a dollop of whipped cream, if desired.

Killer Cocktails from the Quarter

If any town is known for lethal libations it's New Orleans (that's right, you can get them in to-go cups anywhere in the Quarter). The conviviality of cocktails is integral to culture in The Big Easy. And they're served around the clock with enthusiasm, at infamous jazz brunches, martini-soaked lunches at Galatoire's, and in legendary bars throughout the Quarter. At my restaurants, and in most people's homes, the drinks tend to get more creative and personal. The following list of elixirs is plucked primarily off the bar menus of Bayona and Herbsaint. The drinks were created and/or perfected by the two talented beverage directors there, Shannon Skarda at Bayona (don't miss her Cotillion) and Kenny Jackson at Herbsaint. Both these people are old friends, and we've shared plenty of great times—including Bayona staff parties, Mardi Gras, and Jazz Fest fêtes—over the following concoctions.

Simple Syrup

Equal parts sugar and water create what is referred to as a "heavy" simple syrup. It's the one we prefer for cocktails.

1 cup sugar   1 cup water

Heat the sugar and water in a small saucepan over medium-low heat, stirring occasionally, until the sugar melts. Allow the syrup to cool and then store in the refrigerator.

Classic Sazerac

MAKES 1 COCKTAIL

Two types of bitters give this drink its characteristic flavor.

2 ounces Old Overholt rye whiskey or Sazerac bourbon

2 dashes Peychaud's bitters

2 dashes Angostura bitters

Herbsaint or other anise liqueur (such as Ojen)

Lemon twist

Chill a rocks glass with ice water. Put a scoop of crushed ice into a shaker and add the whiskey and Peychaud's and Angostura bitters. Shake vigorously to chill. Empty the chilled glass and dip the glass rim in Herbsaint or another anise liqueur. Strain the chilled rye mixture into the glass. Run a lemon twist around the rim and drop it into the drink.

Bitters

A common ingredient in French Quarter cocktails, and the distinctive flavor in a Sazerac, bitters are a distillation of herbs, barks, and roots. Named after their slightly bitter taste, they are a digestive and appetite stimulant. Angostura and Peychaud's are two of the most popular varieties.

Ramos Gin Fizz

2 ounces gin

1½ ounces half-and-half or milk

1½ ounces orange juice

Splash of fresh lime juice

½ ounce Simple Syrup (p. 376)

2–4 drops orange flower water

Soda water, as needed

Orange slice

Combine all the ingredients, except the soda and orange slice, in a cocktail shaker with crushed ice. Shake vigorously. When you think that you are finished shaking, shake some more. Strain into a chilled Collins glass and top with enough soda water to fill the glass. Garnish with an orange slice.

Fizz Facts

A classic gin fizz is made with gin, fresh lemon juice, sugar, and soda. It's traditionally served in a tall Collins glass over ice. Stirring in a frothy egg white changes it into a "silver fizz," and adding orange flower water and cream or milk makes it a Ramos Gin Fizz, a drink created in the late 1800s by bar owner Henry Ramos.

Pisco Sour

A few years ago Chip and I took a trip to Peru. We started in Lima and then traveled on to Cuzco and Machu Picchu, one of the most beautiful places on earth. While in Lima, we stopped at an outdoor bar in the Barranco neighborhood, an artists' and musicians' enclave rather like a Peruvian French Quarter. We met a salty old bartender who made us these delicious frothy drinks that reminded me somewhat of a gin fizz, but after two, our heads were spinning. Pisco is a spirit made from grapes, and it is quite strong, so beware!

1 egg white

6 ounces Pisco

2 ounces fresh lime or lemon juice

1–2 ounces Simple Syrup (p. 376), or
    superfine granulated sugar

2 cups crushed ice

Angostura bitters

Place the egg white in a blender and blend briefly, until frothy and light. Then add all the other ingredients except the bitters, and blend until frothy and smooth. Taste and adjust to your liking with more citrus or sugar. Pour into two glasses and sprinkle with a drop or two of bitters.

Half Sinner, Half Saint

Kenny Jackson named this drink after his Gemini heritage. Vya vermouth, which is made in California, is his favorite brand for this particular cocktail, but you can substitute other varieties as well. He says using crushed ice (as opposed to cubes) is crucial.

½ ounce dry vermouth
½ ounce sweet vermouth

Light dash of Herbsaint
Twist of lemon, for garnish

Place all the ingredients (except the lemon) and a scoop of crushed ice in a cocktail shaker. Shake vigorously and serve in a chilled rocks glass, garnished with the lemon.

Cotillion

MAKES 1 COCKTAIL

5–6 fresh basil leaves, plus 1 for
 garnish
1 sugar cube
1 ounce Cointreau or Triple Sec

1½ ounces Patrón or other silver
 tequila
5 ounces orange juice, preferably
 fresh-squeezed

Using a wooden spoon or "muddler," mash the basil with the sugar cube and Cointreau in a tall Collins glass. Fill the glass with crushed ice and add the tequila and orange juice. Stir with a long spoon or straw and garnish with a basil leaf.

Lychee Champagne Cocktail

1½ ounces chilled Gewürztraminer

½ ounce chilled Simple Syrup
(p. 376)

1 ounce chilled lychee syrup, from
canned lychees

4 ounces Prosecco or other sparkling
wine

1 stalk lemongrass, sliced into 4-inch
lengths, for garnish

Lychees, for garnish

Combine the Gewürztraminer, Simple Syrup, and lychee syrup in a chilled
martini glass. Top with the Prosecco, stir gently, and garnish with lemongrass-
skewered lychees.

Kaffir Lime Kick

2 ounces Hangar One Kaffir Lime
vodka

4 ounces spicy ginger ale (we use
Boylan's)

Kaffir lime leaves

Combine the vodka and ginger ale over ice in a tall glass and stir. Crush a kaffir lime leaf in your fingers and stir into the cocktail.

Satsuma Margarita

When I first got *Rick Bayless's Mexican Kitchen,* I was so inspired by the recipes that I invited people over and made brunch for the first time in years. It was a warm, sunny New Orleans winter day, and I picked satsumas from my backyard tree and made these margaritas to welcome everyone.

1 cup freshly squeezed satsuma or tangerine juice (about 4 satsumas)
6 ounces good-quality silver tequila (such as Patrón)

2 ounces Cointreau
½ ounce Mandarine Napoleon or Grand Marnier

Place juice, tequila, and Cointreau in a shaker with crushed ice and shake vigorously. Serve straight up in chilled martini glasses or on the rocks. Lace each drink with Mandarine Napoleon, which is similar to Grand Marnier but flavored with tangerine instead of orange.

Passion Fruit Margarita

Watch out for these—they go down easy!

2 ounces silver tequila (such as
   Patrón)

1 ounce lime juice

½ ounce Simple Syrup (p. 376)

1 ounce passion fruit puree

Superfine sugar, for rimming the glass

Combine the tequila, juice, syrup, and puree in a cocktail shaker with crushed ice. Shake vigorously and serve straight up or on the rocks in a sugar-rimmed glass.

Brandy Milk Punch

A favorite from the land of the Jazz Brunch . . . Sometimes this is made with half-and-half, cream, or even ice cream to create a richer drink.

2 ounces brandy or bourbon

4 ounces milk

½ ounce Simple Syrup (p. 376)

Grated nutmeg or Tia Maria liqueur, to finish

Place the brandy, milk, and Simple Syrup with ice cubes in a shaker or blender, and shake or blend until frothy.

Pour into a rocks glass or strain into a martini glass. Top with a little grated nutmeg or lace with a splash of Tia Maria.

Tia Maria is a dark Jamaican rum–based liqueur with a coffee flavor.

Sources

The Louisiana Seafood Promotion Board
504–568–5693
For mail-order seafood sources.

The Bauman Family
610–754–7251
www.baumanfamily.com

Central Grocery
504–523–1620
Mail-order muffulettas, olive salad, Creole cream cheese, and more.

Community Coffee
800–525–5583
www.communitycoffee.com
New Orleans–style dark roast coffee and chicory.

Café du Monde
www.cafedumonde.com
Chip's favorite coffee and chicory.

Hoppin' John
www.hoppinjohns.com
For stone-ground grits, cornmeal, and corn flour.

Louisiana Fish Fry Products, Inc.
800–356–2905
Gumbo filé, cayenne pepper, fish fry coatings, jambalaya and
crab/shrimp/crayfish boil seasoning, sauces.

Mauthe's Dairy
985–796–1001
My favorite Creole cream cheese.

Poche's Market
337–332–2108; 800–3–POCHES
www.pochesmarket.com
Andouille, tasso, crayfish tails, and other Cajun specialties.

Smith Creamery
985–877–4445
www.smithcreamery.com

Stansel Rice Company
www.stanselrice.com
Popcorn rice, grown in Louisiana.

Steen's 100% Pure Cane Syrup
800–725–1654
www.steensyrup.com

Zatarain's
www.zatarain.com
The premier manufacturer of New Orleans seasonings and spices,
plus mixes for things like gumbo, jambalaya, etc.

OTHER USEFUL WEB SITES

New Orleans Fish House
www.nofh.com
For crab, crayfish, etc.

www.allthingsdutch.com
A nod to my Danish heritage! Here's where to order Conimex *ketjap manis*,
other Asian and Indonesian sauces, and even Dutch candy.

www.boiledpeanuts.com
Southern specialties, including stone-ground grits.

www.pataks.com
Curry pastes (mild, hot, and vindaloo) and lime pickle.

www.nueskes.com
Applewood-smoked bacon, smoked duck, and ham.

Index

Page references in *italic* denote illustrations.

A Note About the Type

The text of this book was set in Plantin, a typeface first cut in 1913 by the Monotype Corporation of London. Though the face bears the nname of the great Christopher Plantin (ca. 1520–1589), who in the latter part of the sixteenth century owned, in Antwerp, the largest printing and publishing firm in Europe, it is a rather free adaptation of designs by Claude Garamond made for that firm. With its strong, simple lines, Plantin is a no-nonsense face of exceptional legibility.

Composed by
North Market Street Graphics, Lancaster, Pennsylvania

Printed and bound by
SNP Lee Fung Printers Ltd., China

Designed by
Soonyoung Kwon